Marketing
An Introduction

Marketing
An Introduction

Michael Cant (editor)

JUTA

Marketing: An Introduction

First published 2010

Reprinted 2013

Second edition 2013

Reprinted 2015 (Twice)

Reprinted 2016 (Twice)

Juta and Company Ltd

First Floor

Sunclare Building

21 Dreyer Street

Claremont

7708

PO Box 14373, Lansdowne, 7779, Cape Town, South Africa

ISBN 978-1-48510-216-8

Project Manager: Debbie Henry

Editor: Wendy Priilaid

Proofreader: Pat Hanekom

Typesetter: Unwembi Communications Pty Ltd

Cover designer: Saaleha Bamjee

Indexer: Sanet le Roux

Print administration by DJE Flexible Print Solutions

Typeset in: Myriad Pro Light (10.7pt)

Contents

Preface

The second edition of *Marketing: An introduction* comes hot on the heels of the incredible success of the first edition, which made it clear that there is a place amongst students and lecturers for a book that is written in language that is easy to understand and relate to, and covers all the relevant trends and developments in the field of marketing. The book has been written with the aim of providing students and practitioners with a thorough understanding of marketing, as well as how the theory is applied in a practical sense. The role and importance of marketing in an organisation is explained, with an emphasis on the fact that all functions in an organisation must work together to achieve the greatest success.

It is the responsibility of the marketing function to generate income. To do this, marketing managers need a thorough understanding of the environment in which the company operates; the influence of external factors such as the economy, unemployment and politics on the business; the need for timely information; how to conduct research; the way consumers make decisions; and how to segment the market and target a specific one. Based on this, the company would look at its offering in terms of the marketing mix, or the so-called four Ps – the product to offer (including the brand and service), the price to charge, the place to offer the product (distribution), and how to inform the market of the product (promotion).

The second edition of *Marketing: An introduction* adds new dimensions to the first edition, and is up to date with the latest developments including social media and market trends, thus giving a sound and current foundation of marketing to students and business owners alike. The book was once again well researched to include the inputs from other lecturers and educational institutions in order to ensure that it remains the leading introductory marketing textbook in South Africa. The text has been structured in a logical way that is easy for students to follow, and makes use of practical examples to explain various marketing concepts. Care has been taken to ensure that the text is easy to understand, and that educators and students alike can benefit from the layout and design of the course.

The authors in the team, all well-known academics in the marketing field, trust that you, the reader, will benefit from your interaction with this book.

Michael Cant

Editor

December 2013

Author team

Prof MC Cant Chair of Department: Department of Marketing and Retail Management, Unisa

Prof CH van Heerden Head of Department: Marketing, Logistics and Sport Management,

Tshwane University of Technology

Prof J Wiid Senior lecturer: Department of Marketing and Retail Management, Unisa

R Marchado Senior lecturer: Department of Marketing and Retail Management, Unisa

Acknowledgements

Special acknowledgements to Claudette van Niekerk, Leanne Manley and Catherine Sephapo for their assistance.

Fundamentals of marketing management

CHAPTER 1

✓ Learning objectives

After studying this chapter, you should be able to:

- explain what marketing is;
- explain the concept of change;
- explain the marketing activities;
- define marketing;
- explain the marketing process; and
- discuss the marketing function in an organisation.

Introduction

In spite of the changes in the world of technology and the digital age, marketing is and will always play a central role in most organisations – although this may be in a different manner or role. It is generally recognised that marketing is central to a business because it defines what customers want and need, and because it directs the resources of the business to meet these needs. The rapid change in the marketing environment over the past decade has increased awareness of the importance of marketing. Businesses need to adapt to changes in the environment, which are not all uncontrollable, and ensure that in spite of them their offerings stay relevant and in line with the needs and demands of the consumer. Successful marketers will be those who can best define and satisfy consumer requirements in the context of an ever-changing marketing environment.

In this chapter, we discuss the definition of and basic approach to marketing. As a result of fundamental changes in the field of marketing, emphasis is now placed on marketing tasks, marketing concepts and other new developments, such as relationship marketing, customer service and internal marketing.

What is marketing?

Marketing means different things to different people as each person interprets things in their own way. It is a common assumption that marketing is synonymous with selling. Some see it as advertising on radio or TV, while others regard it as offering the right products to customers at a good price, displaying items on the shop floor, and so forth. It would be wrong to think of marketing as narrowly as being only selling and advertising. Selling and advertising are just two of the many facets that make up the marketing process, and it is important to understand the term 'marketing' as more than just selling. The central focus of marketing is *satisfying customers' needs*.

This does not mean that selling and advertising are unimportant, but that they are part of a larger marketing mix, which is a set of tools that work together to affect the marketplace. Businesses currently face increasing competition, and those that determine customer requirements and deliver the most value to their customers will be successful. Satisfying the customer is what marketing is all about.

DEFINITION

Marketing

Marketing can be defined as the process of planning and executing the conception, pricing, promotion and distribution of ideas, goods and services to create exchanges that satisfy individual and organisational goals. Marketing is therefore about:

- anticipating and satisfying consumer needs;
- creating a mutually beneficial exchange process; and
- doing so profitably and more effectively than competitors by means of efficient managerial processes.

Defining marketing

To be able to define marketing it is important to have a good understanding of the nature and extent of the marketing process. While it is true that no two writers agree on the exact formulation of a good definition of this complicated process, the definition entitled 'Marketing' in the margin best serves our purposes.

Today, marketing must be understood not in the old sense of making a sale – 'telling and selling' – but in the new sense of *satisfying customers' needs*. If the marketer understands the basic activities of marketing, which include understanding consumer needs, developing products that provide superior value, pricing these products correctly, and distributing and promoting them effectively, then the chances of product success are much higher.

As marketing deals with the offering of products or services, it implies that there are exchanges that need to take place – that is, between the place of production and the place of consumption.

Exchange and marketing

One of the key terms in the marketing process is exchange. The notion of **exchange** is rather straightforward: it is the act of giving something up in order to gain something else. Traditionally, we think of money as the medium of exchange. We 'give up' money to 'get' the products and services we want. However, exchange does not necessarily require money. Two people may barter or trade items such as lambs and cows, or clothes and corncobs.

In order for exchange to take place, the following five conditions should exist:[1]

- At least two parties must be part of the process.
- Each party must have something of value that the other party wants.
- Each party must be able to communicate with and deliver the goods and services to the other party.
- Each party must be free to accept or reject the other's offer.
- There must be a willingness to deal with each other.

DEFINITION

Exchange

Exchange refers to all the activities that relate to people giving something up in order to receive something they would rather have.

If the above conditions prevail, a market exists, but this does not mean that an exchange will take place. However, these conditions are necessary for exchange to be possible. For example, you may place an advertisement in *Junk Mail* stating that you have a second-hand iPad Mini for sale at a certain price. Several people may call to enquire about it, some may want to see if it is in a good condition, and others may even make you an offer. Unless you reach an agreement with a buyer and actually sell the iPad Mini, an exchange will not take place.

When an exchange takes place, certain gaps are created between production and consumption. These are discussed in the next section.

Gaps between production and consumption

The place where a product is produced is not necessarily the place where it is consumed, and this causes gaps in the marketing process. Identifying these gaps can be described as core marketing aspects.

Figure 1.1 Core marketing aspects[2]

EXPLANATIONS

Gaps in the marketing process are caused because the place where a product is produced is not necessarily the place where it is consumed. For example, Apple Inc. products are designed in California and assembled in China. These products then have to be shipped from the manufacturing country to other countries, such as South Africa, which will only receive them two to three months after the initial launch in America.

Core marketing aspects identify the gaps that exist in the marketing process.

Figure 1.1 shows that the core marketing aspects are linked, with each aspect building on the one before it.

The gaps as indicated in the marketing process are in essence the interval between the needs of the consumer and the end product to satisfy those needs. In the process of satisfying customer needs, other gaps also need to be filled. For example, let us look at somebody who wants to buy a new laptop. Although the existing laptop may still be 100% functional, the new model offers features such as Windows 8 and has USB3.0, which allows for a faster and top-of-the-range operating system. These advanced features create the need or desire for a new laptop. For this reason an exchange – money – takes place. The gaps that can be identified here lie in the technological development of the product, features, size, transport of the product, availability in colour range, etc.

The successful marketing of a suitable market offering is possible only if all the gaps in the process have been effectively bridged. According to Cant, Van Heerden and Ngambi[3], five types of gaps may be distinguished:

- **Space gap**. Companies such as I&J have other companies catching fish for them all over the world in all the oceans. Their customers are, however, not limited to those living at the coast, but are all over the country. I&J will have processing plans at various strategic places at the coast but still needs to distribute its products throughout South Africa, therefore a geographical space (distance) exists between the manufacturer and the consumer.
- **Time gap**. Apples are seasonal fruit that can only be grown and harvested in the summer months. In order for apples to be available the whole year round, distributors have to keep large numbers in cold storage, or the fruit needs to be processed and canned so that it is available to consumers at any time of the year. The same applies to maize and most other products we buy on the shelves out of season.
- **Information gap**. In order for consumers to be able to buy or use a product or service, they need to know about it. If a new hotel were to open in Cape Town, for example, it would be necessary to advertise it and what it offers in order to attract customers.
- **Ownership gap**. Once the consumer has paid for a new product, the ownership gap is bridged. When the consumer pays Edgars R350 for a pair of jeans, for example, he or she becomes the owner of the product. For large purchases the consumer may require finance from a bank (for example for a house or car) in order to become the owner.
- **Value gap**. The seller and buyer must agree about an acceptable exchange rate (price of the product) when conducting business. If, for example, the consumer regards the price of R350 for the jeans as too high, he or she will not buy them. This implies that the buyer and seller do not attach the same value to the product. If a product is purchased, this means that both the buyer and the seller attach the same value to it.

Historically, the increasing gap between the buyer and the seller resulted in the development of an acceptable medium of exchange which symbolised the value (or price) of bartered products. This enabled participants to exchange products not for other products of equal value, but rather for the acceptable medium of exchange (gold coins or other forms of payment).

Transporting products and conveying information became increasingly complicated over time, creating an opportunity for the specialised services of *middlemen*. These persons acted as go-betweens to participants who were no longer in close contact. They were paid for their trouble by means of an acceptable exchange medium. The first middlemen were probably hawkers who traded in a variety of products and also conveyed vital information about potential markets and desirable new products. The participants in these activities were the *seller, middleman* and *buyer*.

The activities intended to bridge the gap between buyer and seller usually involve intermediaries, of which there are three main kinds:

- **Middlemen** are those businesses that bring the producer and user together in the marketing channel.[4] Clicks, for example, acts as a middleman for various brands and products, such as Pantene, Garnier, L'Oréal and Revlon, as it offers customers a range of products all under the same roof.
- **Sales intermediaries** are agents who do not take title of products they sell. They provide services to facilitate the sales process, for which they are paid.
- **Auxiliary enterprises** are not directly involved in the transfer of title but provide support services to facilitate the selling process. Examples are Spoornet, advertising agencies and commercial banks.

Without modern society's desire for new and enjoyable things, stagnation and decline are inevitable, and so these desires play a crucial role in economic development. Exchange media, such as paper money, credit cards and eBucks, were developed, and hawkers made way for large wholesalers and retailers to facilitate exchanges between buyers and sellers. Communication media such as the press, radio, television and the Internet helped on a wide front to spread information on the availability of competing products. Because of these developments, services gained in importance. These days there are many specialists offering desirable services instead of products.

There is a big market consisting of people with a wide variety of needs who create a demand for all kinds of need-satisfying products and services. Sellers try to fulfil these needs to satisfy their own needs, which include a profit objective.

Price reflects the value of a specific product to the buyer. The **perceived price** of a product is not only its monetary value, but also includes factors such as the time cost (amount of money that could have been generated in the time spent to attain the product) and emotional cost

DEFINITION

Middlemen
Middlemen refer to individuals who purchase products from producers or suppliers and then sell them to retailers or customers.

DEFINITION

Sales intermediaries
Sales intermediaries are agents, distributors or wholesalers that link producers to other intermediaries or the ultimate buyer, but do not take title of the goods.

DEFINITION

Auxiliary enterprises
Auxiliary enterprises provide support services to facilitate the selling process and are not directly involved in the transfer of title.

DEFINITION

Price
Price reflects the value of a specific product to the buyer.

DEFINITION

Perceived price
The perceived price of a product is not only its monetary value, but also includes factors such as the time cost and emotional cost.

CASE STUDY

@126[5]
@126 is a professional services company specialising in branded design, combining strategic input, interior and architectural design with a keen business outlook. We are presently operational and active in South Africa, Nigeria, Germany, Kenya and Tanzania. Having worked extensively in South Africa, Nigeria and Kenya, @126 has established excellent working relationships with these areas. Our approach is international in quality and pan-African in appropriateness – delivering world-class solutions that are relevant, impactful and successful in their respective environments. The company started as a one-man business in 1994. The challenges and lack of experience in such a small business led to it being shelved for six years and reborn in 2004, with a new identity, shareholders and vision.

(the emotional exertion the consumer had to go through to obtain the product, for example frustration with an unprofessional shop assistant), among others. Today, the consumer does not simply buy a physical object: he or she buys a market offering which combines the physical object with other need-satisfying qualities. Consumers who, for example, pay a premium price for a Porsche or a Ferrari pay not only for a means of transportation, but also for the status connected to those particular brands.

To fill the gaps created by the exchange process, certain actions or activities must take place. We will look at these marketing activities in the next section.

Marketing activities[6]

Marketing activities can be grouped into three categories, namely primary, auxiliary and exchange activities.

The primary or most basic marketing activity is that of *transport*. Transportation has evolved from using donkeys and camels as a means of travel to include pipelines and land, water and air traffic, each with its own unique advantages and disadvantages. The main aim or focus of transport is to ensure that the product is delivered to the consumer in the quickest and safest way possible.

Auxiliary marketing activities refer to those additional activities that are required in the marketing process, and include the following:

- **Sourcing and supplying information**. The seller must know who and where potential buyers are. This information can be obtained by conducting marketing research. Thereafter the seller can supply information to potential buyers by using marketing communication methods such as advertising and personal selling.
- **Standardisation and grading**. To close the gap between seller and buyer, manufactured products must be designed to conform to specific norms or standards. Agricultural products are graded according to certain qualities. Meat, for instance, is graded according to the quality and tenderness of the cut, and there are grades AAA, ABAB, and so on. Accommodation establishments are graded according to their quality, facilities and services by means of a star-grading approach. This method of standardisation and grading facilitates the buying process, and makes it easier for the buyer to distinguish between the ever-increasing varieties of products available.
- **Storage**. This is an activity that closes the time gap. The seasonal aspect of agricultural products necessitates storage to ensure a regular supply of these products throughout the year. Warehouses are normally used for storage. For example, maize is stored in silos from where it is delivered to milling companies as needed for distribution of milled products to wholesalers and retailers.

- **Financing**. Costs are incurred in the transfer of products and services from sellers to buyers. These costs must be financed, usually by banks and other financial institutions. All the participants in the exchange process should strive to keep financing costs down so that the product can be offered to the consumer at a viable price.
- **Risk taking**. The owner of the product is exposed to the risk of loss or damage, and can take out insurance as a form of protection against risks such as arson or theft.

The exchange marketing activities are *buying* and *selling*. Ownership is transferred from one person to the other. An organisation's buying activities are not regarded as a marketing task, but rather as the responsibility of the purchasing department. Selling, on the other hand, is an extremely important task of the marketing department of any organisation. Over the years these marketing activities have, however, been influenced by the prevailing marketing orientation of the time. We will look at the different marketing orientations in the next section.

DEFINITION

Marketing activities
Marketing activities can be defined as those activities used to transfer the market offering to the buyer.

'Marketing activities fall into three categories: primary, auxiliary and exchange activities.'

Marketing orientations[7]

Since the days of Henry Ford, to whom the saying that 'a customer can have any colour car as long as it's black' is attributed, the approach to marketing and consumers has changed. Years ago, management did not realise the importance of actively marketing a business's products and/or services. Over time, however, different approaches to marketing developed and each one resulted in a reorientation of management thinking. This can be described as an evolution in marketing thinking. The phases in this evolution process are characterised by different *marketing management philosophies*, which are also referred to as *alternative marketing concepts*.

DEFINITION

Production concept
The production concept holds that consumers will favour products that are available and highly affordable.

Production concept[8]

From the early 1900s, most businesses were focused on production or had a **production orientation**. This means that they were of the opinion that they just needed to produce their products at a reasonable price and in sufficient quantities, and the market would accept and buy them.[9] The focus was therefore mainly on producing or manufacturing the products as efficiently as possible. Products were mass produced by machines in factories. Managers were concerned about solutions to production problems and spent all their time on efforts to facilitate these processes.

As the central notion of the production era was that products would sell themselves, and the major concern of businesses was production rather than marketing, the needs of consumers were largely ignored by businesses. Marketers got away with this largely due to the lack of competition and the high demand for products at the time.

> **DEFINITION**
>
> **Sales orientation**
> A sales orientation focuses on the selling of products and services, rather than on whether or not they are actually needed.

'The exchange marketing activities are buying and selling. Ownership is transferred from one person to the other.'

'The marketing concept can be regarded as an ethical code or management philosophy according to which the tasks of the business are performed. According to this philosophy, a business aims all its efforts at satisfying customer needs and wants – at a profit.'[12]

During the production era, consumers were relatively poor and unsophisticated. They bought new products whenever they could afford to do so. This led to a situation where the supply exceeded the demand, and gradually stocks began piling up, causing management to realise the importance of stimulating demand to dispose of the stockpile. The result was a change in management thinking and the start of the era of sales orientation.

Sales orientation

When businesses started realising that they could produce more products than their consumers could consume, competition became more significant, and the problems related to reaching the market became more complex. Management came to realise that it was not only about producing but also about selling. This led to the focus being shifted from production to selling – that is, persuading consumers to purchase the products.[10] In sales-oriented businesses, advertisements are placed to inform consumers of the availability of products, while sales representatives promote products by means of direct personal contact. Often, a 'hard-sell approach' (selling at any cost) is used.

The main aim of businesses during the sales era was to maximise sales volume – that is, to sell as much as possible at just about any cost. Profitability was not a major concern. The basic assumption was that sales volume was the key to profitability – the higher the sales, the higher the profit. This obviously was not true as higher sales may incur higher costs, bringing economies of scale into play and resulting in a lower profit!

The marketing concept

For most businesses, the sales era continued until at least 1950. By then, sales were growing rapidly in most areas of the economy. Consumers developed more sophisticated needs and were in a better financial position to satisfy them. There was also a variety of competing products from which they could choose, which led management to realise the importance of the **marketing function**. A change from the sales era to the marketing era resulted in an emphasis not only on the sales message and the price, but also on the quality of products, their packaging, the methods of distribution and the necessity of providing information by means of marketing communication. The marketing concept can be defined as a managerial philosophy that an organisation should focus on meeting the needs of customers (customer orientation or focus), and ensure that all departments and people in the organisation are focused on satisfying these needs (systems orientation or integrated approach), and in the process make a profit (profit orientation). The marketing concept emphasises that marketing begins and ends with the customer.[11] Added to this is a fourth component, namely that the organisation should also consider the community in which it operates – that is, it has a social responsibility to uplift the community.

The essence of the marketing concept lies in four principles, namely customer orientation, profit orientation, systems orientation and social responsibility.

Customer orientation

Customer orientation, the first principle of the marketing concept, indicates that all actions should be aimed at satisfying customer needs and wants. We used to say that customer orientation means that 'the customer is king', but the customer is not always king. The customer can be seen as a dictator. The aim of a business must be to delight the customer. In customer-oriented businesses, the requirements of customers come first. Customers are the focal point of decision making, and all other functional areas (operations, human resources, financing, research and development, and so on) are geared towards satisfying their needs and wants. Customer-oriented businesses do not consider the marketing task to be complete once a sale has been made. Such businesses provide after-sales service. They check on how satisfied customers are with the product or service and what can be done to enhance that satisfaction. Current customer-oriented businesses concentrate on maintaining contact with the customer, providing quality, ensuring customer satisfaction and retaining customers.

Research has shown that increased customer delight, and ultimately customer loyalty, result in higher profits, company growth and greater investor commitment, as well as increased employee satisfaction. Customers who rate the service provided by a business as good only, and are therefore merely satisfied, are easily persuaded to switch to a competitor.

A business should therefore examine the expectations of the consumer and compare them to the consumer's perception of the value received. The consumer will be delighted only if the perception of the value received exceeds expectations. Customer satisfaction can be measured by means of Customer Delight Audits (CDA) or the Customer Satisfaction Index (CSI). These measurements have demonstrated that 5 % or more customers returning each year can boost profits by 35 % and higher.[13]

Profit orientation

The marketing concept views customer orientation as a means of achieving the goals of the business – that is, the goal of making profit. By providing market offerings that satisfy customer needs and wants, the business will be able to achieve its own profit goals as well. These goals can be expressed in many ways, for example achieving a rate of return of 24 % on investment, achieving a specified increase in profitable volume of sales, or by increasing market share from 12 to 14 %.

A good example of a profit-oriented strategy business is Harley-Davidson. This world-renowned brand has fiercely loyal customers and a reputation for quality. This allows the company to set pricing based on desired profit margin rather than relying on sales designed to increase volume or matching its competitor's pricing.[14]

DEFINITION

Marketing concept
The marketing concept can be defined as a managerial philosophy that an organisation should focus on meeting the needs of customers (customer orientation or focus), ensure that all departments and people in the organisation are focused on satisfying them (systems orientation or integrated approach), and in the process make a profit (profit orientation).

DEFINITION

Customer orientation
Customer orientation is the focus on meeting all the needs and desires of customers by acting and performing in a manner that will satisfy them.

Example

Sales-oriented businesses

- Managers of some mail-order businesses are still sales oriented. They advertise products that are, in fact, not readily available or are not worth the quoted price.
- Door-to-door sales have acquired a bad reputation because some salespeople do not allow consumers enough time to make responsible decisions. These salespeople, who are very good communicators, can easily persuade consumers to make hasty decisions. For these businesses, sales are the major consideration.
- A political party will vigorously sell its candidate to voters as the right person for the job. A great deal of money is spent on radio and television advertising, posters and mailings. The candidate's flaws are hidden from the public because the aim is to obtain the 'sale' (the vote), rather than worrying about whether 'customers' (voters) are satisfied with their 'purchase' (putting this person into a position of power).

WWW:

Walmart aims to provide customers around the world with higher-quality products and lower prices to enable them to live a better life. Walmart focuses on putting the needs of customers first by following a customer-oriented strategy.

- http://corporate.walmart.com/

Systems orientation (organisational integration)

A system is an integrated whole – a group of units that work together to achieve a joint objective. Systems orientation is also known as *organisational integration*. In a typical business 35 years ago, operations managers thought mainly about manufacturing a new or improved product. Financial people looked after the cash position of the business, and salespeople were mainly concerned with obtaining orders. Each department thought of its own activity as the centre of the business, and people were not concerned with the whole system as long as the business made a profit.

Ideally, all departments should work together to achieve the successful marketing of the market offering of the business. In other words, the efforts of personnel in the different functional areas, such as marketing, research and development, manufacturing and finance, should be coordinated and integrated.

The systems orientation implies that the activities of the business should be coordinated to satisfy customer needs and wants, and to achieve a satisfactory rate of return on investment.

Social responsibility

Social responsibility is a concept that maintains that businesses are part of the larger society in which they exist and are accountable to society for their performance. Marketers should strike a balance between targeted customers' needs and wants, customers' long-term best interests, society's long-term best interests, and the long-term financial goals of the business.

Businesses often demonstrate social responsibility by spending large sums of money on projects contributing to the wellbeing of the community at large, instead of being concerned only with their target markets.

Social responsibility does not only involve external groups such as the public. The business also has a social responsibility towards the welfare of its employees. Social responsibility programmes for employees include housing, health programmes and care centres for their babies and toddlers.

Social responsibility also means that the business will abstain from any action in conflict with current norms and moral or ethical standards. Contravention of the norms of society can result in the loss of goodwill and consumer resistance.

In the new millennium, environmental issues have become more important. There is a belief that life on earth is threatened by the activities of manufacturers polluting the soil, water and air. **Green marketing** is a further example of social responsibility marketing. Many businesses are using environmental terms such as 'environmentally friendly', 'biodegradable' and 'recyclable' in their advertising campaigns. For example, Nedbank has established the *Going Green* initiative where clients can choose whether to donate towards the protection of biodiversity and the promotion of nature conservation in South Africa

(The Green Trust); the development of sports in underprivileged areas (The Sports Trust); the promotion and preservation of South Africa's artistic and multicultural heritage (Arts and Culture Trust) or the Nelson Mandela Children Fund. Nedbank also initiated an internal *Green Strategy*, where employees aim to reduce their carbon footprint in their everyday operations.

All four principles of the marketing concept must be applied in a balanced manner. If these principles are ignored, success can be achieved only in the short term. Sooner or later, problems will be encountered and these may even lead to the demise of the business. A business that ignores the principles of the marketing concept is not customer focused and market driven. The application of the marketing concept will have an advantageous influence on the business as a whole.

Relationship marketing

A broader view of the market

Relationship marketing is a logical development in the gradual evolution of marketing thinking. Relationship marketing places its main focus on the maintenance of long-term relationships between the organisation, the government, the public, the suppliers of raw materials, the employees, and current and potential consumers.

All the efforts of an organisation should be geared towards building these relationships. This is crucial for survival and growth, especially in an economic decline, and to protect its competitive position.

Relationship marketing represents a broader view of the market and the marketing task, and evolved because of consumers' need for honest and open communication from management, and not just lip service to the marketing concept.

Expansion of the market offering

Relationship marketing acknowledges that different marketing strategies must be used for consumer acquisition and retention.[15] Relationship marketing implies that the four marketing instruments (product, place, promotion and price) alone are inadequate to ensure full consumer satisfaction, and that there is more to marketing than just these elements. The aim should be on the establishment of a relationship with customers and in this way ensure loyalty and long-term profitability.[16] The authors therefore conclude that two further variables must be added to the four marketing instruments, namely *people* and *processes*.

The **people** are the employees who should be well trained in customer service, and who must realise that their own job satisfaction ultimately rests on the success of the organisation in the market. **Processes** are integral parts of the production, administration and marketing functions.

Synergy means that the whole is more than the sum of its parts. When all the variables support each other, they reinforce the quality image of the product. The TQM principle underlies relationship marketing: TQM refers to 'total quality management', which in principle strives

Example E

Social responsibility

- By sponsoring the development, funding, conservation and relocation of rhinos, hippos and elephants in the Kruger National Park, Total succeeded in establishing its brand in the market as a brand that cares for the environment.
- By sponsoring Takalani Sesame, Sanlam shows its commitment to the development and upliftment of proper education in South Africa.
- By sponsoring the Orange African Cup of Nations, Orange African Youth Championships, Orange CAF Confederation Cup and Champions League, Standard Bank has established itself as a brand that cares for sports and its development in South Africa.

towards consumer satisfaction. However, this can only be an ideal of perfection and is closely related to the corporate culture where everybody must make an effort to realise this ideal.

A bigger market

Relationship marketing also entails a wider view of the market itself. In the total market there are various smaller groupings, all with a greater or lesser influence on the marketing effort. These groupings include, among others, current and potential customers, as well as suppliers. Close relationships, especially with the important groupings, must be maintained.

Even though relationship marketing implies a wider view of the market, it also requires that companies adapt to an individual customer approach once they have finalised their exact market. Relationship marketing is different from traditional marketing in the sense that it entails a company building a long-term relationship with its customers in order to generate loyalty and repeat purchases. Organisations are adapting to *micro-segmentation* because of three important changes that have rendered traditional segment-based marketing inappropriate. These changes are as follows:

- Consumers are more sophisticated and knowledgeable, which means that they have higher expectations.
- Technology has changed dramatically.
- Competition between vendors and products is increasing.

A change in company focus is evident in the explosion of a recent trend to market for a segment consisting of one consumer. One example is the use of a mass-customisation approach by companies who cater for the individual needs of consumers through the use of new technology. Adidas, for example, allows for customers to take a photo of themselves and to place it on their website, and then fit their clothes and shoes to the image to assist them in evaluating how the product will look on them.

Handling customer complaints is an important facet of an internal marketing programme. Some car manufacturers have a customer care number with a direct line to the managing director. It is important for companies to research the reasons for complaints. The best and cheapest solution is to ensure that there are no complaints – well-founded ones must receive immediate attention. There must be ample opportunity for customers to direct complaints to responsible people who are able to take appropriate corrective action, and in so doing prevent the loss of customers.

Consumers who are reluctant to complain but tend rather to avoid the unsatisfactory product or situation in future are a grave threat to successful marketing. Consumers who are unhappy and who receive no satisfaction can also direct their complaints to the many consumer action programmes in the mass media (for example *Hellopeter* or the

DEFINITION

Green marketing

Green marketing is the promotion of products and services based on environmental factors or awareness, and incorporates a broad range of activities (such as product modification, changes to the production process, packaging changes, alternative distribution methods and modifying advertisements), which are aimed at taking advantage of the changing consumer attitudes towards a brand. Green marketing focuses on the environmentally friendly marketing efforts businesses use, such as corporate social responsibility plans and sustainability efforts.

Example

Green marketing

- Green labels on products indicate that the products and packaging are environmentally friendly.
- Businesses often sponsor campaigns such as 'Save the Seals' or National Tree Planting Day.
- Incredible Connection advertises that it recycles empty cartridges, old printers, computers, scanners, etc.
- Mondi collects paper and cardboard from residential areas and corporations for recycling.

Continue to next page

'Consumer Watch' column in *The Star*), thereby causing unwelcome negative publicity for the organisation.

Relationship marketing is, in fact, the essence of a market-driven approach to marketing management. It was mentioned previously that marketing philosophy is an evolutionary process which will probably continue, necessitating further adaptations in marketing thinking.

Example E

Continued from previous page

- Collect-a-Can was created in order to ensure that all used beverage cans exist in harmony with the environment.

CASE STUDY i

Discovery – Corporate social investment[17]

Discovery is committed to contributing to the socioeconomic growth of South Africa, making it a better place to live for all inhabitants. As a national asset, healthcare is an area in which Discovery helps to make a difference. The company's corporate social investment projects focus on building an infrastructure that will strengthen South Africa's healthcare system over the long term, and will help make more communities healthier. The following are merely some of the social investment initiatives Discovery has implemented:

- The Discovery Fund was established in 1999, and R800 000 was contributed towards helping poor communities in the public healthcare sector.
- In 2011, more than R40 million was earmarked to help expand healthcare delivery in South Africa. The Discovery Foundation was established to assist in the education and training of medical specialists and the development of academic and research centres.
- Discovery has contributed to academic and clinical research and sub-specialist training in a range of medical disciplines.
- The Discovery Employee Volunteer Programme enables Discovery employees and other stakeholders to support the company's project. Employees take part in national initiatives and also commit to long-term involvement with community projects.

The marketing process[18]

After discussing the general marketing aspects above, we now need to explore what the marketing process entails. This involves a number of issues that have to be addressed, based on the needs of the market and the objectives of the organisation. There are primarily four variables about which the marketing management team has to take decisions: the *product* itself, the *place* where it is to be sold (distribution of the product), *promotion* (the marketing communication methods to be used to inform the consumer) and the *price* of the product, which should reflect its value to the consumer. These four variables combine in a market offering, which the consumer may decide to buy if it satisfies his or her needs.

The so-called four Ps of marketing (product, place, promotion/marketing communication and price) are also known as the *marketing instruments* or the *marketing mix*. Decisions regarding the four marketing instruments combine to form part of an integrated *marketing strategy* (or marketing plan). The marketing strategy for a specific market offering is directed at a group of consumers in a specific environment.

The larger the company's target market, the more advantageous it usually is for the manufacturer and the intermediaries. In the total consumer market there are many different groups. The members of each of these groups (also called *market segments*) have more or less similar characteristics, needs and product preferences. After careful consideration, the marketing management team selects a specific *target market* (or markets) from many different market segments. The market offering is often changed in some way or another to meet the

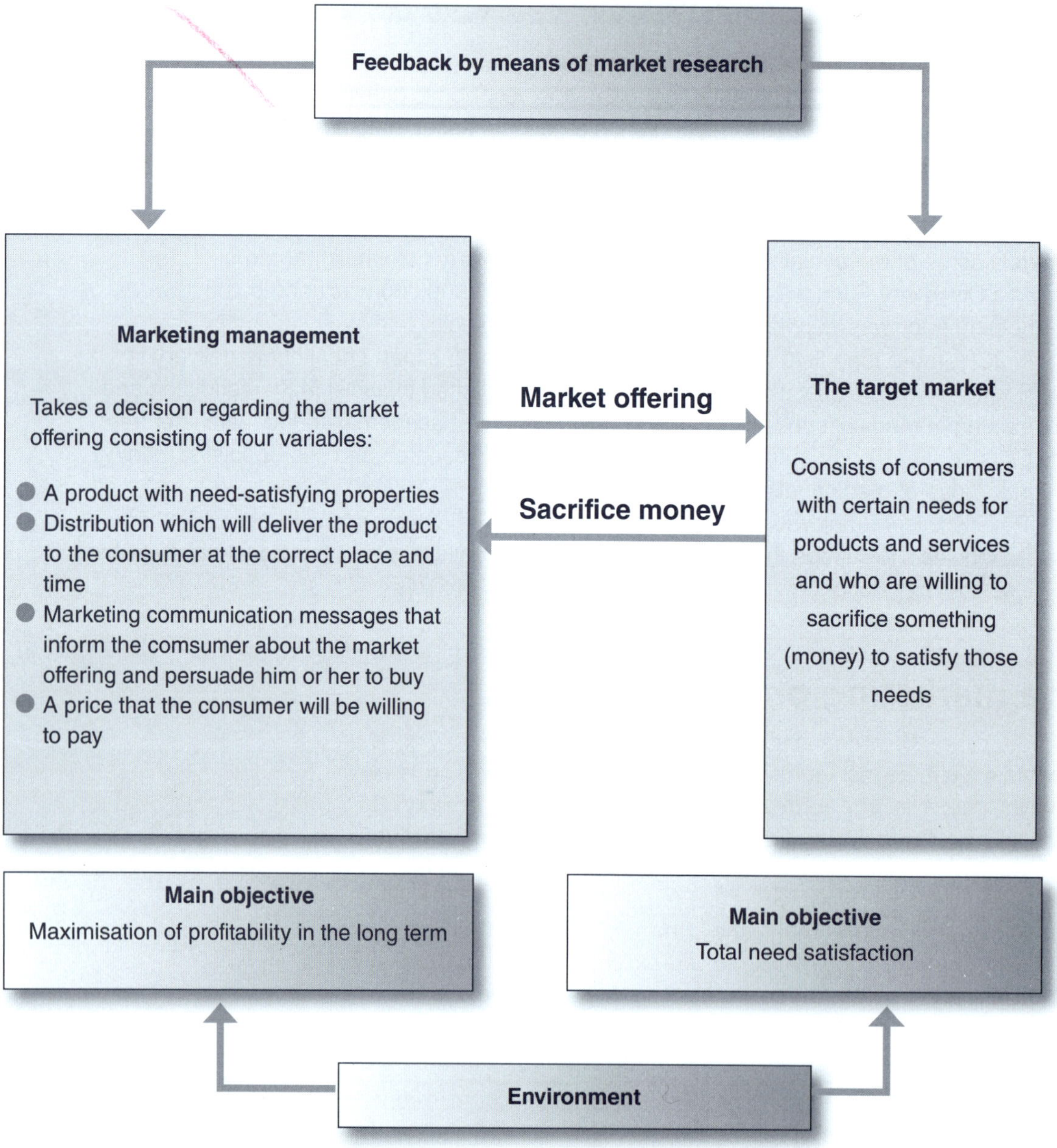

Figure 1.2 The marketing process[19]

preferences of different target markets. It seldom happens that an organisation has only one single target market. Recent trends in marketing have introduced new concepts such as mass customisation, e-marketing and e-tailing, which imply that the Internet can be used to develop a marketing strategy for a single consumer or, in other words, markets of one.

There are usually also a number of competitors marketing similar products and competing for the patronage of the same target markets. Market offerings often differ only slightly from one another, perhaps only in the fact that they have different brand names. Consumers select – and purchase repeatedly – those brand names that afford them the greatest need satisfaction in terms of the sacrifice that they must make. Often, the sacrifice is not only in monetary terms; sometimes consumers are also willing to suffer some degree of inconvenience to obtain the desired brand name product. It is important to place the marketing function as performed in a modern organisation in the correct perspective.

The marketing function in the organisation[20]

The place of the marketing function

At least seven different functional departments can be identified in today's large organisations of which the marketing function can be regarded as a key function due to its contribution to profit and its closeness to the consumer. The managers heading these seven departments must work together to realise the organisation's objectives and goals. Figure 1.3 shows a typical functional organisational structure.

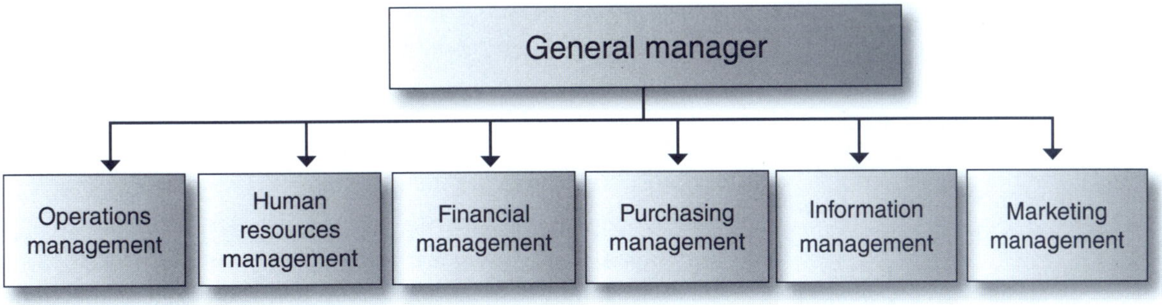

Figure 1.3 Functional organisational structure

The functions of these departments are as follows:

- The **operations function** comprises the physical utilisation of raw materials and their conversion into manufactured materials and finished products, and is usually performed in a factory.
- The **human resources (HR) function** involves the acquisition, training, utilisation and retention of a sufficient number of competent personnel.
- The **financial function** includes the acquisition, utilisation and control of the funds necessary for running the business. The main

Example

Instances of poor customer service

- Ignoring customers and rather talking to friends or colleagues.
- Sales personnel with an uninterested or condescending attitude, or those who make the customer feel unwelcome in any way.
- Employees who are unhelpful or incompetent.
- Failure to deliver on promises or not keeping the customer informed.
- Inadequate or incorrect information in advertising messages.
- Receptionists who are unwilling or unable to handle telephone enquiries.
- Personnel in banks and other services organisations drinking and eating in full view of long queues of people.
- Appointments not kept on time.
- Employees being overly friendly with customers.

There are many other examples of poor customer service, some of which can be regarded as blatantly dishonest, such as padding repair costs. Disreputable acts like these are not marketing and therefore not worthy of discussion in this book.

activities here are the acquisition and application of funds for the profitability, liquidity, solvency and continuity of the organisation.

- The **purchasing function** ensures that the materials necessary for production are bought at the right places, at the right times, in the right quantities and at the right prices.
- The **public relations function** maintains and cultivates a favourable and objective image of the organisation among those whose opinion is important to the achievement of the business objectives.
- The **information function** makes available internal information for planning and control.
- The **marketing function** generates income from sales, and is responsible for managing the marketing process.
- **General management** includes the activities of persons in managerial positions. These persons in top, middle and lower management have to plan for, organise, lead and control the organisation as a whole, as well as its individual functions. The general manager is at the head of the management team.

In practice, there are also other functions and structures, and other names may be used. It is important, however, to realise that the tasks of the different functional departments are performed in both large and small organisations. The resources (capital) and abilities of various functionaries determine the existence and size of formal departments.

In very large multi-product organisations, there can even be more divisions than those shown in Figure 1.3. For example, there may be a marketing director controlling several marketing managers for different products or product ranges. The marketing director provides leadership, and coordinates the activities of several different marketing departments. There are also many different organisational structures that can be identified, of which the functional structure is only one example. Examples of different organisational structures include the matrix structure, and the line and staff structure.

What does a manager do? The workers tend to think that managers spend their working hours sitting and talking while there is real work to be done! In the next section, we will look at the three management tasks that must be performed by the management team.

Management tasks in marketing

On their website, the American Marketing Association describes marketing management as 'the process of setting marketing goals for an organisation (considering internal resources and market opportunities), the planning and execution of activities to meet these goals, and measuring progress toward their achievement'. They also note that this is an ongoing and repetitive process within the planning cycle to enable an organisation to continuously adapt to internal and external changes in the organisation's environment.[21] These changes continuously create new problems and new opportunities, thus, with effective management, an organisation can stay ahead of its competition by using changes in the company environment to its advantage.

The management task, therefore, consists of a continuous process of *planning, organising, leading* and *controlling* marketing activities.

Marketing management:

- identifies opportunities and threats in the marketing environment;
- identifies those opportunities which can be used in terms of internal strengths and weaknesses;
- compiles marketing data;
- chooses a specific target market;
- decides on the products to be produced to satisfy consumer needs;
- decides on the selling price of the product to attain the objective of profitability;
- decides on specific distribution channels;
- decides on marketing communication methods whereby consumers are informed, reminded and persuaded;
- decides on the selection, training, remuneration and motivation of marketing personnel;
- organises and leads activities of the marketing department; and
- controls the marketing process.

These responsibilities are part of the three management tasks which are summarised in Figure 1.4 and discussed below.

WWW:
Visit the American Marketing Association website for more information.
- http://www.ama.org

DEFINITION

Adaptive planning
Adaptive planning is an iterative process framework for organising numerous information flows, analyses, issues and opinions that leads to joint strategic decisions.

Planning

Planning by marketing management entails examining and choosing between various ways of using marketing opportunities, countering marketing threats, and achieving marketing objectives. **Adaptive planning** is a framework for organising information, analysis, issues and opinions that form part of strategic decision making. A situation assessment is done to identify the internal and external factors impacting

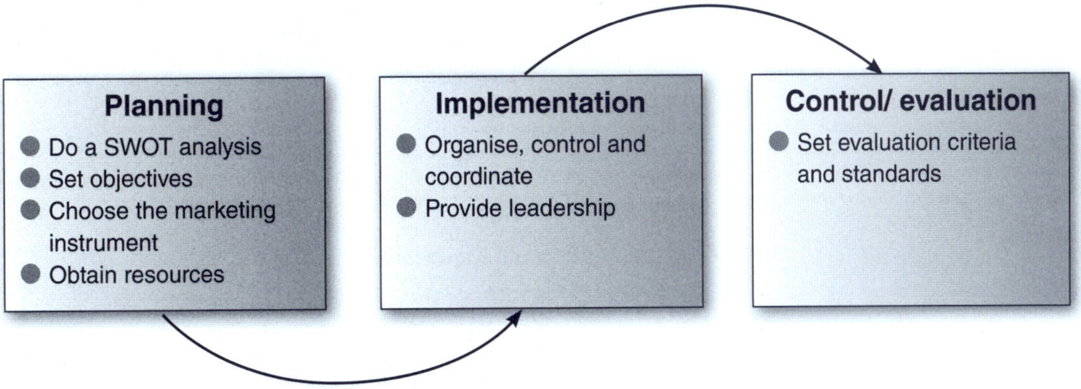

Figure 1.4 The management task of marketing managers

the organisation, as well as the organisation's past performance concerning these factors. The next step is to conceptualise creative and strategic solutions to address these factors. Marketing decisions thus begin with the identification and evaluation of marketing opportunities and threats, and internal strengths and weaknesses.

Contingency planning is another subdivision of planning that entails developing plans to provide an alternative to the main plan in the event that an unlikely, but possible, external factor impacts on the original plan. It is the 'what will we do if ...' of planning. The contingency plan 'deals not with unforeseen events, but with events that were foreseen but considered unlikely to occur'.[22] For example, caterers always cater for a higher number than was specified in case, for example, more people arrive than were expected, or a waiter drops a plate while serving, etc.

> **DEFINITION**
>
> **Contingency planning**
>
> Contingency planning is a plan devised for an outcome other than the expected plan. Contingency planning therefore entails the development of plans to provide an alternative to the main plan in the event that a dubious, but possible, external factor impacts on the original plan.

Organising

Organising and **coordinating** call for the creation of an organisational structure best suited to the implementation of the marketing decisions to achieve marketing objectives. Marketing activities are grouped rationally, and individual divisions and managers are tasked with carrying them out. Finally, the levels of authority, areas of responsibility, lines of communication and methods of coordination between the divisions and individuals are determined. Cooperation is achieved by integrating the interests of divisions, individuals, consumers, investors, suppliers and the community as a whole.

Figure 1.3 shows a typical organisational chart of the different divisions in an organisation under the leadership of the general manager.

Leading

Leading involves a wide range of tasks, such as staffing, communicating and motivating. From a marketing viewpoint, leading embraces all the marketing decisions for putting preparation (planning, organising, coordinating, controlling) into practice. Briefly, once the marketing strategy has been formulated, people have to be found to perform the required marketing activities (staffing); they have to be instructed as to what they should do and told how well they are doing it (communicating); and a positive attitude towards work and the organisation must be carefully cultivated and maintained (motivating). Leading is therefore of paramount importance in the effective performance of the other management tasks.

> **DEFINITION**
>
> **Leading**
>
> Leading involves a wide range of tasks, such as recruitment, communicating and motivating.

> **DEFINITION**
>
> **Controlling or evaluation**
>
> The purpose of controlling or evaluation is to align actual performance with marketing plans.

Over time a few contemporary leadership styles have emerged. These include the following:[23]

- **Contingent reward leadership** is a leadership style where management closely supervises the personnel, and facilitates all staff activities and tasks.
- ***Laissez-faire* leadership** is the opposite of contingent reward leadership in that management is minimally involved in the daily

activities of personnel, leaving them to manage their own activities and tasks.

- **Management-by-exception leadership** is a leadership style where managers intervene only when personnel's performance standards have not been met.
- **In transformational leadership**, leaders use inspiration and charisma, they seek to stimulate the sales personnel intellectually, and they treat each employee as an individual. The ultimate goal of transformational leadership is to move personnel beyond their own self-interest toward that of the organisation

Controlling

Controlling or evaluation is the regulatory task of marketing management, and its purpose is to align actual performance with marketing plans. In order to exercise control, it is essential first to set standards; this requires determination of what has to be controlled and where marketing control is necessary. Secondly, actual marketing performance has to be measured and compared with these standards. Thirdly, the differences between actual performance and standards have to be evaluated. Finally, if necessary, corrective measures should be taken to ensure that future performance is in line with marketing plans.

If the marketing management tasks are not properly performed:

- purchasing management will not know which raw materials and components to purchase;
- public relations management will not know how to perform or improve its liaison function;
- financial management will not know how much funding is required; and
- human resources management will not know how many people to employ.

Summary

A business does not operate in isolation, and many factors contribute to a company's success. Marketing is a managerial process aimed at satisfying the needs and wants of customers. These needs and wants are met by creating the correct products and services.

Marketing operates within a dynamic global environment and is constantly facing new challenges. The success of the marketing concept is now widely understood, spurring growth in non-profit marketing as these organisations begin using the tools and techniques of marketing management. The environment is changing as well, with almost every company being affected by rapid globalisation. The changing world economy, which went into recession in late 2008 and was still struggling in 2013, has resulted in more difficult times for both consumers and marketers. These challenges are intensified by demands that marketers conduct all their business with stronger emphasis on ethics and social responsibility. Taken together, these changes define a new marketing landscape. Companies that succeed in such an environment will have a strong focus on the changing marketplace and a total commitment to using the tools of marketing to provide real value to customers.[24]

References

1. Lamb, C.W., Hair, J.F. & McDaniel, C.D. 2011. *Essentials of marketing*. 7th ed. USA: Cengage, pp. 3–4.
2. Adapted from Cant, M.C. 2010. *Marketing: An introduction*. Cape Town, South Africa: Juta & Co., p. 3.
3. Cant, M.C., Van Heerden, C.H. & Ngambi, H.C. 2010. *Marketing management: A South African perspective*. Cape Town, South Africa: Juta & Co., p. 5.
4. Pride, M., Hughes, P.J. & Kapoor, J.R. 2012. *Business*. 11th ed. USA: Cengage, p. 401.
5. Van Heerden, C.H. 2013. *Contemporary retail and marketing case studies*. Cape Town, South Africa: Juta & Co., p. 1.
6. Cant et al., op. cit., p. 6.
7. Lamb, C.W., Hair, J.F. & McDaniel, C. 1998. *Marketing*. 4th ed. Ohio: South-Western College Publishing, p. 4.
8. Cant et al., op. cit., pp. 7–8
9. Shumasaki, C.D. 2009. *The business of bioscience: What goes into making a biotechnology product*. USA: Springer, p. 98. Available from: http://books.google.co.za/books?id=GQe9xozuENUC&pg=PA98&dq=production+concept&hl=en&sa=X&ei=quFjUdODM5KDhQf924CgAw&ved=0CFUQ6AEwBw#v=onepage&q=production%20concept&f=false.
10. Faarup, P.K. 2010. *The marketing framework*. Denmark: Academica, p. 23. Available from: http://books.google.co.za/books?id=kzm5SUVLJX4C&pg=PA24&dq=sales+concept+in+marketing&hl=en&sa=X&ei=e-1jUd72I4a5hAfnwIGYBQ&ved=0CD8Q6AEwAw#v=onepage&q=sales%20concept%20in%20marketing&f=false.
11. Pride, W.M. & Ferrell, O.C. 2012. *Marketing*. 16th ed. USA: Cengage, p. 11.
12. Cant et al., op. cit., p. 8
13. Strydom, J.W. (Ed.). 2004. *Introduction to marketing*. 3rd ed. Cape Town, South Africa: Juta & Co., p. 8.
14. Barten, L. 2013. *Definition of profit-oriented price strategy*. [Online] Available from: http://www.ehow.com/about_6592703_definition-profit_oriented-price-strategy.html [Accessed: 2013-06-07].
15. Du Toit, M. 2011. *Fundamentals of sales and marketing*. Cape Town, South Africa: Juta & Co., p. 9
16. Cant et al., op. cit., p. 10.
17. Adapted from Van Heerden, C.H. 2013. *Contemporary retail and marketing case studies*. Cape Town, South Africa: Juta & Co., pp. 47–48.
18. Van de Walt, A., Strydom, J.W., Marx, J. & Jooste, C.J. 1996. In Cant, M. 2010. *Marketing: an introduction*. Cape Town, South Africa: Juta & Co., p. 12.
19. Taken from: Cant, M.C., Strydom, J.W., Jooste, C.J & Du Plessis, P.J. 2006. *Marketing management*. 5th ed. Cape Town, South Africa: Juta & Co., p. 21.
20. Cant, op. cit., p. 14.
21. American Marketing Association. 2013. Dictionary. [Online] Available from: http://www.marketingpower.com/_layouts/Dictionary.aspx?dLetter=M [Accessed: 2013-04-4].
22. Cant et al., op. cit, p. 25
23. Cant, op. cit., p. 17.
24. Ibid.

The marketing environment of business

CHAPTER 2

✓ Learning objectives

After studying this chapter, you should be able to:

- explain what the components of the micro-environment are;
- indicate how the variables in the market environment will influence the business;
- demonstrate the impact the macro-environment can have on a business; and
- conduct a SWOT analysis.

Introduction

No environment stays the same, and in the business world this is particularly so. The past few years bear testimony to this as the world as a whole has been plunged into a deep economic crisis since 2008. Think about the high price of petrol in South Africa in 2013, when it cost more than R13 per litre. The rand against the dollar fell to record lows and in July 2013 traded at R10,20 to the dollar. The uprisings in many Middle Eastern countries also led to instability in the region, escalating oil prices and other problems. Looking at all these happenings it is easy to understand why the business environment is never static. It is the responsibility of management to be aware of these changes and how they may influence the business. In some instances the impact of certain changes will affect some companies or industries more severely than others.

This environment in which a business operates refers to both the internal and the external factors or variables. Furthermore, this environment is constantly changing, which means that the business has to monitor these variables constantly to determine their impact on the business, its customers and its competitors. Society largely depends on businesses to satisfy its wants and needs. Businesses, on the other hand, depend on their environments to supply them with resources such as labour, capital and raw materials. Businesses and society therefore influence each other through this exchange, and depend on each other for their existence.[1]

This mutual dependence makes it important that businesses establish sound relations with the community, and vice versa. The outside environment is, however, highly complex and the business has little or no control over most of the variables in it.

> **DEFINITION**
>
> **Marketing environment**
> The marketing environment includes various factors that directly or indirectly affect the activities of an organisation in developing and maintaining successful customer relationships with their targeted customer group. These factors should be considered when new products and services are developed.

Components of the marketing environment

The **marketing environment** consists of three sub-environments or components that all influence one another. These are as follows:

- **Micro-environment**. This environment includes all those internal variables that can be controlled by management, such as the staff to be appointed, funds to be used, the mission and the marketing objectives of the organisation.
- **Market environment**. This environment can be influenced or partially controlled by management, and refers to those forces outside the business such as consumers, competitors and suppliers.
- **Macro-environment**. This environment refers to the external forces the individual business has no control over, but which directly or indirectly influence the business, such as economic, political and technological factors.

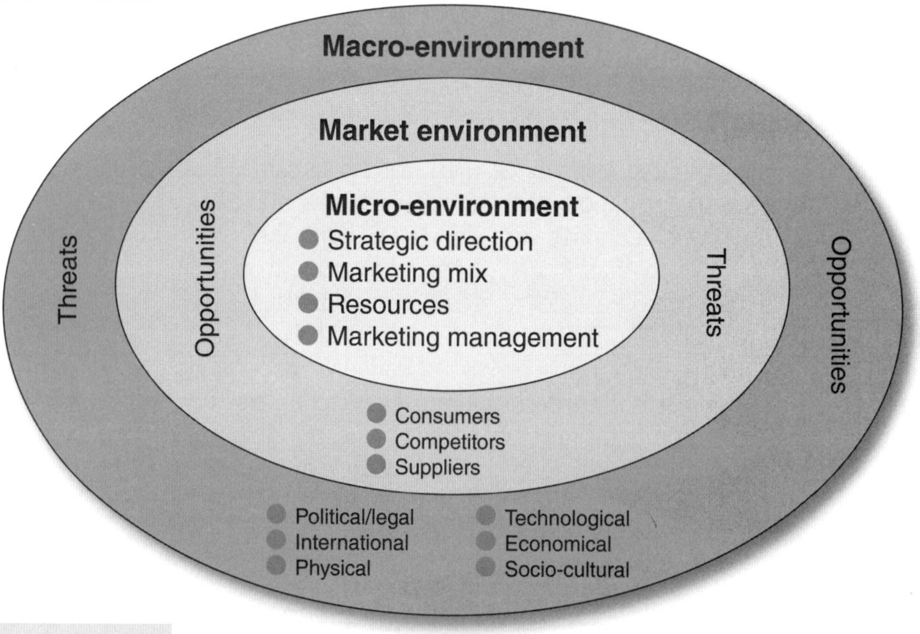

Figure 2.1 The components of the marketing environment

Figure 2.1 shows the major forces that impact on the business and its activities. In order to be successful, the organisation must evaluate the impact and effect changes in these elements will have on the successful operation of the business. It is the task of management to be aware of, evaluate and assess the impact these variables may have on the organisation and to take the necessary steps to steer the business in the right direction. Marketing management should therefore not only look inwards at the micro-environment to identify internal environmental variables, but they should also look outwards to identify external variables. They must understand the effect of such variables on decision making, and conduct a SWOT analysis to determine internal strengths and weaknesses (both internal and in the micro-environment), and external opportunities and threats (in the market and macro-environment).

The variables in the micro-environment

We will begin by defining the **micro-environment**.

The micro-environment refers to those variables the organisation has control over. This, however, does not imply that marketing management on its own exercises direct control over all the variables in the internal environment – this environment is made up of various functional areas and so a number of management members will take decisions regarding these variables and the best way to apply them given the changes in the overall marketing environment. The marketing manager is usually a member of top management and will be able to influence decisions regarding the use of resources. Similarly, the functional heads of finance, human resources, and so on can and will influence decisions of the other functional heads – all based on the aims and goals of the organisation and considering the impact of changes in the overall marketing environment on the business. The marketing manager has direct control only over the activities of the marketing department, and especially marketing instruments. Marketing instruments and activities are therefore under the direct control of the marketing manager. Figure 2.2 lists the internal variables that are the responsibility of the marketing department.

DEFINITION

Micro-environment
The micro-environment can be described as consisting of those elements in the organisation over which the organisation has control or influence.

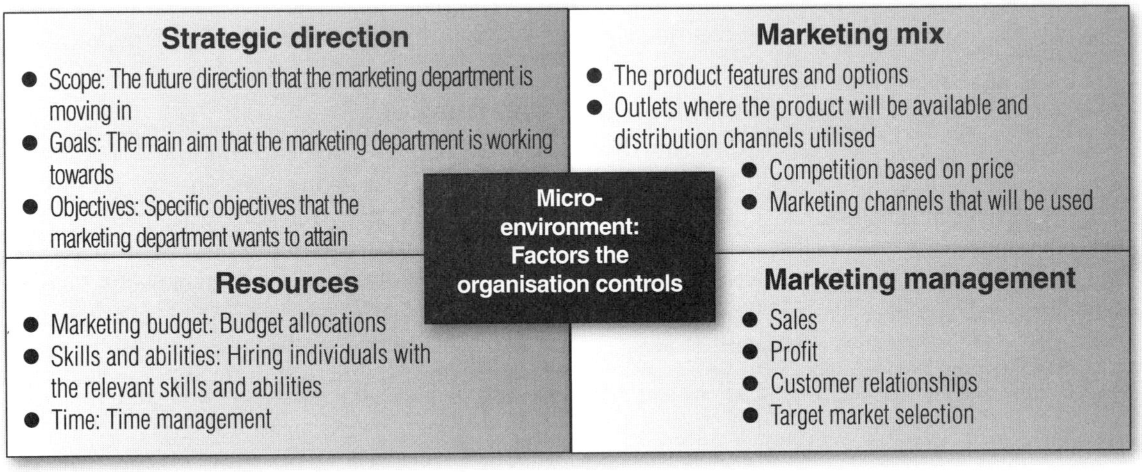

Figure 2.2 Micro-environmental factors that the organisation controls

DEFINITION

Mission statement

A mission statement defines the fundamental, unique purpose of a business, and identifies its customers and products or services. It is a declaration of the 'reason for being' of a business.

Example

Mission statements

- *Data Pathway*
  What puts us at the leading edge of the Internet industry is our ability (and willingness!) to deliver unsurpassed service levels, product innovation and superior management systems to our customers.
- *Microsoft*
  To help people and businesses throughout the world realise their full potential.
- *The Foschini Group (TFG)*
  To be the leading fashion lifestyle retailer in Africa.
- *SAS*
  We deliver proven solutions that drive innovation and improve performance.

Strategic direction

Figure 2.2 shows the first area which the organisation controls which is the strategic direction of the company. This consists of a number of variables, which are described below:

Mission statement

A business is not defined by its name, association or articles of incorporation – it is defined by its mission statement. For an organisation to be able to set clear and realistic business objectives, it needs to be certain about its mission and purpose. A business simply cannot survive if it does not know where it is going and what products or services it will offer. The marketing department's mission statement should be based on, and coincide with, the organisation's mission statement.

The marketing department's **mission statement** provides a concise statement of the current product market position (products offered and markets served) of the department. It also gives clear guidelines on where the resources of the department should be applied to achieve this mission. A mission defines the fundamental purpose that sets a company apart from others of its kind and identifies the scope of its operations in product and market terms. The mission of a marketing department is defined by a customer's satisfaction with its products and/or services. Defining the mission of a marketing department therefore starts with a clear description of its customers. Questions that need to be answered when formulating the mission are as follows:

- Who is the customer?
- What does the customer buy?
- Where is the customer located?
- How does the customer buy?
- How can the customer be reached?
- What does the customer regard as value for money?

A marketing department's mission statement should clearly be more concerned with its customers than with other processes or problems.

Selection of target market

In line with the mission and objectives of the company, a target market must be selected. This target market must be big enough for the company to meet its stated objectives and to ensure the long-term survival and growth of the business. Sometimes a company will deliberately focus on a smaller segment of the market (niche market) which shows potential and which the company can exploit profitably with its available resources.

Each market selected has specific characteristics of which the marketer must be aware in order to develop its marketing strategy to secure the highest possible return. See the example box entitled 'Target market for low-kilojoule, low-alcohol beer'.

Marketing objectives[2]

The mission statement and the objectives jointly set out the purpose of the marketing department. The objectives provide employees with a target for which to aim, and without this target there is no reason for the company to exist. Objectives flow directly from the mission statement and should be applied to the overall organisation as well as the various management departments such as marketing, financial, human resources and product development. An objective is a statement of what needs to be accomplished through the business activities. There are, however, certain guidelines that should be followed when setting up objectives, which include the following:

- Objectives should be *simple, clear* and *concise*, making them easy to understand by employees both from the specific functional area (such as marketing) and outside it.
- Objectives should be *measurable* by allowing the organisation to quantitatively determine whether they have been achieved or not.
- Objectives should be developed based on a specific *time frame* within which they should be accomplished.
- Objectives should also be *consistent* with the *overall mission and strategy* of the organisation.
- Objectives should be *realistic* and *achievable* by the organisation, which will be motivation for the employees who are involved with achieving them.
- Objectives should be *compared to a benchmark* – a baseline against which they are to be measured should be known.

This definition implies that different kinds of objectives are encountered at different levels of the organisation. The next two sections will look at the organisation's long- and short-term objectives.

Business or long-term objectives

The first group of objectives is the *business* or *long-term objectives*. These objectives present a picture of a certain desirable future for the business. The objectives of the business also serve as a standard or norm according to which the actual achievement or performance of the business can be measured. Top management, which usually includes the marketing manager, financial manager and human resources manager, is responsible for setting business objectives. According to Drucker (in Du Toit),[3] there are eight major areas in which a business should set business objectives. These objectives refer to the whole enterprise, and are as follows:

- **Market standing**. A business should decide which products and services it wants to sell and to whom it wishes to sell them. The business should also define the share of the target market it aims to capture.

DEFINITION

Objective

An objective can be defined as something the organisation wants to achieve over a set period of time.

Example E

Target market for sports cars

The manufacturer of sports cars will see its target market as predominantly males, in the age group 25+, in more urban geographical areas, who like excitement and prestige, and fall in the higher income group with a high disposable income.

Example E

Target market for low-kilojoule, low-alcohol beer

A distributor of a low-kilojoule beer will probably see its target market as predominantly female, 18 years and older, in all geographical areas, who are sociable, health conscious and in the middle to higher income groups.

- **Productivity**. This is the ratio of the inputs and outputs of a business. Productivity improvement objectives can be set in several areas, such as work methods, machinery and equipment advances, and increased worker efficiency.
- **Innovation**. A business that plans to remain competitive in today's environment should be innovative and should plan new products.
- **Physical and financial resources**. Objectives should be established with regard to plant equipment and supply of raw materials. Objectives should also be set in terms of how financial resources are to be generated and used.
- **Profitability**. Profit is the reward for the capital investor or the entrepreneur. Profit objectives should be set in terms of a particular financial index – for example 'to achieve a return on investment (ROI) of 21 % during the next financial year'.
- **Manager performance and development**. Businesses should set objectives that relate to the quality of management performance and ensure the development of people at all levels of management.
- **Worker performance and attitudes**. Objectives should be set regarding factors such as output per employee and quality of product.
- **Public and social responsibility**. Objectives should be set that will address the public and social responsibility initiatives of the business.

Functional or short-term objectives[4]

The second group of objectives are the *functional objectives*. Functional objectives refer to those objectives set by functional managers in each functional area, for example marketing objectives for the marketing department. These are *medium-* or *short-term objectives*.

As mentioned previously, marketing objectives should relate directly to the business objectives of the company. The most important marketing objectives are as follows:

- **Profit**. To maximise profitability and to achieve the highest possible rate of return on investment (ROI).
- **Customer orientation**. This marketing objective was discussed as the first principle of the marketing concept (see Chapter 1). It was emphasised that the marketing strategy must be based on the satisfaction of customer needs and wants. If this is not achieved, the business will cease to exist.
- **Survival and growth**. Marketing management must continuously strive to survive, particularly in difficult circumstances. It should furthermore encourage growth by promptly responding and adapting to an ever-changing environment.
- **Increase in sales and market share**. A large market share relative to that of competitors ensures a high sales volume and lower unit costs with regard to production and marketing.

- **Efficiency motive**. All companies strive for efficiency. For example, non-profit organisations strive towards maximum efficiency instead of increasing market share or sales.
- **Marketing instrument objectives**. Other marketing objectives can be set for the different functions in the marketing department, depending on environmental circumstances.

Resources, skills and abilities[5]

The resources, skills and abilities of the organisation are controllable elements of the micro-environment (see Figure 2.2) and are employed to take advantage of external opportunities and to counter threats. The strategic use of these elements is important and is the responsibility of management. These resources include available capital and the skills needed to create an effective organisational structure in which employees are able to function to the best of their ability. They also include the marketing skills needed to compete successfully in the marketplace. An efficient marketing information system that supports decision making, as well as experience and intuitive foresight, are internal strengths that will put the organisation a step ahead of its competitors.

The marketing mix

The marketing instruments (see Figure 2.2 on page 23) are under the direct control of marketing management. How these instruments are used, however, depends on the target market and the expected impact of the macro-environmental factors on the organisation. Marketing management has to make decisions regarding these instruments against its background, while keeping other environmental factors in mind.

The marketing instruments are also known as the marketing mix or the four Ps of marketing. These are as follows:

- **Product**. Which product or products can be offered to meet the perceived needs of the consumer, given the resources and skills available in the company as well as the broader business climate or environment?
- **Price**. The price of the product must reflect its value to the consumer. Another aspect to consider is the relative price versus quality level that the product maintains against competing products. When setting the price, marketing management has to consider the economic climate, customers' willingness to pay a specific price, prices of competitors' products, and so forth.
- **Place**. Customers' buying patterns will determine where a product should be available. Management must decide which outlets should carry the product, based on whether these outlets will reach the organisation's customers. However, customer preference is not the only factor to consider here. Let us take a pharmaceutical company as an example. Even though customers may prefer to buy cough syrup at a supermarket such as Pick n Pay, management may decide rather to approach pharmacies to distribute the product because they feel that this

Marketing mix objectives

- To respond to all queries within 24 hours (product objective).
- To ensure delivery within two days of the finalisation of the order (distribution objective).
- To increase the number of sales representatives by 10% (marketing communication objective).
- To reduce credit sales by 20% and increase cash sales by 12% (price objective).

will create the perception that it is a more effective product because it is only sold through pharmacies.

- **Promotion**. Promotion concerns the marketing communication methods used to inform the target market of the product. This decision is made by the marketing manager and will be influenced by factors such as the target audience to be reached, and the cost and frequency of advertisements in the media.

How these instruments are combined will determine whether the consumer buys a marketing offering or not. The business must ensure that it has the right *product*, at the right *price*, at the right *place* (at the right time), and that the product is *promoted* by informing the target market about it and where and how to obtain it. *These four variables are discussed in more detail later in this book.*

Marketing management

As is shown in Figure 2.2, the third element is marketing management where management takes a decision regarding the market offering. There are four variables to consider:

- **Sales**. Marketers should be committed to attaining their company's sales goals and objectives, which will lead to securing profit and revenue objectives. The sales department should work closely with the marketing department in order to formulate strategies. Factors such as sales forecasts, revenue forecasts and account policies should be taken into account as these will influence the sales plan for a specific period. Sales management should be proactive in the selection and training of sales employees as well as giving constant guidance, support and motivation to its sales teams and departments. Individual and group sales monitoring and evaluation methods should be put in place in order to track the performance of employees, analyse behaviour patterns and monitor costs.[6]
- **Profit**. Profits are the financial gain that is achieved by the business while meeting the needs of the market. Profits are what remain after expenses have been paid in order to meet the needs of the market. The main objective of any business is to make a profit. The marketing and the sales department should therefore work together to ensure sales targets are reached so that a profit can be made in the organisation. It is the task of management to continuously look for ways and means in which profits can be achieved and how to operate more economically by keeping business costs as low as possible.[7]
- **Customer relationships**. Establishing good relations with customers will always be in the best interest of a company. A successful business will understand the importance of identifying and satisfying the needs of both current and potential customers, as well as striving to accomplish these tasks more efficiently and effectively as time passes. Systems and

processes should be put in place to identify, target, acquire and retain the best and most profitable customers. If a business can successfully manage their customer relationships, it will increase both the loyalty of customers and their retention. Customer relationship management (CRM) is therefore important as it will ensure that customers are categorised into appropriate profiles that will correctly describe their needs and the most suitable products and services to offer them, as well as ensuring a superior level of customer service.[8]

- **Target market selection**. Management is aware that it is impossible for them, as well as their products or services, to satisfy every need a customer may have. It is therefore necessary for management to identify the most profitable target market(s) to which it will direct its time, money and efforts. A target market can be defined as the group of customers to which management aims to sell its products and services. This process is supported by focused marketing activities set up by management which are directed to a specific group. In order for marketing management to generate a successful marketing plan for its target market, it needs to develop customer profiles and segments in order to get a good idea of who its customers are. Profiles can be drawn up using many difference factors, for example demographics, geographics and psychographics. For example, a target market profile for a new energy drink may consist of customers between the ages of 18 and 30, with a middle to high income, living in an urban area. Products and services can be altered or produced from scratch in order to meet the needs of a specific target market. Marketing activities can also become more focused and be customised to reach a greater part of the target market.[9]

The variables in the market environment will be discussed next.

The variables in the market environment

The market environment (see Figure 2.1) refers to those variables in the market over which the organisation has limited control and which it can influence in some instances. This environment consists of competitors, consumers and suppliers. Competitors refer to those organisations that offer the same or similar products, while suppliers are those companies that supply the company with their products and services. Lastly, consumers are those who purchase the products or service the organisation offers.[10]

To understand the interaction between the business and its market environment, we need to examine the variables in the market environment more closely.

DEFINITION

Market environment
The market environment refers to those elements or variables that may be influenced by the organisation but which cannot be directly controlled by the organisation.

DEFINITION

Suppliers

A supplier is a business entity that supplies goods or services that are integral to the receiving business's production or delivery of goods and/or services.

Example

Needs competition

Lerato is a student who has R1 500 in her purse to spend. Let us say you sell shoes. Who would your competitors be? Would it be other shoe retailers, restaurants, clothing stores, supermarkets or educational institutions? In fact, they all compete with you for Lerato's R1 500 because she not only has a need for shoes, but for all the products or services listed above.

Suppliers

It has become increasingly important for organisations to ensure that their sources of supply meet their requirements in terms of delivery, quality, prices, and so forth. Having the right **supplier** may mean the difference between success and failure of the organisation as suppliers are an important link in the organisation's overall customer 'value delivery system'. Without reliable suppliers, the business will not be able to meet its obligations to its customers.

In South Africa, the purchasing function is increasingly being managed as part of the overall supply chain. The purchasing function is therefore regarded as part of the supply process. It includes all the activities in the materials flow chain, starting with the supplier, and includes all intermediate activities up to the stage where the requirements are delivered to the end user

The supply of materials and services is extremely important as it has a direct influence on the profit of the business and the price charged to customers. A large part of the cost of a product is directly related to the purchase of materials, which can ultimately mean the difference between success and failure. If the organisation pays too much for its supplies, it will not be competitive and will therefore not be able to survive. Ultimately, this will influence the acceptability of the product in the market.

Consumers

Consumers are the reason why a business exists, and the organisation must focus on their needs, purchasing power and behaviour patterns if it wants to be successful.[11] We will briefly touch on the topic here as consumers and consumer behaviour will be dealt with in more detail in Chapter 3.

In simple terms, a market can be defined as consisting of people with needs who have money to spend and the willingness to satisfy their needs.

It is the responsibility of marketing management to analyse the consumer market in order to see how it functions. Changes in the market composition or in consumer needs may create certain opportunities which, if taken advantage of, could influence the long-term growth and survival of the business.

Businesses operate in *five types of customer markets*,[12] which are as follows:

- **Consumer markets** are individuals and households who buy goods and services for personal consumption.
- **Industrial markets or business-to-business markets** are made up of organisations that buy goods and services for further processing or for use in their manufacturing process.
- **Reseller markets** buy goods and services, and resell them at a profit.
- **Government markets** are made up of government agencies that buy goods and services to produce public services or transfer these goods and services to others who need them.
- **International markets** are foreign buyers, including consumers, producers, resellers and governments.

Competitors[13]

It is seldom, if ever, that a product or service will not experience competition. This fact at the end of the day will determine the price at which a product will be sold. The more unique a product, the less competition it might experience and the more control the organisation may have over its selling price. However, the more intense competition becomes, the more market forces will determine the price.

It is essential that the business does not define its market too narrowly, as this may limit its target market. It is also important to realise that consumers have many different needs, which means there will be *needs competition*.

As soon as the consumer decides to buy a specific product, the competition moves to **product competition**. In Lerato's case, this would be other shoe retailers (see the example on 'Needs competition' on the previous page).

Competition also has positive aspects. It can help to keep excessive profits in check, stimulates higher profitability, promotes better service, and encourages technological innovation.

Competitive market structures

The number of businesses that sell a product may affect the strength of the competition. When many businesses sell a particular product, price considerations and product differences are more important than when only one business sells that product. Furthermore, the number of businesses selling a similar product determines the structure of the market. The advent of the Internet has also led to a change in the total competitive structure. One of the fastest-growing advertising media is online advertising.

Table 2.1 compares some characteristics of the four general types of competitive market structures.

Example (E)

Product competition

The Foschini Group consists of clothing, home-ware and jewellery retailers with over 1 900 stores countrywide.

Competitors of the Foschini Group include:

- all stores specialising in fashion lifestyle products;
- all fashion and footwear retailers;
- all cellphone and airtime retailers;
- all home-ware retailers; and
- all insurance brokers that sell funeral policies.

The Foschini Group sells all these products, so the businesses who also sell these items are all competitors of The Foschini Group.

Table 2.1 Characteristics of competitive market structures[14]

Type of structure	Number of competitors	Product	Example
Monopoly	One	Almost no substitutes	Telkom (this is, however, changing with suppliers like Neotel entering the market)
Oligopoly	Few	Homogeneous or differentiated (real or perceived differences in products)	Examples include car manufacturers and fuel retailers such as Mercedes-Benz, BMW, Engen, BP
Monopolistic competition	Many	Product differentiation with many substitutes	Computer companies
Perfect competition	Unlimited	Homogeneous product	Farmers' markets

DEFINITION

Competition
Competition refers to the contest between two or more businesses that are acting independently, striving to gain the same customer or market segment by overcoming rival businesses.

WWW:

- http://www.tfg.co.za
- http://www.telkom.co.za

These competitive market structures can briefly be described as follows:

- A **monopoly** exists when a business is marketing a product with no real substitutes. The company essentially has complete control over the supply of the product. In South Africa, monopolies are discouraged, but in some instances the government has allowed them.
- An **oligopoly** exists when there are relatively few businesses marketing a particular product, and they control much of its supply. Products in oligopolistic competition may be homogeneous (or similar), such as coal or steel. However, they may be differentiated (having real or perceived differences), such as cars or cigarettes. The furniture and motor industries are examples of oligopolies.
- **Monopolistic competition** is found when a large number of businesses are marketing the same or similar products. Each business attempts to differentiate its product to persuade consumers that its product is the one to buy. Soft drinks, coffee, tea, soap powder, TV sets and computers are typical examples of products of these types of businesses.
- **Perfect competition** is the ideal situation, but it does not exist. If it did, it would be a market with an unlimited number of sellers, not one of which could significantly influence the price or supply of the products. The closest example of perfect competition is the market for agricultural products, sold informally at roadside stalls or at farmers' markets.

The variables in the macro-environment

DEFINITION

Macro-environment
The macro-environment refers to those factors or variables in the environment over which the individual business has no control. These factors influence the business, and need to be constantly monitored as they change continuously. These variables are found just outside the market environment.

The third and last component of the marketing environment is the **macro-environment** (see Figure 2.1).

The macro-environment is dynamic in that it changes rapidly, and in today's global society the impact of such changes may be felt very quickly. The result of this interaction is often a changed business environment with new opportunities and new threats.

The different variables in the macro-environment will be discussed in the paragraphs that follow.

Political and legal environment

Politics plays a major role in the stability of a country and therefore has a profound impact on the way other countries and businesses view the country. Any uncertainty regarding the political stability of a country may lead to a halt in, for example, foreign investment and tourism, which will cause a ripple effect such as inflation, higher interest rates, and lower credit ratings for the country. In Third World countries especially, political instability in terms of constant wars, faction fighting, corruption and other issues can cause major economic disruptions. It is therefore important that governments take great care in terms of how they communicate contentious policy issues, as news travels around the world in the blink of an eye. In South Africa, labour unrest in the mines and the Marikana debacle in 2012 cost the country dearly, and sparked a sharp decline in the value of the rand, and also a drop in share prices of the mines.

Management must also be aware of international laws and regulations regarding business and trade. In addition, businesses need to keep up to date with changes in legislation, both at national and provincial levels. New regulations are continuously implemented in order to effect change. The BRICS (Brazil, Russia, India, China and South Africa) partnership has influenced South Africa's trading agreements with the other countries in the partnership. Political measures guide the economy in a specific direction. For example, if the government wants to increase the level of involvement of social responsibility of South African businesses, regulatory guidelines need to reflect this. Decisions taken by government impact on the running of businesses and cannot be ignored at will. If the government, for example, decides to implement an additional levy on imported goods, businesses importing products will have to comply. This may lead to their being unable to sustain their businesses, and they may even have to close down. Such an action by government will have serious implications for the profitability of companies, and many businesses will start to retrench staff if they cannot afford these increased duties. In the same way, if government were to pass legislation that would lead to the nationalisation of mines, or measures restricting operations of businesses, or suppression of freedom of speech by means of the media tribunal, this will have far-reaching implications for South African companies, as well as for foreign investment. The new political party started by Julius Malema, the Economic Freedom Fighters (EFF), for example, could do untold damage to the country's reputation if it were to become a serious threat to the current situation as it stands for the nationalisation of banks and mines, the reclaiming of land without compensation, and other issues that would be unacceptable on an international level. Individual companies have to comply with such changes if they were passed by parliament and become law.

International environment

The world has become one big market due to advances in technology and the advent of the Internet, e-commerce and communication technology. In the past, news travelled relatively slowly, and reaction time was even slower. Today, communication is instant. What happens anywhere in the world is reported virtually immediately, and people and markets react to these events instantaneously. It is now much easier to source suppliers for products than it was in the past, and competitors are not limited to local stores or outlets, as seen in the exponential growth of online shopping.

Walmart (the world's largest retailer) expanded into the South African market via a buyout of the Massmart group in 2011. This event required other retailers in the country to evaluate this challenge and react to it.

WWW:

- http://www.walmart.com

The changed political dispensation since 1994 has opened new doors for South African businesses – both big and small – which may be seen as a threat or an opportunity. South African businesses compete on an equal footing internationally, which benefits both importers and exporters. New opportunities are also becoming available through partnerships such as the BRICS group, which is an economic partnership for development, integration and industrialisation.

Businesses that intend marketing their products abroad and those intending to import goods must understand all the relevant regulations and conditions that apply in the countries with which they do business. They should also be aware of the implications of any cultural differences that may affect trade. Organisations such as the Industrial Development Corporation (IDC) and the Department of Trade and Industry (DTI) can assist businesses in this regard.

Physical environment

Natural resources such as water, coal, oil, gold and other minerals are not available in infinite quantities. Businesses must be aware of these limitations as various factors can lead to a shortage of raw materials and rising costs. When, for instance, the supply of an ingredient for a specific pharmaceutical product becomes scarce, that product's price will skyrocket, or it could even be taken off the market completely. All businesses need to be aware of the availability of raw materials used in the manufacturing process as this can and will have an effect on the regular supply of the product.

There is general consensus that oil reserves will run out in about 30 years. Companies that manufacture vehicles, engines, and so forth will have to start looking seriously at alternative sources of energy to power their machines.

Technological environment

The one area where change has been taking place at an alarming pace and virtually on a daily (and some even say an hourly) basis is the advancement of technology. One just has to look at the increasingly sophisticated features on cell phones, the growing use of the Internet, new applications of software, better and faster computer hardware, and so on to realise how rapidly technology is changing. These advances manifest in all areas of business, including advertising media, the development of new products, the delivery of products, and many other ways. Most products that are bought today, with the exception of a few basic commodities, originated during the past 70 years. The most recent inventions, which have already become indispensable in modern society – such as laser surgery, silicon protein molecules, fibre optics, and 80 % of the medicines available today – were developed during the past five to 10 years! These extreme changes in the environment are largely as a result of technological innovation.

Technological innovation may be described as the process that expands people's capacity. It originates in research and development by enterprises and the state, resulting not only in new machinery or products, but also in new processes, methods and even management approaches, which in turn bring about change in the environment. Technological innovation also influences other environmental variables. Economic growth is affected by the number of new inventions and also by social change. For example, the introduction of a new product, such as the cell phone, causes major changes in the way people live. Environmental variables in turn impact on technology, so that the process of innovation and change is constantly repeated.[15]

'It can be said that the economy is the heartbeat of a country as it affects every consumer and business.'

Economic environment

The economy is the heartbeat of a country as it affects every consumer and business, and in turn is influenced by various variables of which politics is a major force. Since the great economic collapse in 2007/2008, the European Union has been under tremendous pressure with a number of countries having to be bailed out of their financial difficulties, the American economy has reached record deficit heights, and many countries, including China and South Africa, have experienced a slowdown in economic growth. Mismanagement of the economy by any government can lead to serious complications on a global scale for that country.

The economic forces in a country in general and in the specific area in which a business operates will have certain implications for the business. Management must be aware of these economic forces as any changes will affect other variables in both the market environment and the micro-environment.

The economic environment includes the following:

- **Inflation**. The inflation rate in a country has a direct influence on consumer prices and spending. In South Africa, the fiscal policy of the government aims to keep inflation between 3 and 6 %, and it has largely been able to do so with its strict monetary policies. In July 2013, however, inflation was above 6,3 % on a year-to-year basis.
- **Interest rates**. An interest rate is the price of lending money. Since 2009, the interest rate has been dropping steadily in South Africa, and in January 2012 it was recorded as 5,5 %. In January 2013 the Reserve Bank dropped its rate to 5%, with the prime lending rate of banks dropping to 8,5 %. Businesses set up with borrowed funds are particularly sensitive to interest rate fluctuations. A sharp rise in the interest rate can easily result in a business being unable to meet its commitments. Many countries have an interest rate of between 0,5 % and 1 %, with the objective in mind to stimulate business activity. By keeping interest rates low, governments want to encourage businesses to rather use the money to grow their businesses and in so doing, encourage economic growth.
- **Unemployment**. The tough economic situation that still faces the world after the recession of 2009 has left over four million

South Africans without jobs, bringing the unemployment figure of the economically active population in the country in the third quarter of 2012 to 25,5 %. This state of affairs has a direct effect on consumer expenditure and the demand for products and services. In such times, people tend to cut back on more expensive products and postpone purchases of durable goods as long as possible.

- **Consumer income**. The structural changes in the income of the various consumer groups are of great importance to businesses since they give rise to changed spending patterns with regard to products and services such as food, clothing, housing and insurance. As mentioned above, during hard economic times, people have less money to spend (or have less disposable income).
- **Exchange rate**. The rand has strengthened in the past few years but in July 2013 it was trading at an average of about R10,20 to the US dollar, which is a significant weakening compared to the previous years. A strong rand means that imports are cheaper but exports earn less money than would be the case if the exchange rate were stronger. The price of petrol and diesel, for example, is directly linked to the price of oil per barrel and is adjusted on a monthly basis. This means that as the price of oil increases, for example as a result of a weak exchange rate, the price of petrol and diesel is adjusted accordingly. The exchange rate therefore has a direct influence on transport costs, the cost of imported goods and raw materials, and so on. Companies need to be aware of the impact of these fluctuations on their products and services.
- **Monetary policy**. Another variable affecting all businesses is the government's monetary policy. This policy regulates the money supply, interest rates and the level of the rand relative to other currencies. Fiscal (taxation) policy affects both businesses and consumers through tax reforms and the level of taxation.
- **The business cycle**. The business cycle also plays an important role in the performance of businesses. During a downturn in the business cycle, less disposable income is available. This has a negative effect on businesses, which react by buying fewer products from the manufacturer. In other words, a decrease in stock is a direct result of a downturn in the business cycle.

It is clear from the above discussion that economic trends therefore require continuous and vigilant attention from management.

The socio-cultural environment[16]

The integration of the South African population since independence in 1994, the focus on women in business, black economic empowerment (BEE) and other actions have led to changes in all areas of business. The socio-cultural environment has an impact on marketing techniques, media used, types of advertisements, organisational structures, and products designed and offered for sale across all types of businesses and industries.

Example (E)

Internet for South Africa

The ICT market in South Africa is growing rapidly and constantly changing. An increasing number of South Africans are adopting data services, especially broadband. This allows ICT companies in South Africa to adopt new strategies and differentiate themselves from the competition in order to become the preferred supplier of Internet in the country.

Example (E)

High-income males and females are a growing market for KFC

The market for high-income males and females is growing in the fast-food industry. This has led to an increased demand for:

- a sophisticated and neat way to eat fast food for high-income females; and
- filling meals that are simple and uncomplicated for high-income males.

SWOT is an acronym:

S = Strengths
W = Weaknesses
O = Opportunities
T = Threats

Social and cultural change is strongly influenced by the economy and technology. Social trends directly affect the marketing strategies of a business as they help to determine consumer needs and purchasing decisions. These trends include demographics, lifestyles, cultural values and subcultural influences. Demographics describe the objective characteristics of an individual: age, education, occupation, income, marital status, and so on. Consumers' lifestyles are defined by their activities, interests and opinions. For example, we can talk about an outgoing lifestyle, a health-conscious lifestyle, and a liberal or conservative lifestyle. Cultural values can be defined as beliefs shared by a large number of people in a society that lead to common patterns of behaviour. Subcultural influences involve the values and behaviour that distinguish subcultures from society as a whole. See the example box entitled 'High-income males and females are a growing market for KFC'.

SWOT analysis

A SWOT analysis is a useful instrument for helping managers to identify the internal strengths and weaknesses of a business, and the external opportunities and threats facing it.

A SWOT analysis is based on the assumption that an effective strategy maximises the strengths and opportunities of a business, and minimises its weaknesses and threats. Strengths should be matched to opportunities, and threats should be seen as challenges.

However, not all factors in a SWOT analysis are of equal value. The aim is therefore to identify those critical factors that can have a major effect on the business. Management should then build on vital strengths, correct obvious weaknesses, exploit significant opportunities and avoid potentially disastrous threats. Let us take a closer look at the components of a SWOT analysis.

Strengths

A **strength** is a resource, skill or other advantage relative to competitors and the needs of the market which the business serves, or expects to serve. It is a distinctive competence that gives the business a competitive advantage in the marketplace. A distinctive strength of a business is more than what it can do; it is what it can do particularly well.

Strengths may exist with regard to financial resources, image, market leadership, buyer or supplier relations, expertise, skills and intuitive knowledge. In many industries, the service, efficiency and personal attention offered to customers make a crucial difference in gaining leverage in the marketplace. Businesses that deliver superior service over their competitors have a real competitive strength.

Weaknesses

A **weakness** is a limitation or deficiency in resources, skills and capabilities that seriously impedes the effective performance of a business. Facilities, financial resources, management capabilities, marketing skills and

DEFINITION

Strength
A positive internal factor which helps an organisation to succeed or make progress by distinguishing it from competitors, and increasing its competitiveness in the marketplace. A strength may include a resource, capability or core competency.

DEFINITION

Weakness
A weakness is an organisation's internal factor that is not strong or successful, and prevents the organisation from fully achieving its objectives. It could be a limitation, fault, defect or inferior capability.

DEFINITION

Opportunity
An opportunity is a favourable external factor in the organisation's environment that makes it possible for the organisation to improve its competitiveness.

> **DEFINITION**
>
> **Threat**
>
> A threat is an unfavourable external event, trend or change that may currently or potentially cause damage, injury or harm to an organisation's ability to compete.

brand image can be sources of weaknesses. For example, a business short of cash cannot afford to undertake a large-scale marketing communication campaign.

Sun Tzu, a Chinese military strategist, had the following to say on exploiting the weaknesses of a competitor: 'When your competitor shows his weakness, move rapidly to take advantage of it. Seize what the competitor values most.'[17]

Opportunities

An **opportunity** is a favourable element in a business environment that can be exploited by management. The identification of promising opportunities is an absolute prerequisite for the profitability, survival and growth of a business. Identification of a previously overlooked market segment, changes in competitive or regulatory circumstances, technical changes, and improved buyer or supplier relationships could present opportunities for the business.

An opportunity should not be assessed in isolation, but should be evaluated on the ability of the business to capitalise on it. This implies that the business must have adequate resources to support the action required to take advantage of an opportunity.

Threats

A **threat** is a major unfavourable element in a business environment that can lead to the failure of a product or service, or ultimately the business itself. It is the responsibility of management to identify any such threats, real or potential, and to take the necessary steps to counteract them.

Threats can take different forms, for example changes in the consumer market, an unexpected increase in competition, problems with suppliers, punitive legislation, recession, or an unfavourable exchange rate. These threats should not be accepted as a matter of course, but should rather be seen as challenges, or possibly even as opportunities.

> **DEFINITION**
>
> **Environmental scanning**
>
> Environmental scanning refers to the systematic monitoring of an organisation's marketing environment whereby information is gathered, analysed and evaluated in order to detect early signals that indicate opportunities and threats, which may influence the organisation's current position or future course of action in terms of strategic decision making.

Environmental scanning

To adapt to changes in the environment, the internal and external environments should be continuously monitored. We have seen that a SWOT analysis can be a useful tool in shedding light on those environmental variables that in some way either have a positive or negative impact on the success of the business.

The importance of **environmental scanning** or analysis may be summed up as follows:

- It helps the business to capitalise on early opportunities rather than lose to competitors. In other words, it helps the business to obtain a 'first-mover' advantage by taking action before the competition.

- It provides an early signal of impending problems or threats, which can be defused if recognised well in advance.
- It sensitises a business to the changing needs and wants of its customers.
- It provides a base of objective information about the internal strengths and weaknesses of a business that determine its ability to counter threats or use opportunities.
- It improves the image of the business by showing that it is sensitive and responsive to its environment.

Monitoring the internal environment (in other words, analysing the internal strengths and weaknesses of a business) is part of the strategic management process. It should take place while management keeps an eye on the external environment.

It is not important whether the internal or the external analysis is done first. It is, however, of the utmost importance that this exercise is undertaken regularly. It is very important to do a thorough internal analysis as it is only then that workable strategies can be developed and realistic objectives formulated. The following two pertinent questions can be asked:

- How does management *identify* strengths and weaknesses in a business?
- How must strengths and weaknesses be *evaluated*?

For top management to identify the strengths and weaknesses in the micro-environment, they need to isolate the key success factors for the business. These success factors will depend on conditions in the industry, the market and the position of the business in that industry and market.

Finally, what methods can be used to scan the internal and external environments? Marketing research methods are used to analyse environmental variables. These methods are controlled by the marketing department. Market research is discussed in Chapter 4, and control methods in Chapter 10.

Example *E*

Taking advantage of threats[18]

South Africa is known for its high crime rate, including cash robberies, which causes havoc for businesses and individuals alike. Cash robberies are especially detrimental to the small and informal businesses, which are key targets. A new mobile point-of-sale (mPOS) device was developed in order to assist with fighting these cash robberies. This device allows for a cashless sales transaction, thereby providing an increasingly secured transaction. It may be hired out to small businesses for a set fee, and has been adopted on a global scale. This illustrates how businesses can create an opportunity out of a threat in a marketing environment.

Summary

This chapter describes the micro-, market and macro-environmental variables. The marketing activities that take place in these environments and are influenced by environmental changes are also discussed. This means that a business should continuously adapt itself to the changing environment. The marketing environment should be closely monitored by means of a SWOT analysis. Internal strengths and weaknesses should be pitched against external opportunities and threats in the continuous battle against competitors.

Few businesses have the necessary resources, skills and abilities to serve the total mass market. For this reason, smaller sub-markets or segments are identified, and suitable ones are selected as target markets. The products of the business are positioned in a niche in the market where they are protected to a degree from competitors.

References

1. Cronjé, G. De J., Du Toit, G.S. & Motlatla, M.D.C. 2000. *Introduction to business management*. 5th ed. Cape Town: Oxford University Press, p. 56.
2. Cant, M.C. (Ed). 2010. *Marketing: An introduction*. Cape Town, South Africa: Juta & Co., p. 24.
3. Du Toit, M. (Ed). 2011. *Fundamentals of sales and marketing*. Cape Town: South Africa: Juta & Co., p. 19.
4. Koontz, H. & Weihrich, H. 2009. *Essentials of management: An international perspective*. 8th ed. Delhi, India: Tata McGraw-Hill, p. 87.
5. Business Dictionary.com. 2013. *Sales management*. [Online] Available from: http://www.businessdictionary.com/definition/sales-management.html#ixzz2hOZdjt8X [Accessed: 2013-10-11].
6. Investopedia. 2013. *Profit*. [Online] Available from: http://www.investopedia.com/terms/p/profit.asp [Accessed: 2013-10-11].
7. Business Dictionary.com. 2013. *Customer relationship management*. [Online] Available from: http://www.businessdictionary.com/definition/customer-relationship-management-CRM.html#ixzz2hOaJcNeA [Accessed: 2013-10-11].
8. Investopedia. 2013. *Target market*. [Online] Available from: http://www.investopedia.com/search/default.aspx?q=target%20market [Accessed: 2013-10-11].
9. Du Toit, op. cit., p. 24.
10. Cant, op cit., p. 27.
11. Du Toit, op. cit., p. 24.
12. Ibid.
13. Ibid.
14. Ibid.
15. Ibid.
16. Smit, P.J., Cronje, G.J., Brevis, T. & Vrba, M.J. 2011. *Management principles: A contemporary edition for Africa*. 5th ed. Cape Town, South Africa: Juta & Co., p.74.
17. Krause, D.G. 1995. *Sun Tzu, the art of war for executives*. London: Nicholas Brearly, p. 95.
18. newsWall.co.za. 2013. *Mobile point-of-sale device could lead to lower insurance premiums*. [Online] Available from: http://newswall.co.za/news/latest/south-africa-insurance-investment/mobile-point-of-sale-device-could-lead-to-lower-insurance-premiums/22pv.29076 [Accessed: 2013-06-06].

Consumers and their behaviour

CHAPTER 3

✓ Learning objectives

After studying this chapter, you should be able to:

- illustrate how marketers should take motivation into account in their marketing messages;
- explain the perception process and the marketing implications of perceptual defence;
- explain and illustrate the nature and elements of learning;
- illustrate the use of the components of attitudes, and how attitudes can be changed;
- explain the characteristics of personality and its value to marketers;
- explain the nature of lifestyle;
- explain decision making in the family in terms of family roles and types;
- explain the nature and implications of culture;
- illustrate the implications of different social classes;
- explain the different reference groups;
- illustrate the types of decision making and the decision-making process; and
- understand the stages of adopting a new product and the categories of adoption of new products.

Introduction

As we are all aware, for a business to be successful it needs to offer products that the consumer wants. Without the consumer there will be no market and no business. It should therefore be clear that the consumer is the centre around which everything revolves. Consequently it is essential for the business to know who their customers are, what their needs and wants are, and what makes them do things the way they do – that is, how they behave in given situations. Without this

Example E

The consumer in action

Michael stays in Pretoria, close to Menlyn Mall. He is married, and has three children, Andy, Peter and Jake. Michael does the weekly shopping on Saturday mornings, usually at Checkers in Menlyn Mall. He enjoys going to this particular store as he feels the prices are reasonable, the variety is good, and he can do the whole week's shopping in one place. Armed with his weekly shopping list, Michael starts in the toiletries section, where he chooses Sensodyne toothpaste as he knows his teenage son, Jake, prefers this brand because he has sensitive teeth. At the same time, he buys Colgate with cavity control for his seven-year-old, Andy, who eats a lot of sweets. Michael hopes that this toothpaste will help to prevent expensive trips to the dentist.

In the aisle with the cold drinks, he selects Sparberry for Andy, Sprite for Peter, and Lipton's Ice Tea for Jake, who is on a health kick. He also purchases an apple juice for his wife as he knows that it is her favourite flavour, and a Coke for himself. Michael then continues to the next item on his list – cereal.

Continue to next page

knowledge it will be extremely difficult to make the business a success. It is, however, not enough to know only what the customer wants, but also to know how the customer makes his or her buying decisions. Consumers have also become more globalised and knowledgeable due to technology. The marketer must be aware of how the customer thinks, what influences his or her decisions, and how these elements can be used to persuade the consumer to purchase a specific brand or patronise a particular store. Consider the example entitled 'The consumer in action'.

It is clear from the basic example in the margin that Michael is continuously influenced by his own needs and preferences as well as those of his family and friends, and the advertisements he has seen. This is known as **consumer behaviour**. Marketers need to be aware of their customers' needs in order to meet their own goals and targets. They need to know the needs and preferences of consumers and why they have them in order to try to satisfy them with their particular products.

A customer's buying decision is not determined by only one factor but mostly by a number of them. The study of consumer behaviour is concerned with all the activities and influences that occur before, during and after the purchase itself. It therefore includes not only the buyers and consumers of products, but also those who influence the buying decision.

In this chapter we first look at the determinants of consumer behaviour, namely individual factors as well as group factors that influence behaviour. Then we deal with the consumer decision-making process. Figure 3.1 (on page 43) provides an overview of consumer behaviour.

The *individual factors* in Figure 3.1 are also known as the *internal* or *basic determinants* of consumer behaviour. Consumers' needs, motives, attitudes, perceptions, learning abilities and their personality determine their consumption decisions and behaviour. However, consumers do not live in isolation and are influenced by other factors as well. These include cultural and social influences from the external environment which also shape an individual's behaviour. These external determinants are known as *group factors*, and include the cultural group, reference groups, the family and the social class system. If marketers wish to formulate a successful marketing strategy (consisting of product, price, promotion and distribution strategies), they need to be familiar with the influence of internal and external determinants on the behaviour of consumers in a specific target market.

Let us first investigate the individual factors that influence consumers' buying behaviour.

Individual factors influencing consumer behaviour

Individual factors refer to those factors which are inherent in human behaviour. Why do consumers buy certain products? Why do they buy these products at certain stores? Why do they buy certain products

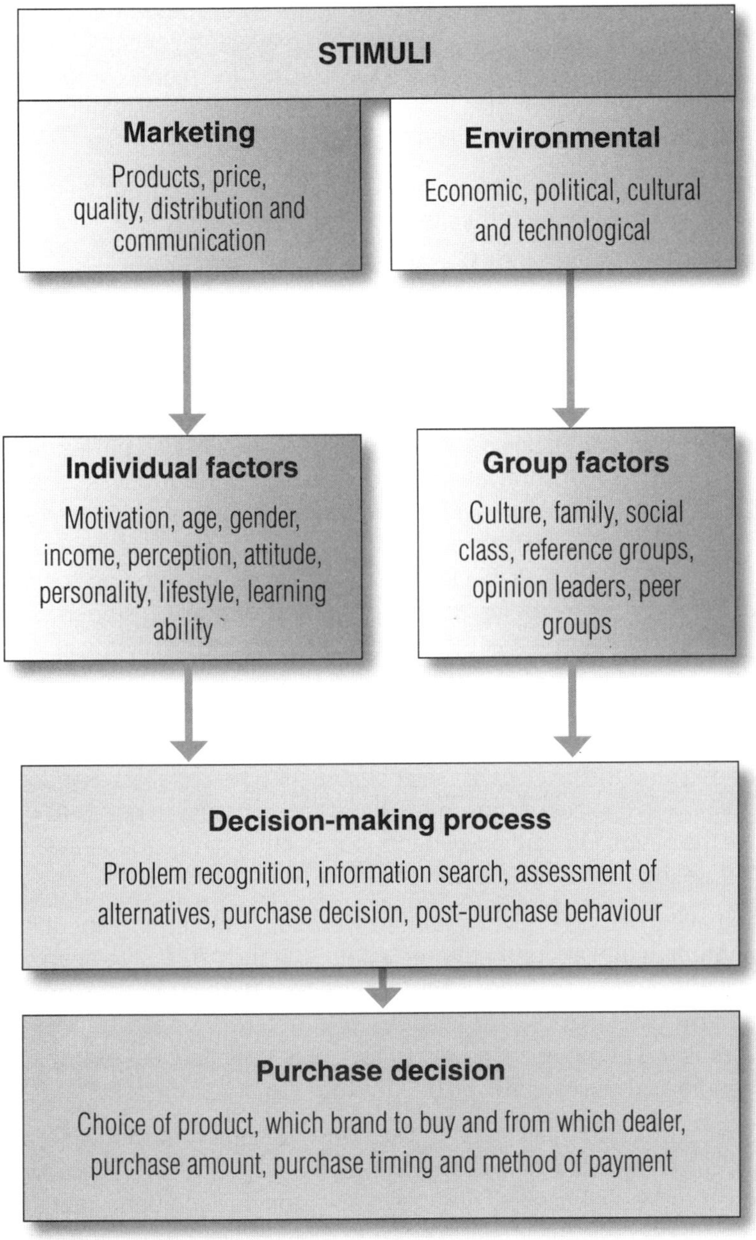

Figure 3.1 Model of consumer behaviour

at certain times? How do they buy? It is not easy to understand all these questions as many factors can and do influence the decisions by customers. Although we have a fair understanding of which factors influence behaviour, our knowledge of how these factors interact to do so is limited. The human mind is often compared to a 'black box' – we know the inputs (stimuli) and the outputs (responses), but not the inner workings (processes) of the mind with respect to the transformation of inputs and outputs.

Example *E*

Continued from previous page
He selects Special K for his wife, as she follows a strict Special K eating plan. He sees an advertisement for the new Nestlé Honey Oaties and decides that it is a much healthier option than the Coco-Pops that he usually buys for himself and the children. Michael continues through the store until he has all the items on his shopping list. Just before moving to the counter to pay, Michael notices a display of engine oil on special offer at a 25 % discount. He remembers that a close friend of his mentioned that the particular brand of engine oil is the best and that his car is due for oil change, so he adds this to the trolley.

DEFINITION

Consumer behaviour

Consumer behaviour is the decision-making process used in selecting, evaluating, using and disposing of products and services.

> **DEFINITION**
>
> **Needs identified in the market**
>
> - In response to consumers' needs Woolworths has now included other branded products in its range on offer.
> - Owing to the increased consumer emphasis on more flexible banking services, banks have increased the use of technology in most banking services, making it easier for customers to use some of the facilities/ services at all times.

Human needs, in particular consumer needs, are the basis of all modern marketing. Needs are the essence of the marketing concept. The key to a company's survival, profitability and growth in a highly competitive marketing environment is its ability to identify and satisfy unfulfilled consumer needs better than the competition does.

Marketers who base their offerings on recognition of consumer needs find a ready market for their products or services.

The first individual factor we will look at is motivation.

Motivation

What drives or motivates a person to do something or buy a product is not always easy to establish. If the marketer knows this, it will be easier to sell to that person as the marketing message can be designed to appeal to that motivating factor. To understand motivation is to understand why consumers do what they do. People do things for a reason or purpose. They may be motivated by a need to feel loved by others, to protect their feet from damage when rock climbing, to relax in a movie theatre, or just to quench a thirst. Marketing students are taught from day one that the goal of marketing is to satisfy consumers' needs. However, this insight is useless unless we can discover what these needs are and why they exist. Motivation is what moves people to action. Marketers need to 'look behind the behaviour' in order to understand the motives of their consumers. When retailers examined the buying choices of consumers, they found unsatisfied needs. Needs are the basic sources of buyer behaviour, but they have to be stimulated before the consumer is driven to action.[1]

To have a need is one thing, but to want to do something about it is another matter altogether. When a person wishes to satisfy a need, we call this *motivation*. There is thus a close relationship between **needs** and **motives**. Needs lead to motives; a motive is a need sufficiently stimulated to move an individual to seek satisfaction. For example, if people are hungry, they will be motivated to buy some food.

The stimulation mentioned in the above definition of motivation, is produced by a state of tension which exists as the result of an unfulfilled need. Individuals strive to reduce this tension through behaviour that they expect will fulfil their needs and thus relieve them of the stress they feel. The specific goals they select and the patterns of action they undertake to achieve their goals are the result of individual thinking and learning.

'Needs are the essence of the marketing concept.'

'Motivation is what moves people to action.'

Motives can be classified in various ways and these classifications offer the marketer useful insight into human behaviour. Two classifications that are particularly relevant to the marketer are Maslow's hierarchy of needs, and the economic and emotional classification.

Maslow's hierarcy of needs

Abraham Maslow identified specific human needs and classified them in a hierarchy of importance. At the bottom level are the most basic needs. Higher-order needs do not emerge before lower-order ones have been reasonably satisfied. The lowest-order needs are physiological, which help to ensure the survival of the individual. The highest level is reflected in the desire for self-actualisation. According to this theory, the individual is motivated to fulfil whichever need is most strongly felt at any given moment. Maslow's hierarchy of needs is shown in Figure 3.2.

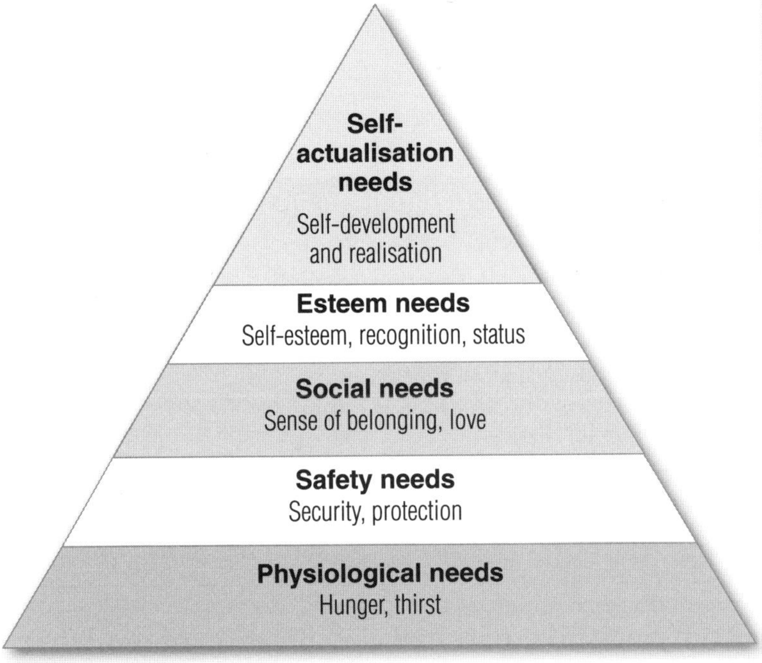

Figure 3.2 Maslow's hierarchy of needs

Let us look at each motive in more detail:

- **Physiological needs**. These are the most basic needs and refer to the need for breathing, food, water and sleep. Hunger impels the consumer to purchase food.
- **Safety and security needs**. These needs are aroused after physiological motives have been minimally satisfied and include the need for security of body, health, family, economy and employment. Security needs would motivate a consumer to erect a security fence, for example.
- **Belongingness or social needs**. These needs are reflected in a desire for friendship, family, a sense of being loved and approval. Many products, such as cosmetics and deodorants, are purchased because of social motives.
- **Esteem needs**. These needs include the desire for recognition, confidence, self-esteem, reputation and respect. These motives impel consumers to purchase luxury products as symbols of status and success.

DEFINITION

Need
We can define a need as the gap that exists between the actual state the consumer is in and the state he or she would like to be in.

DEFINITION

Motives
Motives are a psychological drive or urge that compels individuals towards actions that satisfy their needs.

DEFINITION

Motives that lead to behaviour

Lauren lives in Pretoria, and just got a job that requires her to travel to Johannesburg every day. This is a motive to buy a car.

- **Self-actualisation needs**. These involve the desire for self-fulfilment, new experiences, morality and personal growth, to become all that one is capable of becoming. Not many people are in a position to satisfy this need. An example is to become a top tennis player or artist, or to summit Mount Everest.

These needs are often used in advertising to appeal to specific consumer motives. Examples of product appeals tailored to each level are provided in Table 3.1

Table 3.1 Maslow's hierarchy and marketing strategies

Level of hierarchy	Relevant products	Example of an appeal
Self-actualisation	Hobbies, travel, education	Club Med – 'Where happiness means the world'
Esteem	Cars, furniture, credit cards	Audi – 'Vorsprung durch Technik'
Social	Clothing, grooming products, drinks, gaming	Xbox 360 – 'Life's short, play more'
Safety	Insurance, alarm systems, retirement investments	1st for Women – 'Get cover with care, get 1st for Women'
Physiological	Medicines, staple items	Sunbake bread –'The taste we love'

Example E

Motives that lead to behaviour

The types of houses people live in, the cars they drive, the clothes they wear and the very food they eat are often chosen because symbolically they reflect the individual's self-image while they satisfy specific needs. A man who perceives himself as older and successful may drive a Mercedes-Benz, while a young computer geek making good money may drive a VW Sirocco.

Economic and emotional classification of motives

Consumers are not always motivated by physiological needs in decision making. When a person purchases products, he or she is also concerned with aspects such as price, quality, performance and reliability. A person can satisfy these *economic motives* by applying economic criteria in decision making, as shown in Table 3.2. (Also see example boxes on pages 47 and 48.)

The economic motives are rational in nature and are often expressed by the advertiser in quantifiable terms.

Table 3.2 Economic criteria in consumer decision making

Cost	Performance
• Price • Cost of maintenance • Cost of installation • Operating costs • Additional cost	• Competence • Durability • Reliability • Economy • Resources

The *emotional motives* represent those motives that involve emotions and correspond with Maslow's social and esteem motives. Remember, satisfaction of emotional needs is not a non-rational act – it is almost impossible to make any decision on a purely rational basis as emotional motives invariably influence the consumer's decision. People are usually reluctant to admit that their buying behaviour is influenced by economic motives.

Perception

Perception is influenced by what we have learned. The way in which we perceive things is influenced by what we know about them; in other words, what we have learned about them.

Perception can be a very difficult thing to change once it is engraved in the mind of the consumer. If the consumer perceives a shop to be expensive or poor on service and quality, it will be extremely difficult to change this perception. For decades, marketers have been asking questions such as: What makes a consumer prefer one supermarket to another, or one brand of beer to another, or a specific type of car? Why does a consumer prefer to shop at Woolworths and not at Checkers, or vice versa? The answer can usually be found in the way a consumer perceives the available brands or stores.

Consumers are exposed to marketing communication stimuli such as advertising, store displays and packaging. The perceptions that come from these stimuli often act as triggers and influences in buying behaviour. Consumers make decisions and take actions based on what they perceive to be reality, hence it is important that marketers understand the notion of perception so that they can more readily determine what influences consumers to buy. Knowledge of the principles of perception enables the astute marketer to develop messages that have a good chance of being perceived and remembered by the target consumers.

The perception process

Now that we know what the nature of perception is, we can examine what occurs during the perception process. The *perception process* consists of four distinct steps, namely *exposure, attention, interpretation* and *recall.*

Exposure

Initially, perception begins with exposure to stimuli. Exposure occurs when the stimuli come within range of one of the five primary receptors, namely vision, hearing, taste, smell and touch. Most of the stimuli to which an individual is exposed are deliberately selected – that is, certain stimuli are sought out, others are avoided and the meaning of some is distorted. This is known as selective exposure.

To ensure that consumers in their target market are exposed to a marketing message, marketers often put advertisements in unconventional places where there will be less competition, for example on the back of shopping trolleys, on walls in sports stadiums, and even in restrooms where the marketer has a 'captive audience'.

Retailers use shelf position and amount of shelf space to ensure that consumers are exposed to certain brands. Point-of-purchase displays

Economic motives

If the consumer buys a BMW, he will not easily concede that the underlying motive was his need for recognition (esteem motive). He rationalises by alleging that the reason for his purchase is, in fact, the maintenance plan (economic motive) of the product.

Example (E)

Economic motives

'Buy three, pay for two'

'50 % discount'

DEFINITION

Perception

Perception is how individuals see (select, organise and interpret information) a product, brand or organisation based on their senses of sight, hearing, smell, taste and feel.

Example (E)

The power of perception

A 16-year-old girl sees her favourite pop star, Taylor Swift, endorsing an energy drink. Her interpretation is that the energy drink is healthy so she buys it.

> **Example** Ⓔ
>
> **Selective exposure**
>
> When listening to the radio, an individual might change to a different station when an advertisement comes on.

> **Example** Ⓔ
>
> **Selective attention – physical characteristics**
>
> - Larger stimuli are more likely to receive attention than smaller ones. A full-page advertisement is more likely to be noticed than a half-page one. Some advertisers often set their advertisements off from others by showing their products in colour against a black-and-white background. A large billboard on the highway is more likely to receive attention than a poster.
> - Sudden silences in TV advertisements, drastic changes in music, sudden changes from black and white to colour and the way in which prices are announced and displayed all serve as methods of enhancing attention. Grocery stores display and announce the prices of their products in TV commercials.

also attract attention to sale items. Stores are designed with highly visible shelves and overhead signs to make locating items as easy as possible.

Attention

Attention is activated when one or more of the sensory receptors are stimulated and the resulting sensations are processed in the brain. However, individuals are exposed to more stimuli than they can process, therefore, they have to be selective in attending to marketing and other messages. This is known as *selective attention*, thus the stimuli will be processed only when the individual makes a deliberate effort. Normally, a person will attend to a stimulus if he or she is interested in it. For example, someone who rarely notices car advertisements will become very much aware of them when he or she is planning to buy a new car. The physical characteristics of the stimulus likewise determine whether a person's attention will be activated. The marketer attempts to overcome consumers' selective attention so that they will attend to the marketing message.

Interpretation

Interpretation is the meaning that people assign to sensory stimuli. Just as people differ in terms of the stimuli that they perceive, the eventual assignment of meaning to these stimuli varies as well. Two people can see or hear the same event, but their interpretation of it can be like night and day. Consumers usually interpret information on the basis of their own attitudes, beliefs, motives and experiences, which is known as *selective interpretation*. They often interpret information in a manner that supports their own position. Marketers rely heavily on symbols in marketing messages to promote the correct interpretation.

Recall (or memory)

Consumers do not remember all the information they see, hear or read, even after attending to and interpreting it. *Selective recall* refers to the fact that consumers tend to forget the marketing message. To ensure full and correct recall of the message as well as appropriate purchasing action, the marketer must use point-of-purchase promotion to remind the consumer of the message and product.

Learning ability

Any facet of a person's behaviour is dependent on what he or she **learns** and remembers about objects and situations. How individuals learn is of immense importance to marketers who want consumers to learn about their particular products.

The definition makes it clear that an individual learns as a result of acquired knowledge or experience.

Elements of learning

All individuals learn, but not all individuals learn the same things, nor do they learn at the same speed or in the same way. The *basic elements of learning* are *stimulus, response* and *reinforcement*. These elements are found in all learning.[3]

Stimulus

The first requirement of learning is a stimulus. The consumer can be stimulated by physical things such as products, brands and size, or intangibles such as service and quality. Once the consumer has perceived the stimulus (object), he or she must be motivated to seek the object before learning occurs. The stronger the motivation is, the quicker the consumer learns.

Response

A response is any action, reaction or state of mind which results from a particular stimulus or cue. The same response to a stimulus may occur several times before one can say that the response is learned. Cues stimulate response: marketers who provide consistent cues, as in advertising messages, to a consumer may succeed in creating a favourable image of their product in the consumer's mind.

Reinforcement

Reinforcement increases the likelihood that a particular response will occur in the future as the result of particular cues or stimuli. Positive reinforcement is a pleasant experience, while negative reinforcement involves the avoidance of an unpleasant experience.

Repetition

Repetition refers to the act of repeating past actions or experiences. This action of repetition enhances learning, which is why repetitive advertising is effective in communicating positive images about products to consumers. To aid reinforcement, marketers often hand out free samples and have demonstrations in stores, thus guiding the consumer's learning process towards the retailer's products.

The capacity of learners is important in determining what can be learned and how long it will take. An advertisement should thus not be too complicated. Practice distributed over several periods is more economical in learning than the same amount of practice concentrated into a single period, thus advertising campaigns spread over several weeks or months are more likely to achieve higher consumer learning than short, intense campaigns. The rate of forgetting tends to be very rapid immediately after learning. Repetition is necessary to remind the consumer of the product.

Attitude

Every time you are asked whether you like or dislike a product or an advertisement, you are being asked to express your opinion. For example, if you say that you prefer Sunlight Dishwashing Liquid, this means that you have a positive **attitude** towards it. If you say you do not like smoking, you are in fact saying that you have a negative attitude

Example (E)

Symbols promote correct interpretation[2]

- The 'Proudly South African' symbol assures customers that the companies and their products are of a high standard and are socially responsible, and that they support the local economy.
- Santam's yellow umbrella symbolises the extensive cover that the company offers.

WWW:

- http://www.verimark.co.za

Example (E)

Marketers attempt to promote recall

- Marketers often use symbols, rhymes, jingles and association that assist in the learning and memory process. Vodacom used the popular song *Gangnam style* for their 'Vodacom double your summer' TV commercial.
- Eveready puts pictures of its pink Energizer bunny on packages to remind consumers at the point of purchase of its creative advertising.

DEFINITION

Learning

Learning, in a marketing context, can be defined as the direct or anticipated changes in the behaviour of the consumer due to experience gained.

towards it. The marketer therefore has to try to influence the attitude of the consumer, for example by means of advertisements.

Components of attitude

An individual's attitude is regarded as having three components: *cognitive, affective* and *behavioural (conative).*

Cognitive component

This component of attitude refers to a person's knowledge and perceptions that may be acquired by direct experience with the product and other sources of information. For most attitude objects, we have a number of beliefs.

It is important to note that beliefs need not be correct or true; they need only to exist.

Affective component

This component of attitude has to do with the consumer's feelings or emotions with respect to the focus of the attitude. It captures the overall assessment of a product by a consumer. The evaluation may be a mere general feeling that is developed without cognitive information about the product.

Behavioural (conative) component

This component represents the outcome of the cognitive and affective components – to buy or not to buy. What a consumer does about knowledge of and feelings towards a product is most important to a company. The consumer may have positive information about a product and like it, but may not actually buy it for a variety of reasons. For example, habit in respect of another brand may be strong, there may be other brands the customer prefers, or it may be unaffordable.

The cognitive, affective and behavioural components of attitude tend to be consistent. This means that a change in one attitude component tends to produce related changes in the others. Marketers are ultimately concerned with influencing behaviour. Consumers may be influenced by listening to sales personnel, attending to advertisements or examining packages. Marketers can therefore indirectly influence behaviour by providing information that influences a belief about the product if the three components are indeed consistent with one another.

Attitude change[4]

Marketers are able to change or influence consumer's attitude with their marketing strategies in various ways:

- **Changing consumer beliefs of a brand**. Change the way consumers view the brand or product by associating the brand with positive attributes; for example, Milo Cereal gives children enough energy to go through a full day.

Example (E)

Learning about products

Janet has learnt from past experience that Pick n Pay has a wider variety of groceries then the local grocery shops in her suburb.

Example (E)

Motivation aids learning

Because Jake is keen to become a good cricket player, he is motivated to learn all he can about cricket. He may seek information about the prices and quality of a good cricket bat if he 'learns' that a good bat is instrumental in playing a good game.

Example (E)

Positive and negative reinforcement

- When visiting a store for the first time, an individual finds the service to be excellent and the store to be welcoming. As a result, that person will most likely recommend the store to others and visit the store again.
- A family goes to a restaurant and is eventually seated after waiting for half an hour. The waitress is not friendly, they receive their food after an hour and it is not what they ordered. The family is unlikely to return to the restaurant.

- **Changing consumer's behaviour towards a product**. Once consumers start using a product, it is likely that they will continue using it if they are satisfied. Marketers use price discounts to entice customers to switch to their brand.
- **Adding new beliefs**. Adding new benefits or improvements to products which may include newer applications or uses of the product.
- **Strengthening beliefs**. Focusing on the current positive beliefs or attributes that consumers have about a brand and comparing them to a competitor brand can greatly influence consumer attitude.

Personality

You might say that one of your friends is 'fairly aggressive, very opinionated, competitive, outgoing and witty'. What you have described is your friend's **personality**.

A person's personality thus refers to his or her inner characteristics, those specific qualities, attributes, traits and mannerisms that distinguish one individual from another. These deeply ingrained characteristics that we call personality are likely to influence an individual's product and store choices, as well as the way the consumer responds to the marketer's promotional messages.

Characteristics of personality

Let us now look at some of the characteristics of personality.

Personality reflects individual differences

The characteristics that make up a person's personality are a unique combination of factors, hence no two individuals are exactly alike. Many people can be described as very sociable, while others can be described as 'low' in sociability. Personality is a useful concept as it enables us to categorise people into different groups on the basis of a single or a few traits. Individuals have different unique attributes that make up their personality.

Personality is consistent and enduring

An individual's personality usually remains the same, thus it is unreasonable for marketers to attempt to change someone's personality to conform to certain products. At best, they learn which personality characteristics influence particular consumer responses and attempt to appeal to relevant personality traits inherent in their target group of consumers. However, an individual's personality may change because of major events such as the birth of a child, the death of a loved one or as a result of a major career promotion.

The value of personality to marketers

The personality of individual consumers affects the products that they tend to buy. Consumers who are conscious of the environment, for

DEFINITION

Attitude

A consumer attitude is a learned predisposition to behave in a consistently favourable or unfavourable way toward market-related objects, events or situations.

Example

Repeating past experience

Jack goes to the Pick n Pay in his area every day after work to buy bread and milk. He knows the store layout and knows exactly where to find the products he needs. This makes it easier and less time consuming for Jack to make the purchase.

Example

Negative attitude

A person who does not like a specific brand of clothing has a negative attitude towards that brand and would never consider buying it.

example, look for products that are environmentally friendly. Purchase decisions are sometimes also based on a consumer's self-concept. Consumers also differ in the way they react to advertisements to which they are exposed. It is thus important for marketers to design advertisements that appeal to the different personality types.[5]

> **Example** (E)
>
> **Beliefs make up an attitude**
>
> We may believe that Simba chips are popular with younger people, competitively priced, taste good and made by a large company. The total configuration of beliefs about this brand of chips represents the cognitive component of an attitude toward Simba.

Lifestyle

Marketers use **lifestyle** to discover how people spend their time, what they find interesting and important, and how they view themselves and the world around them. Lifestyle is related to values. Those who value fun probably like skiing, dancing and camping, and they are often big alcohol consumers. A person's set of values plays a very important role in consumption activities – many products are purchased because people believe these products will help them to attain a value-related goal. Our desired lifestyle influences our needs and desires, and thus our purchase and use behaviour. The marketer can use lifestyle groups to depict particular lifestyles that the brand is attempting to target.

In the next section we will look at the group factors that influence consumer behaviour.

> **Example** (E)
>
> **Emotions influence overall reaction**
>
> - The statement 'Perrier water is overpriced' implies a negative affective response to a specific aspect of the product which, in combination with feelings about other attributes, will determine the overall reaction to this brand of bottled water.

Group factors influencing consumer behaviour

Most individuals tend to be involved with other people on a daily basis, whether this is the family, cultural group, social class, reference groups, peer groups or opinion leaders. For example, a substantial amount of learning involves interaction with, or imitation of, other individuals such as family and peers. These groups exert a great influence on the individual, and are reflected in Figure 3.1. We will now look at each of these groups.

The family

The family has a major influence on the consumer behaviour of its members. There are two levels of family. The first is the *nuclear family* comprising a husband, wife and children. The second is the *extended family*, which includes grandparents or other relatives who live under the same roof as the nuclear family. A family whose members have lived in close contact with one another for years gradually develops fixed behaviour and consumption patterns. Most children acquire their consumer behaviour norms through observation of their parents who function as role models.

> **DEFINITION**
>
> **Personality**
>
> Personality is those inner psychological characteristics that both determine and reflect how a person responds to his or her environment.

Family roles[6]

There are five roles in the family decision-making process and marketers need to be aware of these roles when designing a marketing campaign.

- **The initiator**. This is the first person to suggest that a specific product should be bought. This is also the person who collects information about the product or service. Teenagers often act as initiators.

- **The influencer**. This person influences the final decision either explicitly or implicitly in the sense that his or her suggestions and wishes are reflected in the family's decision.
- **The decision maker**. This person takes the actual decision and makes the final choice between alternatives.
- **The purchaser**. This is the person who buys the products. Some purchasers are forced to carry out the instructions of the decision maker, whereas others have the authority to choose for family members and thus assert their preferences. They will either purchase the products based on their own preferences or they will follow instructions given to them.
- **The user**. This is the person who uses the product at the end.

Marketers are inclined to direct their marketing messages exclusively at women as though they alone are responsible for the purchasing decision and dominate family decision making. However, there are indications that men are playing an increasingly important role in family decision making and that they even act as purchasers of items previously regarded as exclusively in the female domain. Modern children are very knowledgeable and it is generally accepted that they too have a role to play in family decision making.

Family types[7]

Families are usually classified in terms of the dominant member. The following family types are distinguished:

- **Husband-dominant family**, where the husband makes all or most of the purchase decisions.
- **Wife-dominant family**, where the wife makes all or most of the purchase decisions.
- **Nuclear family**, where decisions are made by both spouses. Today this type of family is coming more and more to the fore.
- **Child-dominant family**, where the children have a major say in the purchase decisions.

Cultural group

Cultural groups share a commonality of cultural values, rules, norms, symbols and experiences that are passed down from generation to generation. A consumer's **culture** further determines his or her overall priorities in respect of different activities and products, thus a product that provides benefits consistent with those desired by members of a culture has a much better chance of being accepted in the market.

The bounds that culture sets for behaviour are called *norms*. Norms are simply rules that specify or prohibit certain types of behaviour in certain situations and are based on cultural values. Violation of cultural norms results in sanctions or penalties ranging from mild social disapproval to banishment from the group.

South African society is fragmented into many cultural groups and subgroups. Marketing management must therefore be careful not to

DEFINITION

Lifestyle
Lifestyle is the characteristics that represent the style of living of a group or individual.

Example

How advertisers use lifestyle
- Castle Lager advertisements advertise South Africans who like having fun, being together and watching sports.
- Virgin Active appeals to the 'health fanatics'.

WWW:
- http://www.virginactive.co.za/

Example

Children influence some decisions
- Children under 12 are most influential in the purchase of breakfast cereal, snack foods, sweets, soft drinks, games and toys, clothing, music and toothpaste.

DEFINITION

Culture
Culture is the system of shared beliefs and behaviours in a society that are learnt and transmitted from generation to generation.

use symbols in advertisements that can be interpreted incorrectly or differently, and must not portray unacceptable behaviour patterns. It is important that communication to the different target groups reflects their specific cultural norms, values, language and symbols.

Social class

Social class refers to groups of people who have the same social standings in society and who show similar behaviour patterns. The behaviour of a social class is a function of, for example, occupation, income and education. In South Africa, the gap in income between the richest and poorest people, as measured by the Gini coefficient, is one of the largest in the world.

A social class structure usually consists of the upper, middle and lower class. During the past 10 years, more previously disadvantaged South Africans have moved into the middle and upper social classes.

Social class strongly influences consumer lifestyles and is, in general, a good indicator of the type of product that consumers would be interested in. Furthermore, consumers buy products to demonstrate their membership of a particular social class and to advance their social standing in society. Marketers know that most consumers aspire to membership of a higher social class. Their marketing messages therefore imply that by buying their product the consumer may attain membership of a higher class.

Some of the marketing implications of social class are the following behaviours:[8]

- **Media usage**. More-educated individuals generally focus more on reading and going to the theatre than the less educated, who would spend more time watching TV.
- **Collection of information**. Higher social groups are more informed and are more exposed to information sources.
- **Store choice**. The types of stores patronised by the different classes differ – the higher social classes shop more at branded stores than at discount stores.
- **Leisure pursuits**. Individuals in the higher social classes spend more time on leisure activities, often related to some level of prestige – for example being part of an exclusive golf club.

Reference groups

In all reference groups there are distinctive norms of behaviour, and members are expected to conform to these norms in order to avoid sanctions being applied against them. We distinguish between the following types of reference groups that influence consumer behaviour patterns:[9]

- **Membership groups**. These are groups to which an individual has gained membership to, for example Nike running club.
- **Automatic groups**. These are groups that individuals fall into as a result of gender, age, race, etc.
- **Negative groups**. These are groups that individuals intentionally avoid being associated with. This can be a group that is always

Example (E)

Cultural norms

- Direct eye contact is the norm in most Western countries, whereas in Japan it is seen as a sign of disrespect.
- In some African cultures, it is the norm for the wife to sit lower than the husband as a sign of respect. For example, the wife would sit on the floor while the husband will sit on a chair.
- In the Indian culture, it is a norm for brides to decorate their hands and feet with henna.

Example (E)

Cultural differences

- Black and white culture groups may interpret advertisements differently. For example, flowers have special significance in the white culture, but in many black cultures, gifts in the form of flowers are frowned upon. The well-known Five Roses advertisement which said 'And the fifth rose is for you' was not successful when used in media aimed at black consumers.
- Cross-cultural mistakes are also made in other countries. For example, the tag line for Parker Pen that reads 'It won't leak in your pocket and embarrass you' translates in Mexico to, 'It won't leak in your pocket and impregnate you'.

negative and critical at work, or those who go out on a regular basis to drink and womanise.

- **Associative groups**. These are groups that individuals work towards being a part of. For example, individuals aspire to be part of a golf club as these groups are of higher status and social standing. Typical members of associative reference groups are often used as models in advertisements in order to show potential consumers the type of person who buys the product and also the way in which the product can be used. In this way consumers are persuaded to follow the example set by these models.

Peer groups

Peer groups are individuals who have the same background, social status in society and similar behaviours. The members of the peer group are likely to influence an individual's beliefs and behaviour. For example, a teenage girl will be influenced by her peer group when making decisions about appropriate clothes to buy.

Opinion leaders

A reference group need not necessarily be a group of persons, but can also be a reference person or individual to whom others will look when forming opinions and taking consumer decisions. The reference person can therefore be regarded as an *opinion leader*. The opinion leader need not be well known or enjoy high status, but can be an ordinary person or even an imaginary one. Think of the well-known advertisement where a homemaker sings the praises of Omo detergent.

The group factors discussed above, as well as the individual factors, influence the consumer's decisions about what products to buy or which stores to patronise. We will now look at the decision-making process.

Consumer decision-making process

Consumers display distinctive behaviour patterns in the decision-making process. Let us first consider the different types of decision making.

Types of decision making

We distinguish between three types of decision making:

- **Real decision making**. This is a complex process and involves extensive problem solving, such as the decision to buy a new house or car.
- **Impulse decision making**. This refers to unplanned action on the spur of the moment as opposed to conscious planning during real decision making, for example deciding to buy a chocolate bar displayed at the till while waiting in a supermarket queue.
- **Habitual decision making**. This occurs when a consumer is brand loyal, for example buying a large tin of a particular coffee automatically without even considering other brands.

DEFINITION

Social class
Social class refers to groups of people who share more or less the same social standing in society.

DEFINITION

Reference group
A reference group refers to a group of people that an individual uses as a standard when making decisions.

DEFINITION

Adoption process
This refers to the different stages in the process by which an individual makes a decision to purchase the new product or not, to keep on using it, or to change to a new product or service.

Phases in consumer decision making[10]

Phases involved in consumer decision making are the following:

- **Need recognition**. This refers to when the consumer recognises or becomes aware of a need. For example, because John's wife is pregnant, he realises that his one-bedroom apartment will be too small for a family, so he recognises a need for a bigger apartment or house.

CASE STUDY

A new approach to business[11]

KFC realised that, in order to connect with its audience, it needed to restructure its business around its customers. The brand had always been a mass-market retail business with a very broad focus across the consumer spectrum. Admittedly, it was segmented across race, dividing its target audience by 'emerging' and 'developed' – euphemisms for 'black' and 'white'.

However, across the globe, marketing was becoming a niche game, with the winners identifying and focusing on very tightly defined segments.

Recognising this, the marketing team, in partnership with Ogilvy, divided that one mass market into the following new segments, which could be individually targeted, using age, income, gender and product-usage occasions:

- **High-income families**. Young families with children, generally headed by the mother.
- **High-income individuals**. Upwardly mobile high achievers, to be further segmented by gender divides – male and female.
- **Affordable-value customers**. Families and individuals who were typically previously disadvantaged and very conscious of the cost of living, but would increase fast-food consumption if the price were right.
- **Teens and young adults**. Students and young adults with busy lives and limited responsibilities.

This was the first time in the history of the KFC group that target markets had been so clearly defined, and that specific offerings were created to target these specific segments tightly.

Questions

- Explain how the consumer behaviour of each segment influences the purchase decision.
- How does KFC benefit from aiming its marketing activities at different segments?

- **Search for information**. The consumer will do research and find information from various sources. For example, John may first use internal sources, such as memory and experience, and then external sources such as the advice of family members and friends, or marketing sources such as real estate magazines or websites.
- **Evaluation**. The consumer looks at alternatives and makes comparisons. John may consider buying a bigger apartment or a house. He now evaluates these two alternatives in terms of certain criteria such as cost, the area and the space.
- **Purchase decision**. A decision is made once the consumer has chosen the best alternative. John also has to decide what he can afford and if he will use a real estate agent.
- **Post-purchase evaluation**. The consumer re-evaluates his decision. If his expectations in his dealings with the real estate agent are met,

this can lead to brand loyalty. If his expectations were not met, he may complain and never consider using the company again. This condition is known as *cognitive dissonance*. The post-purchase phase can be regarded as the beginning of a new decision-making process. Will John, for example, consider using the same agency if he moves again?

In the next section the adoption of new products by consumers is discussed. Also see the case study entitled 'A new approach to business'.

Adoption of new products

When a product is new and unknown, and there is a certain degree of risk attached to its use, it is only adopted gradually as part of a learning process. The microwave, as a new product, was adopted relatively slowly. The perceived risk attending the adoption of a new product includes financial risk (the money spent on the product will be wasted if the product is unsatisfactory); functional risk (there is a danger that the product may not perform as desired); social risk (consumers may feel that others may look down on them if they purchase the product); and physical risk (the potential for personal harm or health hazard). Consumers usually move through the following five stages in arriving at a decision to purchase or reject a new product:

- **Awareness**. During this first stage, consumers are exposed to the product innovation. They know about the new idea but lack sufficient awareness about it.
- **Interest**. The consumer becomes interested in the product and seeks more information about it.
- **Evaluation**. Based on their information, consumers draw conclusions about the innovation or determine whether further information is necessary. This stage represents a kind of 'mental trial' of the new product. If the evaluation is satisfactory, the consumer will actually try the product. However, if the mental trial is unsatisfactory, the product will be rejected.
- **Trial**. At this stage, consumers use the product on a limited basis. Their experience with the product provides them with the critical information that they need to adopt or reject.
- **Adoption or rejection**. The adoption of some products may have minimal consequences, while the adoption of other innovations may lead to major behavioural and lifestyle changes, such as the major impact on society of products like the car and television.

Marketers of a new product must therefore do everything in their power to allay the fears of the consumer. Sufficient information must be provided in the marketing messages to convince consumers the product will satisfy their needs. Let us look at the characteristics of people who adopt an innovation at different points in time:[12]

- **Innovators**. These are younger individuals and are more willing to try new things. They are also more educated.

- **Early adopters**. These are willing to take calculated risks.
- **Early majority**. These adopt after the innovation has been successful.
- **Late majority**. These are sceptical about innovations, tend to be older and have less social status, and often adopt more in response to social pressure.
- **Laggards**. These are more traditional and are the last people to adopt an innovation. They are less likely to try anything new and do not have much social interaction.

Marketers often attempt to identify the innovators – those who are more likely to adopt a new product – in the hope that the product will spread more easily in the market.

Summary

In this chapter, we examined the individual and group factors influencing buying behaviour. We also looked at the different types of decisions, and the consumer decision-making process. We further briefly discussed the adoption of new products and consumer buying behaviour.

References

1. Based on Boundless.com. n.d. *Customer wants and needs*. [Online] Available from: https://www.boundless.com/marketing/an-overview-of-marketing/introduction-to-marketing/customers-wants-and-needs/ [Accessed: 2013-05-15].
2. Santam. 2013. *Logo history*. [Online] Available from: http://www.santam.co.za/about-us/who-we-are/the-yellow-umbrella [Accessed: 2013-05-15].
3. Based on Joubert, P. 2010. *Introduction to consumer behaviour*. Cape Town, South Africa: Juta & Co., p. 61
4. Based on USCMarshall. 2010. *Attitudes*. [Online] Available from: http://www.consumerpsychologist.com/cb_Attitudes.html [Accessed: 2013-05-06].
5. Joubert, op. cit., p. 93.
6. Based on USCMarshall. 2010. *Families and family decision making*. [Online] Available from: http://www.consumerpsychologist.com/cb_Family_Decision_Making.html [Accessed: 2013-05-20].
7. Cant. M.C., Van Heerden, C.H. & Ngambi. H.C. 2010. *Marketing management: A South African perspective*. Cape Town, South Africa: Juta & Co., p. 61.
8. Harrington, C. & Steward, K. 2013. *Social class*. [Online] Available from: http://www.slideshare.net/kas053/social-class-10147687 [Accessed: 2013-05-22].
9. Based on Rao, R.S. 2010. *Reference groups*. [Online] Available from: http://www.citeman.com/9018-refernce -groups.html [Accessed: 2013-05-24].
10. Based on Managementstudyguide.com. 2013. *Stages in consumer decision making*. [Online] Available from: http://www.topentrepreneur.co.za/Pages/Marketing/Consumer%20Behaviour%20The%20Decision%20Making%20Process.html [Accessed: 2013-05-20].
11. Van Heerden, C.H. 2013. *Contemporary retail and marketing case studies*. Cape Town, South Africa: Juta & Co., p. 65.
12. QuickMBA.com. 2010. *Product diffusion curve*. [Online] Available from: http://www.quickmba.com/marketing/product/diffusion/ [Accessed: 2013-05-22].

Marketing information and marketing research

CHAPTER 4

✓ Learning objectives

After studying this chapter, you should be able to:

- explain the information needs of marketing management;
- discuss the nature of marketing information systems;
- elaborate on the types and sources of marketing information;
- discuss the use of marketing research as a major instrument in addressing the information needs of managers;
- introduce the Internet as a new development in marketing research; and
- investigate the techniques used for measuring and forecasting market demand.

Introduction

The need for information has become increasingly more important in the past decade. This is due to a large extent to the level of globalisation taking place and the fact that technology has all but eliminated distances and borders. Marketers need up-to-date and reliable information immediately and not at some time in the future. This new millennium can rightly be called the information age where technology will dictate the speed and availability of information. These developments have also resulted in what is termed 'information overload' – that is, that there is just too much information available for marketing management

'Information management is focused on accessible and available data.'

to digest and disseminate. Much greater emphasis is consequently being placed on the efficient management of information than ever before. The problem facing marketing managers today is not necessarily in the acquisition of information, but in the time spent on processing it so that only relevant and quality information remains and is applied.

This chapter considers, in the first place, the changing information needs of marketing managers. It then briefly discusses the nature of marketing information systems, and information sources in particular. The next section of the chapter deals with the application of marketing research as an important tool for information acquisition and management, with particular attention being paid to the Internet. The last part of the chapter highlights selected techniques for the measurement and forecast of market demand.

Information needs

Information for marketing decision making

Information bridges the gap between the market and the company, and serves as a link between the two.[1] The fact that there are numerous information sources available to marketing managers makes for a complex decision-making environment. Marketing managers, however, need information to reduce the possibility of incorrect or risky decision making, and therefore need it to be timely, accurate and reliable. Without such information, the planning, implementation and control of marketing activities cannot be carried out.

In reality, however, marketing managers find themselves in a situation where the information is often not readily available in order to make an educated decision, or the information is available but is not structured in a useful format. This means that an information gap exists.

An information gap refers to a situation where there is a lack of useful information necessary to make decisions, meaning that managers cannot use the information they have to make informed decisions. Managers must often decide if they have the necessary information at hand and, if so, whether they need more. The major types of marketing information requirements are illustrated in Figure 4.1. From this diagram it is clear that there are many environmental variables about which marketing managers need information.

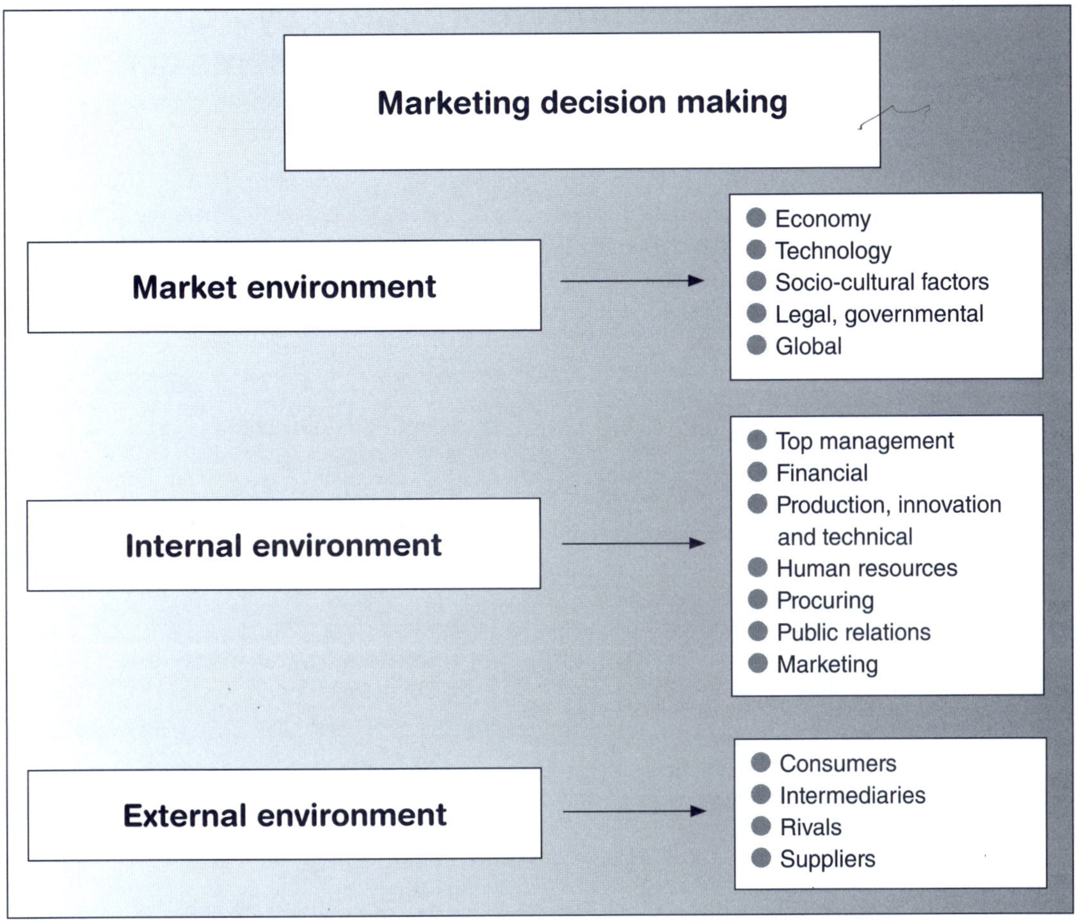

Figure 4.1 Marketing decision making

The role of information in management

The role that information plays in management cannot be overemphasised. In some instances there is either too little or too much information, or there is insufficient time to make a decision, and this creates a need to improve the process in which information is managed in the organisation. Information management is consequently focused on *accessible* and *available data*. For example, managers may encounter a situation where they need information on competitors' marketing plans that is not readily available. Accessible data is, in fact, available, but has to be collected.

Information management also deals with the difference between data and information. *Data* refers to all available statistics, figures, opinions, facts and forecasts, while *information* refers to data that is organised in a fashion that leads to marketing actions. Information management must continuously monitor data sources, and manage data reduction and information transition, as well as a constant flow of information to marketing managers. This can only be accomplished with a marketing information system.

DEFINITION

Marketing information system

A structured process that is used to gather and analyse data regarding a particular opportunity or threat in order to assist marketing managers to make informed decisions.

Marketing information systems

Marketing information systems defined

The marketing information system is a tool that marketers use to manage information effectively.

A marketing information system is a typical input–output system with information sources being the input, and relevant, timely and accurate information the output. It is a system of interactive and interdependent subsystems which function as a whole. The various components of a marketing information system are illustrated in Figure 4.2.

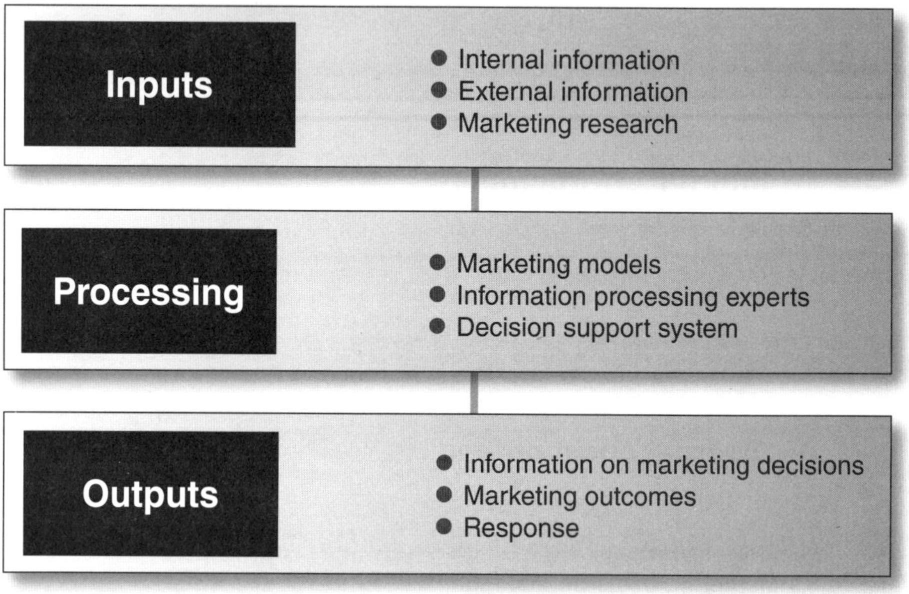

Figure 4.2 Components of a marketing information system

Components of a marketing information system

The basic operation of a marketing information system involves the gathering of data (*inputs*) and the processing of data in a database with the aid of marketing models, information processing specialists and the decision support system (DSS) to produce useful marketing information (*outputs*) (see Figure 4.2). Let us look at each component in more detail.

Inputs

The inputs into the marketing information system consist of the following:

- **Marketing research**. This is the planned collection of information on an ad hoc or continual basis.
- **Internal data sources**. These are all available sources of internal information, such as sales records, accounting reports, production reports, financial reports, etc.

- **External data sources**. These are all sources of information available from outside the company, such as published reports, articles, and syndicated studies and statistical records.

Processing

In the processing section of the marketing information system, the following three components are identified:

Marketing models

Marketing models refer to sets of cause-and-effect relationships built into standardised models. Various models are available to marketers, including the following:

- **Marketing mix models** are models that help in the determination of an optimal marketing mix and take into account the market response to the various marketing mix elements and their interactions.
- **Forecasting models** include time series models, econometric models and judgemental models, which have been used in forecasting sales, shares and other marketing objectives.
- **New product forecasting models** are used for forecasting the performance of new products and services.
- **Advertising models** are used to assist marketers in making advertising decisions, and include decision calculus models and models used for media selection and scheduling.

Decision support system (DSS)

A decision support system (DSS) or marketing decision support system (MDSS) is a computerised system which helps marketing management to obtain and use information that is relevant to specific decision-making situations. The American Marketing Association describes it as a 'coordinated collection of data, system tools, and techniques with supporting software and hardware by which an organization gathers and interprets relevant information from business and the environment and turns it into a basis for making management decisions'.[2]

Decision support systems are made up of the following parts:

- **Data system**. This is the part of the DSS that includes the processes used to capture and store data that originates from a number of external and internal sources.
- **Dialogue system**. This is also called the *language system*, and is the part of the DSS that permits users to explore the databases by using the system models to produce reports that satisfy particular information needs.
- **Model system**. This includes all the routines that allow the user to manipulate the data so as to conduct the kind of analysis desired.

Information processing specialists

Information processing specialists are specialised personnel who help with the information processing of specialised requests and reports.

'A decision support system (DSS) or marketing decision support system (MDSS) is a computerised system which helps marketing management to obtain and use information that is relevant to specific decision-making situations.'

'A marketing manager must weigh the value of information against its costs in deciding which marketing information will deliver the optimum results needed by top management.'

Outputs

The outputs consist of specific information in the form of reports on sales, consumer demand, competitors' reactions and the like, which can be used to answer questions or to solve problems. From the output side of the marketing information system, information on the decisions taken by marketing management provides feedback to the input side where more information is needed to solve a specific problem.

Advantages and costs of marketing information

A marketing manager must weigh the value of information against its costs in deciding which marketing information will deliver the optimum results needed by top management. All information has two important dimensions: *a quality* or *value dimension*, which refers to the value of the information as expressed in the quality of decision making, and the *cost dimension*, which refers to the price of the information.

The *quality* or *value dimension* is a function of the following criteria:

- **Accurate (valid) information**. This refers to the realities of the situation.
- **Timely information**. This simply means recent information that is available when desired.
- **Adequate information**. This means sufficient qualitative and quantitative information to enable better decisions.
- **Availability of information**. This refers to the accessibility of information (that is, can it be obtained?).
- **Relevant information**. This refers to the suitability of information for the decision which has to be taken.

No information can be obtained without a cost implication. The *cost dimension* of information consists of:

- **economic costs** (direct financial or indirect costs in terms of opportunity costs, such as those which result from delaying a decision); and
- **psychological costs** (frustration in searching for information).

The real value of information can only be obtained from a *value appraisal*. A value appraisal involves the assessment of information in terms of its contribution to marketing decision making. Figure 4.3 shows a typical value appraisal expressed as a simplified cost/value formula.

Benefits received — **Cost incurred** = **Value**

Figure 4.3 Value appraisal of marketing information for decision making

It is possible that at times the value of the information cannot be determined by a value appraisal. Nevertheless, marketing management should regularly consider the value of information to develop an efficient information system. This is particularly important to prevent so-called nice-to-know information that does not substantially contribute to marketing decision making from being included in the information system. This, among others, will increase the role that marketing information can play in relationship marketing.

The place and role of marketing information in relationship marketing

The days of companies focusing only on securing the deal or making the transaction are long gone. The focus today has moved to relationship and not transaction marketing. Marketing information therefore contributes to the main functions of relationship marketing, which include customer retention, high customer commitment and high customer contact.

In Chapter 1, the concept of relationship marketing was briefly discussed, and particular attention was paid to the importance of information for relationship marketing. The availability of good and reliable marketing information in relationship marketing offers organisations a number of competitive advantages, which include the following:[4]

- It makes the entry of competitors more difficult.
- It makes changing brands more costly and difficult (brand switching).
- A strong customer database is developed, which assists in the establishing of a long-term relationship with customers.
- It is easier for organisations to meet the needs of the market more efficiently and to deliver products that are according to their requirements. This enhances the relationship that organisations have with their customers.

A number of factors related to information and technology influence relationship marketing decisions directly. Some of these are:[5]

- the provision of information to difficult and demanding customers on time;
- the provision of information with regard to excessive cost that the business incurs, such as unsuccessful products, low customer service, use of disproportionately high transport costs or ineffective marketing campaigns;
- the availability of data in-house such as the buying patterns of customers, customer profiles and their viewing patterns;
- business data, which refers to data that is relevant to the business, for example bar coding, electronic price scanning, etc; and
- the availability of reliable and relevant online information technology from various private and government sources.

CASE STUDY

Customer service in relationship marketing[3]

Dazzling service is one of Discovery's values, and since its inception, the company has sought to differentiate itself from the market based on its service offering. Over the past 20 years, the company has relied on the latest technology and infrastructure models to service high and continuously expanding volumes of client contact and interaction.

The service team structure consists of small teams, each servicing a particular regional client base. This structure offers the efficiencies of a large-scale servicing platform without the associated bureaucracy. Smaller, integrated teams working with defined, smaller sets of clients are able to provide personalised and immediate service.

Continue to next page

CASE STUDY

Continued from previous page

Since the company's inception, Discovery's use of pioneering call-centre technology and highly skilled call-centre agents has set the company apart from other financial services institutions. This focus has been retained over the years, in spite of challenges posed by its ever-expanding scale. There are 24-hour call centres for each brand, and walk-in centres in Cape Town, Sandton, Centurion, Durban and Port Elizabeth.

DEFINITION

Marketing research

Marketing research is the systematic gathering, recording and analysing of data to provide information useful in marketing decision making. The American Marketing Association defines marketing research as follows:[7]

> 'Marketing research is the function that links the consumer, customer and public to the marketer through information – information used to identify and define marketing

Continue to next page

From the above factors, it is clear that relationship marketing is impossible without information technology. The rapid growth of modern computer technology has been responsible for the explosion in information availability and consequently the strategic option of relationship marketing.

The nature of marketing research

Marketing research is performed to answer marketing management's questions of: 'Who are the consumers who buy?'; 'What products are bought?'; 'When are they bought?'; 'Where are they bought?'; 'Why are they bought?'; and 'How are they bought?'.[6]

Marketing research can, in the broadest sense, be classified as informal or formal. *Informal marketing research* involves taking advantage of every valid opportunity to collect information and market intelligence, and is quite effective as a 'first warning' mechanism. *Formal marketing research*, however, follows a methodical step-by-step approach which should result in reliable information for decision making. Formal marketing research focuses on specific problems and phenomena such as marketing actions, marketing performance and a better understanding of the market.

It is also important to distinguish clearly between the terms 'market research' and 'marketing research'. *Market research* is simply research into a specific market. It is a very narrow concept. *Marketing research* is much broader and includes not only market research, but also areas such as research into new products or modes of distribution such as the Internet. (Also see the definition box on marketing research.)

Steps in the marketing research process

Marketing research is referred to as a process, and this process consists of a number of steps which has as their aim to systematically collect, interpret and analyse marketing data. Researchers differ in the number and sequence of steps in the marketing research process, and because every marketing research problem is in some way unique, the procedures followed in the research process will vary to some extent. However, all marketing research processes contain the following basic steps, as illustrated in Figure 4.4.

Each step in the marketing research process will be discussed in detail in the following sections.

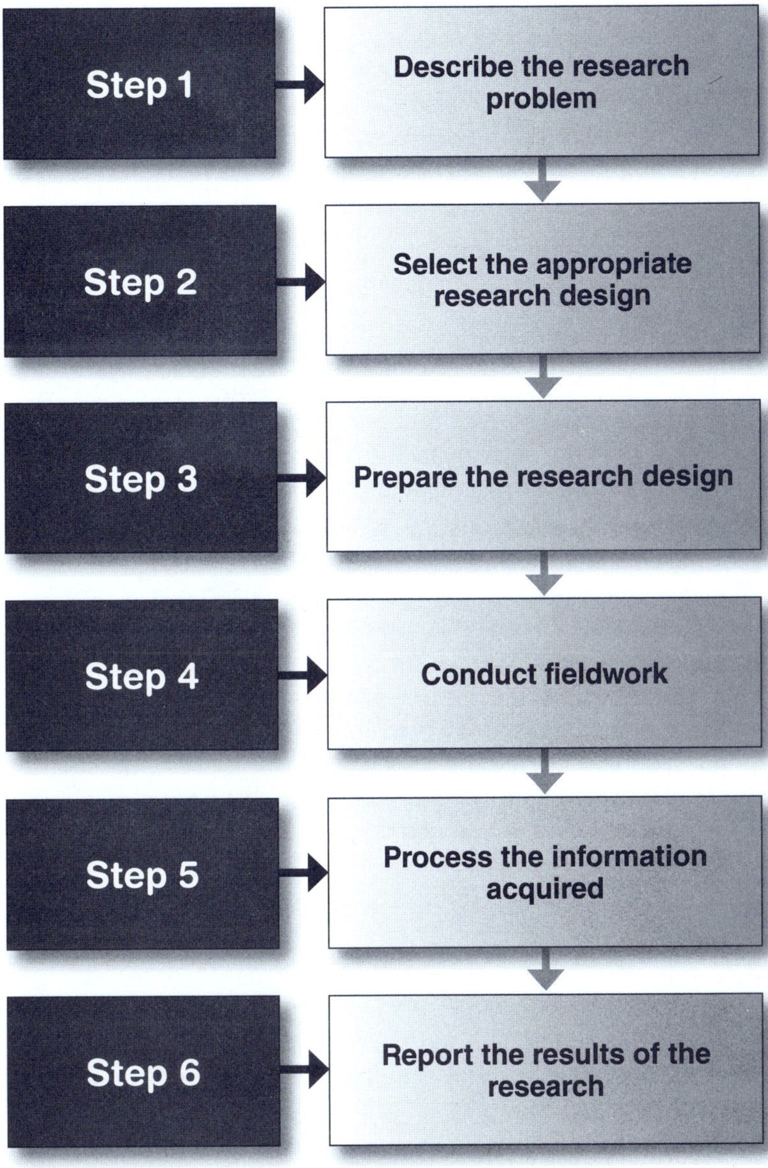

Figure 4.4 Steps in the marketing research process

Each of these steps is discussed below:

Step 1: Describe the research problem

Marketing problems refer to situations that may present real problems to marketing decision makers, as opposed to *marketing opportunities*, which are favourable or unexploited situations in the marketing environment that can be used by key decision makers to the advantage of the organisation.

The first step in the research process is the identification and formulation of the problem to be researched. The marketing problem or opportunity should be clearly defined and formulated to ensure that the results

DEFINITION

Continued from previous page

opportunities and problems; to generate, refine and evaluate marketing actions; to monitor marketing performance, and to improve understanding of marketing as a process. Marketing research specifies the information required to address these issues, designs the method for collecting information, manages and implements the data collection process, analyses the results, and communicates the findings and their implications.'

Put in more simple terms, marketing research can be defined as the systematic search for, recording and analysis of data which is used to solve problems or identify opportunities in marketing and related fields.

'A useful way to identify the research problems is to state the basic research problem as a hierarchy of questions.'

'Once the purpose of the study has been established, primary and secondary objectives should be established that support the purpose of the study and give some direction to the research process.'

obtained through the research are relevant. Both researchers and managers should remember that management problems stated as opportunities or threats are merely symptoms of underlying problems which have to be clearly defined. A weak diagnosis will inevitably lead to an inefficient solution. A useful way to identify the research problem is to state the basic one as a hierarchy of questions. The hierarchy of questions involves the following categories:

- **Management question**. The management problem represents a specific decision that management must make and is usually verbalised in some sort of management question (for example 'Are there changes in consumer preferences?').
- **Research question**. The management question must then be translated into a research question. At this stage the researcher will consider the appropriate research objectives (for example 'What are the reasons for changes in consumer preferences?').
- **Investigative questions**. Investigative questions will enable the researcher to answer the research question and thus answer the management question (for example 'Can changes in income patterns cause changing consumer preferences?').
- **Measurement questions**. The final category in the hierarchy involves the most specific level of the research design. Measurement questions would appear on the actual questionnaire or data collection instrument. (Specific questions could be 'What is your annual income?'; 'What is your occupation?'; and 'How much do you spend on product X?').

The situation analysis is an important part of problem formulation. A *situation analysis* refers to the process of gathering background information about the business and its environment.

The purpose of situation analysis is to assess the current situation, the position of the organisation and what the result will be, if the problem persists. Situation analysis takes the following environmental factors into consideration:

- **Secondary data analysis** (where existing information and forecasts are investigated);
- The **macro-environment** (economic, legal, technological, social);
- The organisation's **product markets** (product types, sales volumes, market shares);
- **Customer markets** and **buyer behaviour** (demographic, lifestyle, buying behaviour, preferences);
- **Marketing strategies** (advertising, pricing, intermediaries, products);
- The **resources and constraints** of the organisation; and
- The **technological skills** of the organisation.

The scanning of these environmental factors is used to complement the problem formulation and to serve as a valuable tool for setting the scene for decisions regarding the research design. Once the purpose of the study has been established, primary and secondary objectives should be formulated that support the purpose of the study and give some direction to the research process.

The specific information that is needed to solve a marketing research problem is refered to as a *marketing research objective*. Researchers should consider the following when stating the research objective:[8]

- The research question that is formulated should be specific in the information that will be needed by the researcher.
- The hypothesis is set in order to allow the researcher to test an unproven statement regarding the relationship between two or more variables. In essence it is a possible solution to the problem.
- The scope of the research is also crucial as it refers to the parameters of the study to be conducted by the researcher.

In this regard, the target segment (subjects of the research) and their accessibility should be considered. It should be determined whether the areas under investigation can be reached and if the level of accuracy will be satisfactory. Available resources should also be assessed. The researcher should then decide if the value of the information gathered is more than the costs that would be incurred.

These factors are illustrated in Figure 4.5.

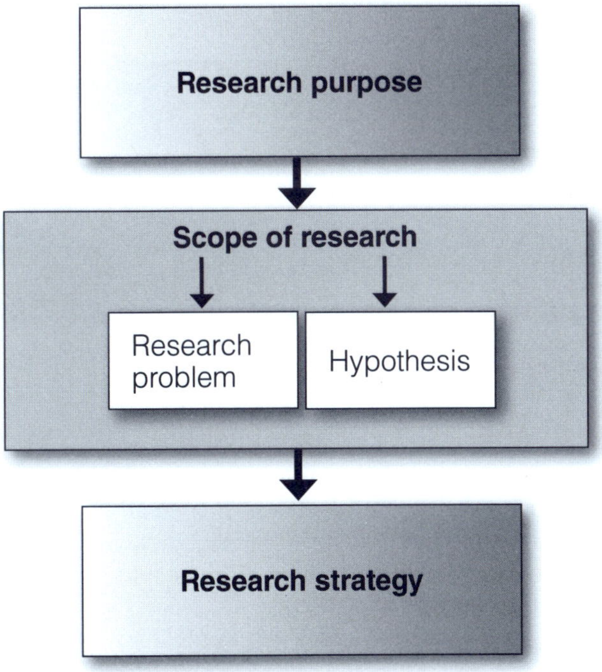

Figure 4.5 Factors determining the research objectives

The next step in the research process involves determining the possible research design that can be used in the study.

Step 2: Select the appropriate research design

A research design is a detailed plan for collecting and analysing data to obtain answers to a specific retail problem. Figure 4.6 describes the different design types and the five basic research design activities.

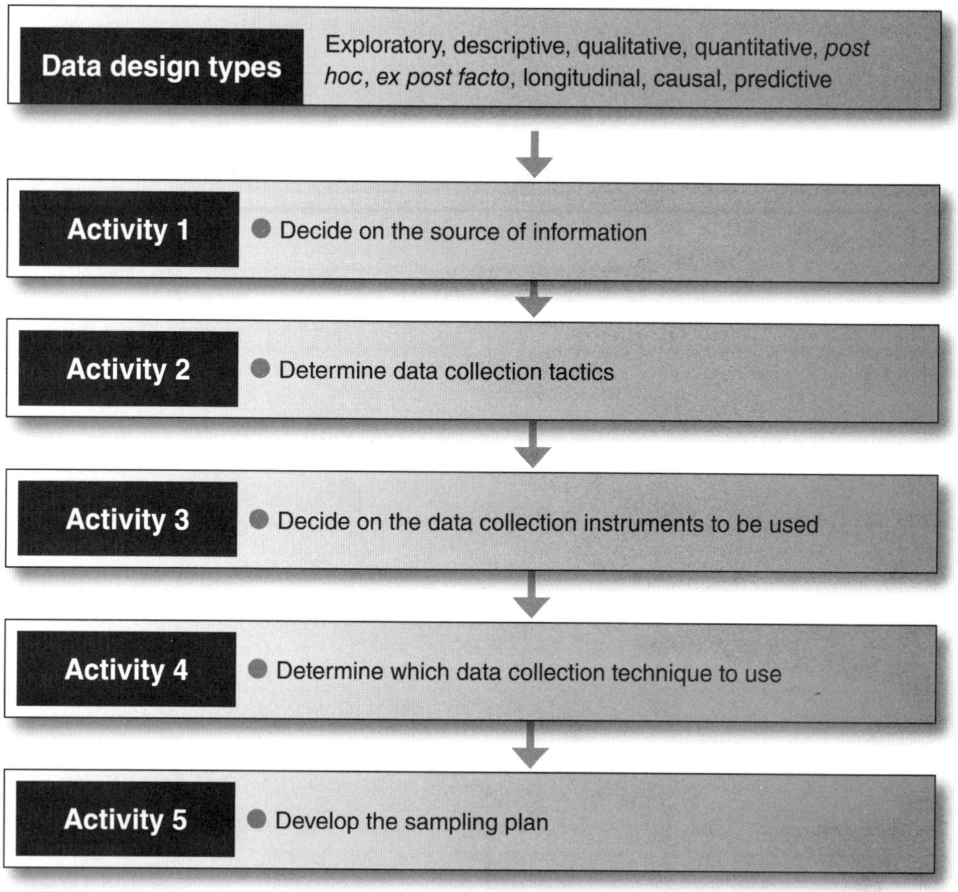

Figure 4.6 Research design types and activities

During the first step in the marketing research process, the general type of information required was established, which in turn shifted the focus towards the research objectives. The definition of the research problem and requirements of the research objectives would therefore determine to a large extent the type of research design that is most suitable for the situation.

The classification of available research designs (as shown in Figure 4.6) in the marketing research methodology is very broad and involves the following types of research designs (note that some of these designs overlap in their basic nature due to the different objectives addressed with each design).

- **Exploratory research**. The word 'exploratory' is clear in what this type of research is – exploring is necessary as very little information is available regarding a specific issue or situation. The main focus is on obtaining more information in order to determine if further research is needed, or if the study should proceed.
- **Descriptive research**. As the name indicates, descriptive research aims to provide a comprehensive and accurate description of the situation. This type of research answers the questions of 'who', 'what', 'when', 'where' and 'how' regarding a topic or situation.
- **Qualitative research**. Qualitative research seeks in-depth, open-ended responses. The aim is to get respondents to speak freely about a chosen subject and to obtain as wide as possible a response.
- **Quantitative research**. The focus of this research is on quantifying the responses obtained in the research process. The approach is descriptive in nature, and usually presents the findings in numbers, figures or statistical parameters.
- ***Post hoc* research**. *Post hoc* research attempts to investigate variables and predictors of future happenings in the marketing environment. It deals with current issues as opposed to past incidents.
- ***Ex post facto* research**. This research explains the phenomenon after it has happened.
- **Longitudinal research**. All other research designs can be described as 'snapshots' of a certain research problem, while longitudinal research designs have the objective of obtaining information over a period of time – in most cases, many years – with the aim of identifying trends which are occurring in the marketing environment over time.
- **Causal research**. Most marketing variables exist in close relationship with other variables, and marketing managers need to be informed of any cause-and-effect relationships that exist between them. The concept of 'cause' is the central objective of causal research designs. It attempts to determine the extent to which changes in one variable cause changes in another.
- **Predictive research**. This research aims at forecasting future values, such as sales, income and market share.

Table 4.1 lists examples of the above-mentioned research designs as well as the type of information the researcher will need.

'A research design describes the plan to be followed in order to fulfil the marketing research objectives and provides the framework to solve a specific problem.'

Table 4.1 Research design examples and information needed by the researcher

<table>
<tr><th>Research design</th><th>Example</th><th>Information needed</th></tr>
<tr><td>Exploratory research</td><td>Literature reviews, experience surveys and focus groups</td><td rowspan="9">The type of research will determine the information needed by the researcher.

Types of information needed include:
• facts;
• levels of awareness;
• opinions and attitudes;
• preferences; and
• motives and behaviour.

Through defining the information needs of the study, the researcher ensures that the data obtained in the study will match the requirements of the research problem and objectives.</td></tr>
<tr><td>Descriptive research</td><td>Personal interviews, postal questionnaires, telephone interviews and questionnaires</td></tr>
<tr><td>Qualitative research</td><td>Focus groups, interviews</td></tr>
<tr><td>Quantitative research</td><td>Questionnaires</td></tr>
<tr><td>Post hoc research</td><td>Perception measurement of a company's service quality</td></tr>
<tr><td>Ex post facto research</td><td>To determine why a company's advertising campaign failed</td></tr>
<tr><td>Longitudinal research</td><td>The seasonal fluctuation in the sales of, for example, cold remedies</td></tr>
<tr><td>Causal research</td><td>Experimentation</td></tr>
<tr><td>Predictive research</td><td>Sales forecasting</td></tr>
</table>

Step 3: Prepare the research design

The following activities are involved in preparing a specific research design, as indicated in Figure 4.6.

Activity 1: Decide on the source of information

The first activity in the preparation of the research design entails deciding between the two main categories of data sources (see Activity 1 in Figure 4.6). These are secondary and primary sources. *Primary data* is the data that is collected by the researcher to solve a specific research problem, while *secondary data* refers to data that has already been collected by, either the researcher, his or her organisation, or an outside agency.

Researchers should always begin their research by doing an in-depth analysis of secondary data. If a researcher's information needs can be fully satisfied by secondary sources of information, then there is no need to conduct further research. The collection of primary data involves a number of accompanying activities associated with most of the descriptive and causal research designs. Since primary data has to be collected, obtaining the data is a relatively expensive and slow process, but the data is usually more relevant to the research objectives than secondary data. Although secondary data is cheaper and faster to obtain than primary data, the researcher has to always consider its relevance, accuracy, reliability and timeousness. The different sources of primary and secondary data are shown in Table 4.2.

Table 4.2 Examples of primary and secondary data sources

Primary data		Secondary data	
Internal sources	**External sources**	**Internal sources**	**External sources**
• Employees	• Consumers • Clients • Retailers • Wholesalers • Competitors	• Company records	• Libraries • Industry associations • Chambers of industry and commerce • Government bodies • Marketing research organisations • Universities

Activity 2: Determine the data collection tactics

After the researcher has determined the research design and that primary data will be collected, he or she has to decide *how* the required data will be collected (see Activity 2 in Figure 4.6). The collection of secondary data is usually a simple process because libraries and relevant government organisations, among others, can be used. Primary data, however, is not always readily available and must be collected for the specific objectives of the research.

Once researchers have determined that the benefits of primary data outweigh the costs, they can proceed by selecting a *primary research method*. Data collection approaches can be classified into three main categories:

- **The observation approach** is simply the process of recognising and noting what is going on rather than asking for information. This may be done by means of people (where certain actions are noted on an information sheet by a person observing the individuals under investigation) or by means of some electronic method (which can be a camera that has been installed in a shop aimed at a specific section, or a recording of conversations).
- **The survey approach** uses direct or indirect questioning of selected individuals (respondents). This problem-specific data is then collected. It is the most widely used form of data collection in marketing research. This approach uses structured questions and response categories which allow the results to be quantified (and is thus sometimes called quantitive research).
- **Experimentation** used in causal research design refers to the process of conducting a controlled test to discover an unknown effect. The objective of controlling and manipulating the

'The questionnaire is the most common way to collect primary data for survey purposes.'

independent variable is to determine the causal relationship with the dependent variable.

Activity 3: Decide on the data collection instruments to be used

The data collection instrument that the researcher should use is the one that will reach the target market most effectively, depending on the research budget. The *questionnaire* and *mechanical /electronic equipment* are the two types of research instruments that a researcher can use to collect primary data (Activity 3 in Figure 4.6).

Questionnaire

The questionnaire is the most common instrument for the collection of primary data for survey purposes. With the design of the questionnaire, careful consideration must be given to the type of questions, their format, wording and sequence. The questions should be relevant and easily understood by the respondent. The questions can be open (respondents reply in their own words) or closed (respondents select one or more alternative responses listed on the questionnaire). The sequence of the questions has to be considered when structuring the questionnaire. For example, the introductory questions should arouse interest and ensure cooperation, while the difficult and/or more personal questions should be asked towards the end of the questionnaire. A good questionnaire has the following criteria:

- *Will it obtain the required information to assist in making decisions?* The primary role of any questionnaire is to provide the required information necessary for management decision making.
- *Is it formulated or structured in such a way that it suits the requirements of the respondents?* One of the most important tasks in designing questionnaires is to have appropriate questions. They should be in plain language which is easily understood and not cluttered with marketing jargon and business terminology.
- *When the questionnaire is designed, are editing and data-processing requirements taken into account?* Editing involves going through the completed questionnaire to check that all the questions were answered and that the instructions were followed. The questionnaire must be developed so that the data can be entered into the necessary software program effectively and efficiently.

On the next page is an example of a questionnaire used in a shopping centre survey.

Example

Questionnaire: Shopping centre survey

Respondent no. | | | |

Dear Respondent

Thank you for your willingness to complete the shopping centre survey. The purpose of the survey is to determine your perceptions about shopping centres in the Johannesburg East area. The survey should not take more than 10 minutes to complete. This is an anonymous and confidential survey. You cannot be identified, and the answers you provide will be used for research purposes only.

Please answer all the questions. There are no right or wrong answers. We are interested in understanding your perception of shopping centres in the Johannesburg East area.

Question 1

Various shopping centres in the Johannesburg East area are listed alongside. Please tick all the centres that you have visited in the past month.

Bedford Centre	
Eastgate	
Festival Mall	
Lakeside Mall	
Northmead Mall	
Greenstone Shopping Centre	
East Rand Galleria	
Bedfordview Shopping Centre	

Question 2

Listed alongside is a set of attributes (reasons) many people use when selecting a shopping centre to visit. Think back to the last shopping centre you visited, and then rank order these attributes from 1 to 7, with 1 being the most important and 7 being the least important reason for visiting that specific centre. Please make sure that you rank order all seven of the attributes (reasons).

Atmosphere	
Convenient location	
Entertainment	
Restaurants	
Safety	
Special events	
Specific store	

Question 3

On average, how often do you visit the shopping centre? (Please tick the most applicable.)

Every week	
Every two weeks	
Once a month	
Once every two months	
Three to four times a year	
Less often	

Mechanical/electronic equipment

Galvanometers, eye cameras, and electronic and mechanical meters are used to measure respondents' reactions, behaviour and opinions. These can be simple counting meters (for example the number of people entering a shopping mall) to sophisticated instruments which measure reactions (for example emotional reaction to a specific advertisement measured with a galvanometer or eye camera).

Activity 4: Determine which data collection technique to use

Once the researcher has decided to conduct research through the use of a questionnaire as a method of survey research, the following methods can be used to distribute questionnaires and collect data: personal interviews, telephone interviews and self-administered surveys.[9]

Personal interviews

These interviews are conducted face to face by a trained interviewer, and can be administered at any venue. The advantages and disadvantages associated with personal interviews are listed in Figure 4.7.

Personal interviews

Advantages

- Interviewer can answer questions that the respondent has
- Interviewer can ask probing questions and follow up on answers
- There is increased cooperation from respondents
- Data can be recorded
- Interviewer can make use of visual aids and scoring devices
- Illiterate or functionally illiterate respondents can be reached
- Computer-assisted personal interviewing (CAPI) can help speed up the interview process, and increases the accuracy of the data collected
- Interviewers can pre-screen respondents to ensure that they fit the target population

Disadvantages

- The cost of personal interviews is very high
- The data collection process takes a lot of time
- If the geographic dispersion of the target population is high, the data collection process takes longer
- Interviewers must be highly trained to conduct personal interviews
- Interviewer bias can occur
- Respondents may be difficult or unwilling to allow interviewers into their homes
- Respondents may not be available
- Follow-up can be labour intensive

Figure 4.7 Advantages and disadvantages of personal interviews

Telephone interviews

These interviews are conducted telephonically by an interviewer.

The advantages and disadvantages associated with this method are listed in Figure 4.8.

WWW:

- http://www.surveymonkey.com

Telephone interviews

Advantages

- The costs are lower
- A larger geographic area can be covered
- Fewer interviewers need to be used
- There is better access to respondents who are difficult to reach
- There is a quicker completion time, and interviewer bias is reduced
- Computer-assisted telephone interviews (CATI) allow the responses to be directly into the computer file, which reduces errors and cost

Disadvantages

- The target group may not be accessible by telephone or may not be listed in the telephone directory
- There is a lower response rate
- Telephone directories may be unreliable
- The interview and questionnaire are limited
- The response rate is lower, and responses may be less complete

Figure 4.8 Advantages and disadvantages of telephone interviews

Self-administered surveys

Self-administered surveys are conducted when respondents are asked to complete the questionnaires in their own time. These may be mailed or delivered either personally or online to respondents, or potential respondents may be intercepted in a mall or restaurant, and asked to complete the questionnaire. The advantages and disadvantages associated with this survey method are listed in Figure 4.9.

Self-administered surveys

Advantages

- This method has the lower cost
- Extended geographic coverage is possible without increasing cost
- Complex survey instruments may be used
- Minimal staff is required for data collection
- Computer-literate respondents have fast access
- There is more time for respondents to think about their answers
- Incentives may be used
- This method also allows for rapid data collection
- Visual illustration may be used
- Respondents perceive this method to be more anonymous
- It is easier to reach inaccessible respondents

Disadvantages

- The questionnaire length is limited, and detailed instructions and details are necessary
- The security of the computer used may be a problem
- It is not possible to probe for answers or explain questions
- This method has a low response rate
- The respondent needs to be in an environment that has few distractions
- Respondents who are not computer literate may experience some anxiety
- Respondents who represent the extremes can skew the data
- The mailing lists being used must be accurate

Figure 4.9 Advantages and disadvantages of self-administered surveys

Because every research project is unique, there is no 'one-size-fits-all' or 'best' survey method. Researchers should consider the available resources and target market, taking into account the advantages and disadvantages of each method, before choosing a suitable one.

Activity 5: Develop the sampling plan

The development of a sampling plan is a crucial stage in the research process and can affect the value of the information gathered by the research. Researchers seldom study the whole population, but usually only a *sample of the population*. Valuable information is obtained from a sample that represents the total population. A sample that is not representative of the total population may not give a true picture of that population and is therefore plagued with problems of validity and reliability.

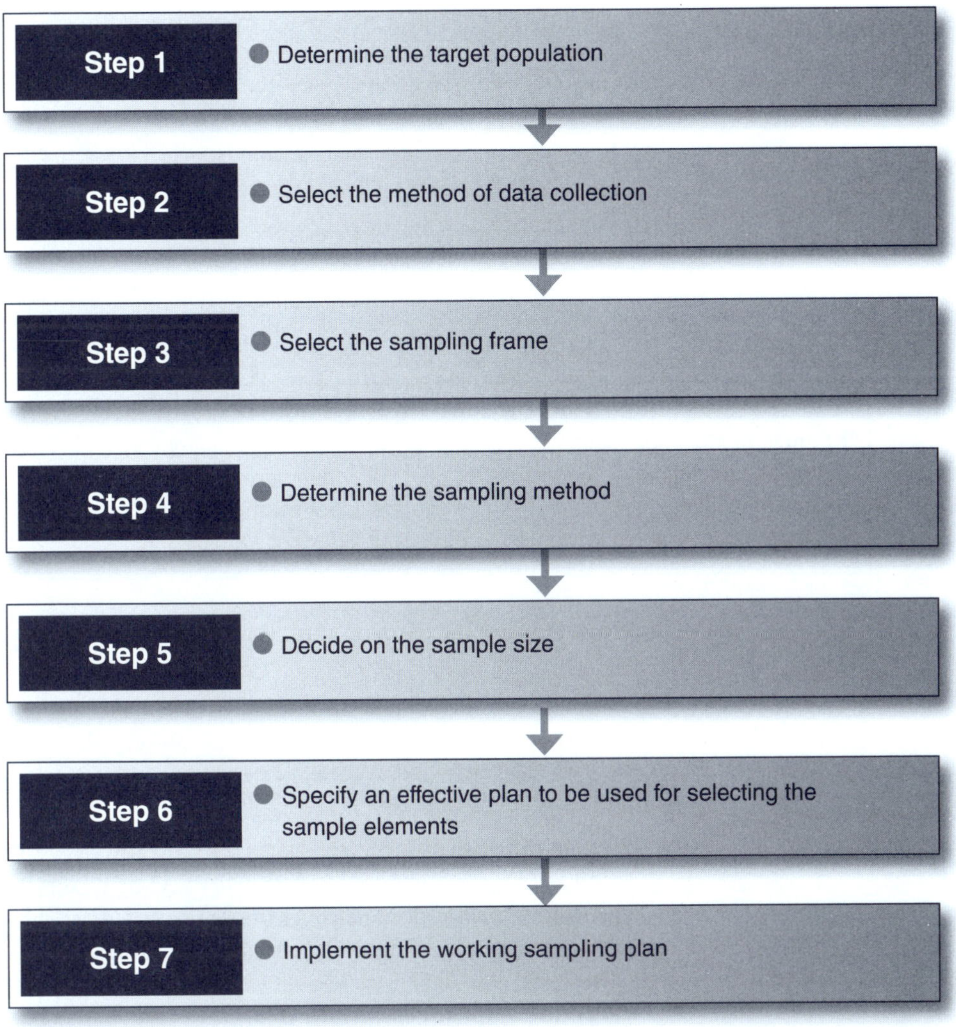

Figure 4.10 Steps in the sampling plan

There are seven steps to follow when developing a sampling plan[10] which are illustrated in Figure 4.10.

Step 1 deals with identifying and defining the target population on which the research is to be conducted. In *step 2*, the data collection method is identified, while in *step 3* a sampling frame is chosen. The sample frame refers to the list of the sample units that will be used, and can consist of any population record.

Step 4 entails determining a sampling method. This depends on the objectives of the study, the available organisational resources, the specific time limitations of the study and the nature of the problem or opportunity under investigation. Probability sampling needs to be conducted where every element of the population has a known and non-zero chance of being selected to participate in the sample. Simple random sampling is the best known and most widely used probability sampling method. Non-probability sampling is when elements in the sample are selected in a non-random manner. These methods are discussed in more detail below. The classification of sampling methods is illustrated in Figure 4.11

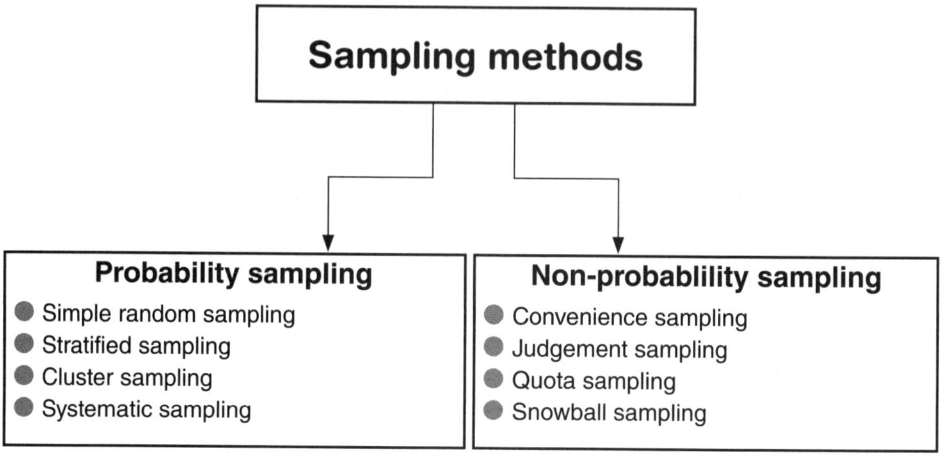

Figure 4.11 Classification of sampling methods

Probability sampling

Probability sampling, also known as *random sampling*, is the best way to ensure a representative sample. The following probability sampling methods can be employed:

- **Simple random sampling**. The principle of this method is the same as picking numbers randomly from a hat. It uses computational random number generators or tables of random numbers. The sampling units are identified by numbers so a comprehensive listing of the population is required.
- **Stratified random sampling**. Where the total population can be divided into unique and distinctive groups and the researcher wants to a make sure that each group is clearly represented, stratified random sampling can be used. It allocates the sample size to each specific group, called stratum, according to size. It does not need a detailed population frame (list of population). Any sampling procedure (such as simple random sampling) can then be used to draw the different sampling units from each respective stratum.
- **Cluster sampling**. Simple random sampling treats each population element individually, while stratified sampling treats elements in groups of the population individually. Cluster sampling groups the population into clusters and randomly selects a few to study. The grouping is done according to availability or ease and should be heterogeneous within subgroups and externally homogeneous.
- **Systematic sampling**. Systematic sampling delivers the most representative samples of all sampling methods. It randomly selects the starting point in the list of population and then

selects respondents at set intervals. For example, the starting point of the sample has been randomly selected as room number 5 of a hotel, every 12th room could then be selected for the total sample.

'Probability sampling, also known as random sampling, is the best way to ensure a representative sample.'

'The sample size involves the number of sampling units that are included in the investigation.'

Non-probability sampling

Due to the high cost and difficulty in obtaining truly random sample, marketing research is often based on *non-probability sampling* (or non-random sampling). Non-random sampling does not give every member of the population a known and equal chance to be included in the sample, and is not representative of the population. This is not to say that non-random sampling is of little value as researchers still employ some method to ensure a form of representation in the sample. The judgement of the researcher can be based on factors such as convenience, relative importance of units and recommendations from experts. Although the degree of representativeness cannot be evaluated statistically, it is still acceptable if the composition is carefully done and is relevant to the particular research situation. The researcher can use one of the following non-probability sampling methods:[11]

- **Convenience sampling** is when the sample population is drawn from whoever is readily available. The sample, however, is not a true representation of the population, and data is not very reliable.
- **Judgement sampling** selects the sample population based on a certain profile. For example a researcher deliberately selects female students between the ages of 18 and 24 who smoke.
- **Quota sampling** is where a certain number of respondents need to be included in the research and the researcher selects the respondents based on the premise that certain relevant characteristics describe population dimensions. Therefore, if a sample distribution of a sample has these specified characteristics, then it is presumed to be representative of the population.
- **Snowball sampling** entails selecting a small group of people who then identify other individuals with similar characteristics required by the researcher.

Step 5 in the sampling plan (Figure 4.10) includes the determination of the sample size. There are some general norms and guidelines involved in choosing the number of sampling units that are included in the investigation. Statistical confidence is one of the best norms for determining the sample size of a known population. There is a greater possibility of unreliable and invalid research results with smaller sample sizes, while the possibility of research errors and bias increases with larger ones.

Step 6 in the sampling plan (Figure 4.10) entails developing the operational procedures for selecting sample elements. If a researcher fails to develop a proper operational plan, the whole study can be jeopardised. The sample selection procedures should specify whether probability or non-probability methods will be used. In the case of probability sampling, the procedures should be detailed, clear and unambiguous. After a proper sampling plan has been developed, the actual research can be conducted.[12]

The final steps in the sampling plan, *step 7*, involve developing the operational procedures for selecting elements and the execution of the sampling plan. There are a number of problems that can occur if the researcher does not develop a proper plan. The sampling methods that will be used must be specified and the procedure explained in detail.

Step 4: Conduct fieldwork

Fieldwork is the actual data collection using the data collection instrument (see Step 4 in Figure 4.4). Aspects to be considered in the planning and control of fieldwork include training of interviewers, distribution of questionnaires, logistical planning of fieldwork execution, fieldwork supervision and follow-up control. Bias is almost always due to badly executed fieldwork. It is therefore important to prevent bias as much as possible to ensure that the research results are reliable and valid.

'Fieldwork is the actual data collection with the aid of the data collection instrument.'

Preventing bias

Researchers should be aware of the following sources of bias as these can cause serious measurement errors:[13]

- **The respondent**. Whenever we deal with people, bias is probable, making them a possible source of error. The main aspect that influences the results will be respondent's characteristics, others could include fatigue, boredom, anxiety and literacy.
- **Situational factors**. Respondents may be influenced by the environment that they are in, for example other people, the weather or the physical environment, such as the place where the interview is conducted.
- **The fieldworker**. The interviewer can distort information by rewording or misinterpreting what the respondent has said. Interviewer bias can also occur where the interviewer influences the respondents. The implementation of the data collection also has its specific sources of error. They are:
  - selecting the incorrect respondents;
  - non-response errors caused by refusals or not-at-home respondents;
  - errors in encouraging questionnaire completion;
  - incorrect interpretation of data; and
  - interviewer dishonesty.

- **The data collection instrument**. The last potential source of measurement error comes from the type of data collection instrument used in the research. For example, a questionnaire with flaws in the design, wording or layout could lead to vague and misleading questions being included. The sampling procedure is another example of error in the data collection instrument. Samples that are not representative of the total population can lead to over- or under-representation of certain groups in the population, and can result from the aforementioned measurement errors.

Important considerations in fieldwork

There are various errors that can occur during the fieldwork process. For example, information can be lost or recorded incorrectly by the fieldworker. The following considerations are important in the implementation of fieldwork:[14]

- **The use of interviewers and fieldworkers**. The first step is the selection of the fieldworkers. The requirements of the fieldworker must be looked at. There need to be sufficient questionnaires and manuals for the fieldworkers to use. The sample population must also be taken into consideration. Researchers are important in determining the quality of information received. It is thus important that fieldworkers receive the necessary training.
- **Administrative procedures**. This refers to the administrative procedures such as recruiting and selecting fieldworkers, scheduling times and conducting follow-up procedures.
- **Quality and cost control**. The evaluation of the fieldworkers and the fieldwork process is important in ensuring that data is accurate, and free of discrepancies and mistakes.
- **Evaluation of interviewers**. Interviewers must be evaluated against the initial objective of the research. Other factors such as training instructions, quality of information gathered, number of refusals, etc, should also be looked at. It is important to have regular meetings with the interviewers to discuss problems and to evaluate their progress.

Step 5: Process the information acquired

After the data has been collected, processing has to take place (see Step 5 of the research process, Figure 4.4). The collected data has to be edited, verified and coded in order to capture it electronically. Although it is possible to process research data by hand, the versatility and power of modern computers as well as the availability of commercial processing software make the researcher's life much easier.

Data preparation[15]

The first step in the analysis of data is to edit the raw data. *Editing* refers to the detection of errors and/or omissions in the data – and the correction of these where possible – and lastly the certification that the minimal data quality standards have been achieved. The process of editing the data collected ensures that it is accurate, consistent, uniform, complete and arranged to simplify the coding and tabulation process.

Editing can occur in the field (*field editing*) or in the central location where all the data is edited at once (*central editing*). After editing, the data needs to be coded. Assigning numbers to answers in the questionnaire is called *coding*. This enables the researcher to group the answers into a limited number of classes or categories and is necessary for the efficient analysis of data. There are four coding rules to be followed:

- The coding categories must be relevant to the research.
- Extensive categories must be used so as to fulfil the research objectives completely.
- The categories must not overlap.
- Each category should be defined as a concept.

'Data entry entails converting the information gathered into a medium which can be viewed and manipulated.'

Data entry

Data entry is the process of converting the data that has been collected to a medium suitable for processing. In other words, the data should be put into an Excel spreadsheet or similar statistical software to allow for statistical analysis. This will enable the researcher to determine whether the relevant hypothesis can be rejected or accepted so that the research question can be answered.

Following the data preparation and coding of open questions, the data is then captured on computer. The data capture should also be audited for possible typing errors or misinterpretation of coding instructions. Techniques used to ensure data integrity include double capture and data file comparisons, field code restrictions and skip patterns. This process and entails a check of internal inconsistencies and all possible allowable and unallowable codes is called *data cleaning*.

Tabulation and analysis

Interpretation of the data set is virtually impossible without the aid of a summarised format such as a table or some type of graphic representation. It is important for the researcher to stipulate the type of tabulation, the format in which the information should be presented and whether items should be tabulated in combination with others (cross-tabulation).

The analysis and tabulation of data is a specialised field in itself and it is preferable to obtain the expertise of a professional at this stage of the research process so as not to jeopardise the actual outcome of the research.

Step 6: Report the results of the research

The final step in the marketing research process (see Step 6 in Figure 4.4) involves the interpretation of the marketing information for decision-making purposes and the reporting thereof to the marketing decision maker. It is important that the decision-making context is thoroughly grasped and that the communication of the marketing information takes place in the appropriate format. This is because communication problems between researchers and marketing decision makers often arise due to their different backgrounds and work environments. Inevitably, the written *research report* is the document that management will use as its information source in making a decision.

In evaluating the quality of the research report, criteria such as intelligibility, relevance, clarity, conciseness, organisation, timeousness, accuracy and comprehensiveness are applied. Management is, in general, not interested in the technicalities of methodology, but wants results. The researcher, however, must clearly demonstrate the scientific nature of the project. The presentation must therefore be technically correct and accurate, as well as understandable and useful.

In the research report, the problem is first defined, and the information from secondary and primary sources analysed and interpreted. Conclusions and recommendations are then made. It is not the researcher's task to make decisions or to implement them – this is the task of marketing management. The articulateness of the researcher is of great importance in the writing of a good research report. Second, the research objectives must be directly addressed in the report. The use of graphics is highly recommended, as most managers do not have the time to go through complex tables to reach a conclusion. The researcher should be selective in the amount of information supplied in the research report. It is advisable to publish all the detailed tabulation and statistical calculations in a separate technical report.

Marketing research on the Internet

The development and phenomenal growth of the Internet and World Wide Web promise great opportunities for creative applications in marketing research.

'The development and phenomenal growth of the Internet and World Wide Web promise great opportunities for creative applications in marketing research.'

Advantages of Internet research

One of the reasons that Internet surveys are popular is because creating and sending out questionnaires to respondents is much faster. A South African Internet supplier reported, for example, that more than 70% of respondents out of a total of 1 850 replied within the first 24 hours of the request being e-mailed to them. Since the data is electronically collected, statistical software can be used to process and analyse it with greater ease than ever before.

A second reason for the appeal of the Web as a medium for marketing research is the cost. Development, distribution and interviewer costs are almost totally eliminated, or reduced to a fraction of the cost of the paper-based versions of similar projects.

The Internet's ability to reach large numbers of people is another major advantage and benefit of Web-based research. It also crosses the usual communication barriers experienced with international research.

Finally, the visual appeal of web-based surveys with attractive fonts, graphics, audio, video and professionally formatted page layouts contributes significantly to increased response rates and the general enjoyment of responding to Web surveys. The capabilities of the Internet make it possible to design and implement creative research projects never before possible with paper-based research (for example the application of adaptive conjoint analysis, which is impossible through paper-based research).

Disadvantages of Web surveys

Even with the many appealing characteristics of Web research, there are also a number of notable disadvantages. The first major problem with Internet research is the lack of representativeness of Internet users. Despite its enormous growth, fewer than 10 % of South African households have Internet access, which causes a distinct bias towards younger, male, well-qualified, technically oriented respondents.[16] A second serious disadvantage is the problem of security, which is a particularly sensitive issue for most Internet users. Spamming (mass-distributed e-mail messages or junk e-mail) and the invasion of privacy through the use of cookie files are a cause of great concern to many Internet respondents.

'The Internet's ability to reach large numbers of people is a major advantage and benefit of web-based research. It also crosses the usual communication barriers experienced with international research.'

Internet survey techniques

Two basic methods of Internet research are currently being used:

- **Conventional website-based surveys**. Respondents are invited (by e-mail, telephone or fax) to visit a specific URL where the website survey is located.
- **E-mail-based questionnaires**. Various versions of e-mail-based research are currently available. For example, the questionnaire is prepared as a self-executable e-mail attachment. Another approach is e-mail speciality software that will enable the automatic distribution and return of e-mail questionnaires to a targeted list of e-mail respondents.

Market measurement and demand forecasting

The need for measurement and forecasting

The last section of this chapter deals with a specific element of marketing information – market measurement and demand forecasting. When an organisation observes a new market trend, based on the information obtained from marketing research or the marketing information system, it is essential that the current size and future potential of the new market demand is determined. Knowledge of market sizes and probable growth patterns provides the basis for the selection of attractive markets and thus helps in the formulation of appropriate marketing strategies for those markets.[17]

Market measurement and market forecasting are management tools through which the markets under investigation are expressed in quantitatively measurable entities. They should be used in conjunction with other marketing information and qualitative management tools. *Market measurement* focuses on the current size and characteristics of the market, whereas *market forecasting* looks at the future market situation.

Levels of market measurement

The size of a market can be measured on at least four levels: a *consumer level*, a *product level*, a *geographic level* and a *time level*. Marketing managers must clearly define the required level of measurement as this would directly impact on the formulation of resulting marketing decision making. The four levels of market measurement differ as follows in the nature of what is measured and can be distinguished[18]:

- **Consumer level**. The consumer level of market measurement is the most popular level used as it provides information on the number of final consumers defined in different market segments. For example, the consumer level of the market for soft drinks would provide measurement information on segments such as schools, sports meetings and private households.
- **Product level**. As most markets are targeted by various formats of the same product, the market measurement can also be expressed in terms of the total number of current buyers for each product type. Product types for soft drinks would, for example, be divided into all sales of soft drinks, sales of small bottles (500 ml) and sales of large bottles (2 ℓ).
- **Geographic level**. The total market can be divided into geographic segments and it is thus possible to express the market measurement in geographic terms. Soft drinks can, for instance, be divided into sales for each of the nine provinces of South Africa or for certain climatic regions.
- **Time levels**. A market measurement should also be specific in terms of the time of purchase and provide information on the sales over different time periods such as monthly sales, seasonal sales and annual sales.

Relevant markets for measurement

The different types of markets that can be measured are not all relevant to a specific business. It depends on whether the business is actively involved or interested in the particular market.

Two important indicators are derived from the market measurement which the company will use for evaluating its competitive position in the market. They are also used to evaluate the efficiency of the marketing effort.

- **Sales potential** refers to the quantitative indication of what the organisation's probable sales in a total market, available market

'Market share is a well-known measure of competitive position, and indicates the relationship of an organisation's sales to those of all participants (competitors) in the same market.'

and/or target market should be in view of various possible marketing efforts. Sales potential should not be confused with *market potential*, which is an indication of the size of the total demand for a product type at an infinite level of marketing input from all participants (competitors) in the market.

- **Market share** is a well-known measure of competitive position and indicates the relationship of an organisation's sales to the sales of all participants (competitors) in the same market. Market share can be expressed in volume as well as monetary terms.[19]

Methods of market measurement

Various practical methods exist for the measurement of market size, of which those listed below are the most widely used in practice:

- **The basic method**. This is the simplest method of market measurement, and entails the calculation of the total number of buyers, the average quantity purchased per time period and the average price of the product for the same time period.
- **The chain ratio method**. This method involves a series of successive calculations to a base quantity. The base quantity is often the total economically productive population (or just the total population). This method usually involves a percentage calculation of the number of people who are expected to buy the product in the future. This is called *buying intention*.
- **Market build-up method**. This method is a special application of the basic method discussed earlier and is used particularly by industrial manufacturers. The method involves the determination of all potential buyers of the product and the quantities they will buy. These two figures are then multiplied to obtain the market potential for the particular product.
- **The market index method**. This method of market measurement is particularly useful for consumer goods. It is based on a statistical index calculated from the number of potential buyers that form part of a specific market, and should be used as a relative measure.[20]

The nature and role of market forecasting

Whereas market measurement relates to the determination of the size of the current market, market forecasting is concerned with the size of the future market. In essence, forecasting involves predicting the future, and the uncertain nature of any prediction should thus be borne in mind. It is of crucial importance for marketing management to be supplied with reliable measures of future sales, as these measures will be used as a key success factor in the planning and implementation of marketing strategy.

Market forecasting plays an important role in the total business forecast, which includes environmental scanning. The *market forecast* of future market demand (usually in terms of forecast sales) is used extensively not only in marketing planning, but also by other functional departments of the company as the basis for their own forecasts and budgets. Note that the market forecast is part of the marketing forecast, which includes aspects such as forecasts on prices, products, distribution and marketing communication. The *market forecast* is thus only concerned with the market demand.

Market forecasting can be done from two different perspectives:

- **Historical basis**. The forecast is based on historical data.
- **Current basis**. The forecast is based on the current situation.

'Market forecasting can be done from two different perspectives, namely a historical basis and a current basis.'

Market forecasting methods

A few methods of market forecasting are discussed below:

- **Time series analysis**. This approach to market forecasting is based on historical data, and involves the careful investigation of past trends and relationships between different variables. It relies heavily on the principles of cause-and-effect relationships.
- **Statistical demand analysis**. This investigates all the possible factors that could have an effect on sales, and allocates relative weights to each of them. It is also based on investigation of sales histories, and attempts to explain sales as a function of a number of independent variables.

Whereas the first two methods are historically based forecasting methods, the last three are based on the current situation and are essentially less mathematical and quantitative. The first of these methods involves a survey of buyers' purchasing intentions.

- **Survey of buying intentions**. Potential buyers of the product are asked to indicate their buying intention on one of several surveying techniques. These techniques include buying probability scales, consumer confidence indices and measurement of buyers' sentiment. Surveys of buying intentions are subject to various problems, the most obvious being the overestimation of buying intention.
- **Opinions of sales personnel**. Sales personnel are at the forefront of the company and in contact with consumers. They are often best equipped to know the market, realise the changes and form a 'gut feel' for future sales. Opinions of sales personnel may be biased by subjective involvement or they may be overoptimistic (or pessimistic) about their products. By offering certain incentives, sales personnel can be motivated to make more efficient estimates.
- **Jury of expert opinion**. This includes dealers, suppliers, marketing agents, industry spokespeople, industry associations, research organisations and consultants.

Summary

This chapter discussed the marketing information system as an integral managerial tool in marketing planning and strategy formulation. The importance and strategic nature of marketing information were outlined, and emphasis was placed on the role of information in relationship marketing. Marketing research was discussed from a management perspective, and the chapter was rounded off with a brief discussion on market measurement and demand forecasting.

In the next chapter, market segmentation, targeting and positioning will be discussed.

References

1. Cant, M.C. 2010. *Marketing: An introduction*. Cape Town, South Africa: Juta & Co., p. 57.
2. American Marketing Association. 2013. *Dictionary of marketing terms*. [Online] Available from: http://www.marketingpower.com/_layouts/dictionary.aspx [Accessed: 2013-05-20].
3. Van Heerden, C.H. 2013. *Contemporary retail and marketing case studies*. Cape Town, South Africa: Juta & Co., p. 38.
4. Boundless.com. n.d. *Marketing information systems*. [Online] Available from: https://www.boundless.com/marketing/consumer-marketing/technology-to-assist-market-research/marketing-information-systems/ [Accessed: 2013-05-22].
5. Based on Cant, M.C., Van Heerden, C.H. & Ngambi, H.C. 2010. *Marketing management: A South African perspective*. Cape Town, South Africa: Juta & Co., p. 121.
6. Ibid.
7. American Marketing Association, op. cit.
8. Entrepreneur.com. 2013. *Market research*. [Online] Available from: http://www.entrepreneur.com/encyclopedia/market-research [Accessed: 2013-05-23].
9. Based on Wiid, J. & Diggines, C. 2013. *Marketing research*. 2nd ed. Cape Town, South Africa, Juta & Co., p. 112.
10. Wiid & Diggines, op. cit., p. 195.
11. LærdDissertation.com. 2012. *Non-probability sampling*. [Online] Available from: http://dissertation.lærd.com/non-probability-sampling.php [Accessed: 2013-05-30].
12. Based on Du Toit, M. 2011. *Fundamentals of sales and marketing*. Cape Town, South Africa: Juta & Co., p. 79.
13. Ibid.
14. Ibid.
15. Ibid.
16. Statistics South Africa. 2012. *General household survey*. [Online] Available from: http://www.statssa.gov.za/Publications/P0318/P0318August2012.pdf [Accessed: 2013-10-10].
17. Kumar, B. & Balhorta, R. [Online] Available from http://www.authorstream.com/Presentation/aSGuest70408-563937-market-measurement-and-forecasting/ [Accessed: 2013-12-19].
18. Ibid.
19. Ibid.
20. Ibid.

CHAPTER 5

Market segmentation, targeting and positioning

✓ Learning objectives

After studying this chapter, you should be able to:

- explain the concept of marketing segmentation;
- indicate how marketers can segment their market;
- highlight the prerequisites for effective market segmentation;
- explain what is meant by the term 'target marketing';
- suggest factors that should be considered when selecting a target market;
- explain the concept of product positioning;
- discuss the positioning process; and
- describe the positioning methods that marketers can pursue in practice.

Introduction

It is not possible for one company to be everything to everybody. Meeting all the needs of a customer is physically impossible by any one company. In fact it is extremely difficult for one company to even meet, for example, all the clothing needs of the market. It is therefore important that companies regularly evaluate their own position and decide on their market strategy – that is, they have to reflect on the markets they are currently in or intend servicing, and to segment them accordingly. To be successful, marketers need to satisfy the demands of the customer, and the more specifically they do so, the greater the chances of success are. To meet their primary objective, however, companies must make a profit. This is the reason why segmentation is needed – to identify those segments that are economically viable and will result in profit for the company.

Marketers are quick to realise that to satisfy an individual customer's need is not economically feasible – it is far too costly and unrealistic. Instead, marketers need to generalise about the needs, demands and preferences of the heterogeneous market, realising at the same time that they cannot be all things to all people. They must focus on satisfying a specific market's needs, concentrating on what they do best to remain competitive in an increasingly cutthroat marketplace. How this can be achieved is the central theme of this chapter.

Segmentation, targeting and positioning defined

> **DEFINITION**
>
> **Market segmentation**
>
> Market segmentation is the process of dividing the market, which is very diverse, into subgroups of consumers with similar needs, wants or demands in order to achieve maximum customer satisfaction by successfully addressing the specific needs, wants or demands of the target group.

For a company to be successful and meet its long-term objectives it has to meet the needs of the target market it has selected to serve. A company cannot keep on doing the same thing over and over as the needs initially met by these actions will change over time. As the customers' needs change, so should the offering of the company. It is the task of marketers to constantly monitor the segments they are serving for any changes or new demands that may arise. If they do not, their competitors will. Although the satisfaction of customer needs is not a goal in itself, it enables the enterprise to achieve its own goals, therefore the greater the need satisfaction customers can derive from an enterprise's products, the easier it becomes for the enterprise to achieve its own goals.

It is assumed that by breaking the total market into segments or smaller units, each of these identified segments will have similar needs, and will respond in a similar way to the market offering and strategy. The market for shoes, for example, can be subdivided into the following sub-segments: babies, girls, boys, teenagers, ladies' formal, ladies' casual, men's casual, men's formal, and outdoor or active shoes, just to name a few. There is a wide variety of shoes, and each of these segments exhibits different characteristics and needs with regard to occasion, use, fashion, and so forth. Shoes were initially created to protect the feet, but as time has progressed, the needs for shoes became more functional and are now increasingly used as a fashion statement. One type of shoe cannot satisfy the unique needs of all the above-mentioned market segments.

The organisation must decide which market segment(s) needs it can best satisfy. The Business Express train service that runs between Pretoria and Johannesburg (Gautrain) has, for example, decided to cater primarily for the needs of the business commuter and has therefore developed its product offering around this segment. Minibus taxis, however, cater for cost-conscious commuters and therefore will have a different approach.

Once the target market segment has been selected, the company must decide how best to compete effectively in it.

There are various ways that a company can compete in the selected segment and it is important that the basis selected from which to compete is based on the company's own strong points. A company can, for example, decide to compete on the basis of a lower price (when compared to competitors) or on the basis of product range, service levels, or the brands it offers.

Segmenting the market

To segment the market is not something that can be neglected or done offhandedly. The future of the company may well depend on the way the market is segmented, and this is therefore regarded as a key task which requires the correct identification of the market to serve and the correct basis on which to segment it. Owing to its importance, the discussion on segmentation will cover the following: defining segmentation; the advantages and disadvantages of market segmentation; the prerequisites of effective market segmentation; and the common bases used to segment consumer and industrial markets.

Advantages and disadvantages of market segmentation

Market segmentation offers the following *advantages* to marketers:

- It forces marketers to focus more on customer needs. In a segmented market, the marketer can fully appreciate the differences in customer needs and respond accordingly. A greater degree of customer satisfaction can be achieved if the market offering is developed around customer needs, demands and preferences.
- Segmentation leads to the identification of excellent new marketing opportunities if research reveals an unexplored segment. Without proper segmentation, such a market segment may remain untapped for years.
- Market segmentation provides guidelines for the development of separate market offerings and strategies for the various market segments.
- Segmentation can help guide the proper allocation of marketing resources. A large, growing market segment may be allocated a greater proportion of the marketing budget, while a shrinking one may be scaled down or eventually abandoned if it becomes unattractive.

However, market segmentation also has the following *disadvantages* which must be considered by the marketer:

DEFINITION

Market targeting
Market targeting is the process of deciding which market segment(s) to pursue by concentrating marketing efforts on the specific segment(s).

- The development and marketing of separate models and market offerings is very expensive. It is much cheaper, for example, to develop only one product for one segment than to develop multiple products for multiple segments and multiple strategies.
- Only limited market coverage is achieved since marketing strategies are directed at specific market segments only.
- Excessive differentiation of the basic product may eventually lead to a proliferation of models and variations, and finally cannibalisation. Cannibalisation occurs when one product takes away market share from another developed by the same enterprise.

Prerequisites for market segmentation

The main aim of segmentation is to enhance customer satisfaction and the profitability of shareholders. For example, to subdivide the market for small delivery vehicles into Western Cape and KwaZulu-Natal farmers would make little marketing or business sense. In this case, geographic location makes no difference since the requirements of the farmers remain the same regardless of location. However, geographic location would be effective as a means of segmenting the market for insecticides since farmers in the Western Cape have to deal with different pests than do those in KwaZulu-Natal.

'The main aim of segmentation is basically to enhance customer satisfaction and the profitability of shareholders.'

For market segmentation to be effective, it must meet the following criteria:

- **It must be measurable**. If it is not possible to measure the size, purchasing power, potential profit and profile of the segment, it would be extremely difficult to compare such a segment with others or to properly assess its attractiveness.
- **It must be large enough**. Pursuing a market segment that is too small is not profitable. A segment must be the largest homogeneous group of people worth exploiting with a tailored market offering and marketing strategy. Although South Africa boasts a large variety of cultures, some of them, such as the Chinese community, may be so small that they do not warrant special attention by marketers.
- **It must be accessible**. Marketers must be able to reach the market segment with their market offering and strategy. How is it possible, for example, to reach rural people if they cannot read or do not listen to the radio? Such a segment is largely inaccessible to the marketer.
- **It must be actionable**. It must be possible to develop separate market offerings for different market segments. Smaller enterprises are often unable to develop different market offerings or marketing strategies, even if they realise that there are distinct differences between various segments.
- **It must be differentiable**. Different market segments must exhibit heterogeneous needs. In other words, people in different segments must have different needs, demands and desires.

People in the same segment, however, must exhibit similar characteristics and needs. The marketer should also be able to distinguish the segments from each other without too much difficulty.[1]

Once marketing management is satisfied that a specific segment conforms to these conditions, it can be considered as a possible target market.

Bases for segmenting consumer markets

Variables used in segmentation

The marketing manager can use different variables to segment a market. These variables can generally be classified according to *psychographic, geographic, demographic* and *behavioural* bases. Table 5.1 provides a detailed analysis of these classification bases, and lists the various bases for segmenting consumer markets, and examples of the possible variables to be taken into consideration. In the following sections, we offer a brief explanation of each approach.

'For market segmentation to be effective, it must be:
- measurable;
- large enough;
- accessible;
- actionable; and
- differentiable.'

Table 5.1 Bases for segmenting consumer markets[2]

Psychographic segmentation	
Lifestyle	People are classified according to their values, beliefs, opinions and interests, for example conservative, liberal or active.
Personality	Personality is the amalgamation of physical, emotional, social and behavioural characteristics that a person may possess, for example outgoing (extrovert versus introvert), impulsive or optimistic.
Social class	The population is divided according to socioeconomic groupings. People are grouped into various classes, for example lower, middle or upper.
Geographic segmentation	
Geographic region	Segmenting the market geographically may be divided into world regions, countries, cities and suburbs. A marketer for a high-end fashion outlet boutique may target the richer suburbs in South Africa, for example Clifton in Cape Town, Sandhurst in Johannesburg, and Woodhill in Pretoria, or generally in Pretoria East.
Size of city or town	This could influence the location of a company targeting major city centres such as Johannesburg and Cape Town.
Density of the population	This refers to population numbers within a region, which may be classified as urban, suburban or rural.
Climate	This refers to the climate within a region, such as summer rainfall, hot and humid, or cold and windy. For example, a restaurant owner who wants to open a beach restaurant in Cape Town will have to consider the prevailing wind when designing it.

Continue to next page

Behavioural segmentation	Continued from previous page
Attitude to product	A customer may have a certain regard for a product, which may be positive, neutral or negative.
Purchase occasion	Consumers' frequency of using a product may vary, for example regularly or only on special occasions.
Benefits sought	The benefits that customers may need from a product vary; for example in a car these may be economy, convenience, prestige or speed.
User status	This relates to the frequency that a customer uses a product; for example the customer may be a non-user, a potential user, a regular user or an ex-user.
Usage rate	This may be heavy, medium, regular or occasional.
Loyalty status	This may range from no loyalty to medium or strong.
Readiness stage	The customer may be unaware or aware of, informed about, interested in or intending to buy the product.
Demographic segmentation	
Race	Customers may be segmented according to their race, such as Caucasian, African, coloured, Asian or Indian.
Education	This refers to the qualifications that consumers have, such as matric, diploma, degree or postgraduate.
Age	Customers fall into one of the following age groups: 0–4 years old (babies); 5–12 years old (children); 13–18 years old (teenagers); 19–24 years old (youths); 25–34 years old (young adults); 35–64 years old (adults); 64+ years old (seniors).
Gender	Gender segmentation is necessary as females may have different needs and wants of a product than males.
Family size	Segmentation is done according to the family dynamics, such as number of people in the household.
Family life cycle	These are, for example, young married couples without children, married couples with children, married couples without children, or single parents.
Annual income	This influences, for instance, loans or credit approval that customers may need.
Occupation	This influences buying decisions that consumers may have. Occupation categorisation includes student, housewife, retired, manager or owner.
Religion	This may be, for example, Catholic, Jewish, Muslim, Hindu, Protestant or Buddhist.

Regarding the bases identified, the following must be noted:

- A mutual relationship may exist between some of these bases. It is possible, for example, that there is a strong relationship between income, occupation and education on the one hand, and between family size and geographic region on the other. In the online industry, for example, there is a relationship between gender, age, salary and job description, and the likelihood of shopping online.[3]

- Needs seldom relate to one segment base only. A specific marketing strategy is unlikely to be directed only to people with an income of R130 000 per year. A better description of a particular market segment often uses more than one segment base, for example young females between the ages of 18 and 24, who like sport, are socially active, earn R15 000+ per month, and live in Gauteng.
- The market segmentation bases described in the diagram are not exhaustive, and many others may be identified by marketers. In the online industry, for example, marketers also use type of products or services offered, buyer needs and benefits sought as segmentation bases. The number of possible segmentation bases is, to a great extent, determined by the creativity of the marketing manager.

Geographic segmentation

In segmenting a market geographically, the marketer divides the total market into different geographic areas, such as countries or regions. Variations such as the size of the city or town, or population density, may also be appropriate bases. The enterprise can then decide to target only one or a limited number of geographic areas. If customers in different areas exhibit diverse needs, these differences can be addressed at local level. The assumption is that people with similar characteristics tend to live in the same area and therefore have similar buying patterns.

'In segmenting a market geographically, the marketer divides the total market into different geographic areas, such as countries or regions.'

Demographic segmentation

Demographic segmentation is probably the most common base for segmenting consumer markets because it is clearly identifiable. This may be because of the relative ease with which the approach can be applied or because consumer needs are often strongly associated with these variables.[4]

Traditionally, companies in South Africa, with its diverse population groups and cultures, used race heavily as a basis for market segmentation. Increasingly, however, and specifically more so since 1994, companies are moving away from this approach and making more use of other segmentation variables such as income, education, lifestyle, living standards, and so on. In 1993, the South African Advertising Research Foundation (SAARF) published its first Living Standards Measure (LSM) report, explaining how it arrived at eight LSM categories, using 13 variables such as degree of urbanisation and ownership of cars and major appliances instead of the outmoded category of race.[5] Since then, the SAARF LSM has become the most widely used marketing research tool in South Africa. The most recent LSM classification divides the population into 10 LSM groups, 10 (highest) to 1 (lowest). In Table 5.2 we provide a brief description of each of these groups.

Note that even in the 1990s, culture and religion remained powerful segmentation bases, primarily because the different cultures and religions have vastly different traditions, beliefs, taboos and preferences

WWW:

- For more information on the LSM, go to http://www.saarf.co.za

that must be accommodated. Differences include the languages that people speak, the food they eat, the clothes they wear, and the sport they watch or participate in, to mention a few.

Table 5.2 Description of selected LSM groups[6]

<table>
<tr><th colspan="2">Brief description of LSM 1–10</th></tr>
<tr><th>LSM 1: 1,9 % of adult population</th><th>LSM 2: 5,1 % of adult population</th></tr>
<tr><td>Demographics
● Male and female
● 50+
● Primary completed
● Small urban/rural
● Traditional hut
● R1 369 average household income per month
Media
● Radio: A major channel of media communication; mainly African Language Services (ALS) – Umhlobo Wenene FM, Ukhozi FM and community
General
● Minimal access to services
● Minimal ownership of durables, except radio sets
● Mzansi bank account
● Activities: Minimal participation in activities; singing</td><td>Demographics
● Female
● 15–24 and 50+
● Some high school
● Small urban/rural
● Squatter shack, matchbox and traditional hut
● R1 952 average household income per month
Media
● Radio: Commercial, mainly ALS-Ukhozi FM, Umhlobo Wenene FM
General
● Communal access to water
● Minimal ownership of durables, except radio sets and stoves
● Mzansi bank account
● Activities: Minimal participation in activities; singing; attending burial society meetings and traditional gatherings</td></tr>
<tr><th>LSM 3: 6,1 % of adult population</th><th>LSM 4: 12,2 % of adult population</th></tr>
<tr><td>Demographics
● Female
● 15–34
● Some high school
● Small urban/rural area
● Squatter shack, matchbox and traditional hut
● R2 545 average household income per month
Media
● Radio: Mainly ALS stations, Ukhozi FM, Umhlobo Wenene FM
General
● Water on plot or communal
● Minimal ownership of durables, except radio sets and stoves
● Mzansi bank account
● Activities: Singing</td><td>Demographics
● Male
● 15–34 and 50+
● Some high school
● Small urban/rural area
● Squatter shack, matchbox and traditional hut
● R3 141 average household income per month
Media
● Radio: Commercial, mainly ALS, Gagasi, Motsweding, Ukhozi, Umhlobo Wenene FM, community radio
● TV: SABC1
General
● Electricity, water on plot or communal, non-flush toilet
● TV sets, electric hotplates
● Mzansi bank account
● Activities: Attending gatherings; going to nightclubs</td></tr>
</table>

Continue to next page

Continued from previous page

<table>
<tr><th>LSM 5: 17,4% of adult population</th><th>LSM 6: 22,4% of adult population</th></tr>
<tr><td>Demographics<ul><li>Male and female</li><li>25–34</li><li>Some high school</li><li>Small urban/rural area</li><li>House, matchbox/matchbox improved</li><li>R4 200 average household income per month</li></ul>Media<ul><li>Radio: Commercial mainly ALS stations, Lesedi FM, Motsweding FM, Ukhozi FM, community radio</li><li>TV: SABC1,2,3, e.tv, Top TV</li></ul>General<ul><li>Electricity, water on plot, flush toilet outside</li><li>TV sets, hi-fi/radio set, stove, fridge</li><li>Mzansi accounts</li><li>Activities: Singing; baking for pleasure; going to nightclubs; attending gatherings; buying lottery tickets</li></ul></td><td>Demographics<ul><li>Male</li><li>25–49</li><li>Matric</li><li>Large urban area</li><li>House/townhouse, cluster house</li><li>R6 454 average household income per month</li></ul>Media<ul><li>Wide range of commercial and community radio</li><li>TV: SABC1,2,3, e.tv, Top TV, Community TV</li><li>Any AMPS newspaper</li><li>Outdoor</li></ul>General<ul><li>Electricity, water in home, flush toilet in home</li><li>TV set, stove, fridge/freezer, microwave oven</li><li>Savings and Mzansi accounts</li><li>Activities: Hiring DVDs; going to nightclubs; buying takeaways (in past four weeks); attending gatherings; buying lottery tickets; going to gym</li></ul></td></tr>
<tr><th>LSM 7 Low: 4,9% of adult population</th><th>LSM 7 High: 5,8% of adult population</th></tr>
<tr><td>Demographics<ul><li>Female</li><li>35+</li><li>Matric and higher</li><li>Urban</li><li>R9 768 average household income per month</li></ul>Media<ul><li>Wide range of commercial and community radio</li><li>TV: SABC1,2,3, e.tv, DStv, Top TV, Community TV</li><li>All print</li><li>Accessed Internet in past seven days</li><li>Outdoor</li></ul>General<ul><li>Full access to services</li><li>Savings accounts</li><li>Increased ownership of durables plus DVD player and motor vehicle</li><li>Participation in all activities</li></ul></td><td>Demographics<ul><li>Male</li><li>35+</li><li>Matric and higher</li><li>Urban</li><li>R12 311 average household income per month</li></ul>Media<ul><li>Wide range of commercial and community radio</li><li>TV: SABC1,2,3, e.tv, M-Net, DStv, Top TV, Community TV</li><li>All print</li><li>Accessed Internet in past seven days</li><li>Cinema and outdoor</li></ul>General<ul><li>Full access to services, including cheque and savings accounts</li><li>Increased ownership of durables plus DVD player and motor vehicle</li><li>Participation in all activities</li></ul></td></tr>
</table>

Continue to next page

Continued from previous page

LSM 8 Low: 4,2 % of adult population	LSM 8 High: 4,1 % of adult population
Demographics ● Male ● 35+ ● Matric and higher ● Urban ● R14 275 average household income per month **Media** ● Wide range of commercial and community radio ● TV: SABC1,2,3, e.tv, M-Net, DStv, Top TV, Community TV ● All print ● Accessed Internet in past seven days ● Cinema and outdoor **General** ● Full access to services and bank accounts ● Full ownership of durables, incl. PC ● Increased participation in activities	**Demographics** ● Male ● 35+ ● Matric and higher ● Urban ● R15 499 average household income per month **Media** ● Wide range of commercial and community radio ● TV: SABC2,3, e.tv, M-Net, DStv, Top TV, Community TV ● All print ● Accessed Internet in past seven days ● Cinema and outdoor **General** ● Full access to services and bank accounts ● Full ownership of durables, incl. PC ● Increased participation in activities
LSM 9 Low: 4,6 % of adult population	**LSM 9 High: 4,6 % of adult population**
Demographics ● Male ● 50+ ● Matric and higher ● Urban ● R18 444 average household income per month **Media** ● Wide range of commercial and community radio ● TV: SABC2,3, e.tv, M-Net, DStv, Top TV, Community TV ● Accessed Internet in past seven days ● All print ● Cinema and outdoor **General** ● Full access to services and bank accounts ● Full ownership of durables ● Increased participation in activities, excluding stokvel meetings	**Demographics** ● Male ● 35+ ● Matric and higher ● Urban ● R22 887 average household income per month **Media** ● Wide range of commercial radio ● TV: SABC2,3, e.tv, M-Net, DStv, Top TV, Community TV ● Accessed Internet in past seven days ● All print ● Cinema and outdoor **General** ● Full access to services and bank accounts ● Full ownership of durables ● Increased participation in activities, excluding stokvel meetings

Continue to next page

Continued from previous page

LSM 10 Low: 3,3 % of adult population	LSM 10 High: 3,0 % of adult population
Demographics ● Male ● 35+ ● Matric and higher ● Urban ● R27 807 average household income per month **Media** ● Wide range of commercial radio ● TV: SABC 3, M-Net, DStv, Top TV, Community TV ● All print ● Accessed Internet in past seven days ● Cinema and outdoor **General** ● Full access to services and bank accounts ● Full ownership of durables ● Increased participation in activities, excluding stokvel meetings	**Demographics** ● Male ● 35+ ● Matric and higher ● Urban ● R33 590 average household income per month **Media** ● Wide range of commercial radio ● TV: M-Net, DStv, Top TV, Community TV ● All print ● Accessed Internet in past seven days ● Cinema and outdoor **General** ● Full access to services and bank accounts ● Full ownership of durables ● Increased participation in activities, excluding stokvel meetings

Psychographic segmentation

Psychographics and lifestyle

Psychographic research is the psychology behind why customers make purchase decisions. It assesses customers on a psychological dimension, instead of only focusing on demographics. Motives determine a person's behaviour and their lifestyle. Psychographics is the study of individuals based on characteristics that describe them. It uses demographics to study consumer attitudes, behaviours, opinions and lifestyles.[7]

Consider a team of marketers who want to target a student population. They identify their ideal customer as 'an 18-year-old, first-year economic management student living at home with his or her parents'. You may know many people who fit this description. Do you think they are all the same? Would they all be likely to share common interests and buy the same products? Probably not, since their lifestyles are likely to differ considerably. In other words, customers may share the same demographic characteristics and still be very different people, hence retailers need to find a way to 'breathe life' into demographic data to really identify, understand and target customer segments that will share a set of preferences for their products and services.

The term 'psychographics' is often used interchangeably with 'lifestyle' to denote the separation of customers into categories based on differences in choices of consumption activities and product usage. There are many psychographic variables that may be used to segment customers, but they all share the underlying principle of going beyond surface characteristics to understand customers' motivations for buying and using products. Demographics allows us to describe who buys, while psychographics allows us to understand why they buy. This is largely based on the values of the customer concerned.

Values determine lifestyle

'Lifestyle' refers to how consumers and society live, their attitudes, behaviours, values and norms.[8] Values are the goals we live for. They are the core beliefs that motivate us. Customers are motivated to purchase products to satisfy their needs and wants, which are based on their values, therefore their personal values determine product choice. Customers buy products that they perceive will achieve a value-related goal.[9]

Psychographic profiles

In South Africa, the now known Nielsan Sociomonitor Value Groups Survey is one of the most expert psychographic profiles that exists. Respondents are asked to answer an extensive array of psychographic questions, which is used to create the value groups. The respondents' answers are grouped and scored. Depending on their answers, each respondent is given a different score and position on the 'social map'. The value groups are the result of the grouping of customers with similar values, attitudes and motivations. [10]

The uses of psychographics

Psychographics can be and is used extensively in market segmentation. Psychographics allows marketers to go beyond the simple demographic or product usage descriptions. Sometimes marketers create their strategies with a typical customer in mind. This stereotype may not be correct, because the actual customer may not match these assumptions. For example, marketers of a body lotion for women were surprised to find their key market was composed of older, widowed women rather than the younger, more sociable women to whom they were pitching their appeals.

Psychographic information can allow marketers to emphasise features of the product that fit in with a person's lifestyle. Products targeted at people whose lifestyle profiles show a high need to be around other people might focus on the product's ability to help meet this social need.

Psychographic information can offer very useful input in advertising, communicating something about the product. The advertiser obtains a much richer mental image of the target customer than that obtained through dry statistics, and this insight improves the advertiser's ability to talk to that customer. For example, it was found that heavy drinkers of brandy tended to feel that life's pleasures were few and far between. Commercials were developed using a theme that told these drinkers: 'You only go around once, so reach for all the gusto you can'.[11]

Understanding how a product fits or does not fit into customers' lifestyles allows marketers to identify new product opportunities, design media strategies and create environments most consistent and harmonious with these consumption patterns.

Behavioural segmentation

The market can also be segmented on the basis of their buying behaviour. This may take the form of the following:

Purchase occasions

Some buyers may use a product regularly, while others may use it only on special occasions. Bread and cake are two examples of products that fall into this category. Bread is a staple food item which is generally consumed on a daily basis as lunch, whereas cake is usually consumed on special occasions such as birthdays, weddings and other celebrations.

Benefits sought

Some market segments may be specific in what benefits they seek when buying a specific product. Some may seek economy in a car, while others may prefer speed or a good maintenance plan. When consumers are very specific with regard to the benefits they seek, marketers can respond with products that address these needs, and in so doing, satisfy them.

User status

Consumers can be segmented into groups consisting of non-users, ex-users, potential users or regular users. A balanced approach would require that an enterprise focus on both regular as well as potential users. While the regular users guarantee survival in the short to medium term, potential users who can be enticed to become users represent future growth.

Usage rate

Marketers can make provision for different market segments based on how frequently buyers purchase their products. Heavy users should receive special attention by marketers, since they may represent the bulk of sales revenue. It is therefore common to see hotels, casinos and airlines develop special clubs or frequent flyer programmes to appeal to this important segment of the market.

Loyalty status

Consumers vary in the degree of loyalty they have towards the organisation or its brand names. At one extreme are the switchers, or those consumers who show no loyalty toward any brand. They can be attracted through frequent sales and promotions, but attracting them may sometimes not be worthwhile. On the other hand, there are very loyal consumers. Hardcore loyals insist on a particular brand and go to great lengths to acquire it. Ideally, they should be retained and, where possible, encouraged to become spokespeople for the organisation's products and services, as suggested by the relationship marketing philosophy. Loyalty is the reason why companies follow the 80/20 principle, that is, that 80% of the profit is made from 20% of the loyal customers.

Buyer readiness stage

Different marketing approaches have to be followed, depending on the consumer's readiness to buy. Potential customers who are unaware of the product must first be made aware of it, while those who may buy the product must be persuaded to do so. When tablets were introduced to the South African market, most people were either unaware, or aware but uninformed, of the product. Initially, awareness had to be established, and as it increased, more aggressive strategies were followed in the marketing of tablets.

Attitude towards the product

'Potential customers who are unaware of the product must first be made aware of it, while those who may buy the product must be persuaded to do so.'

By segmenting customers according to their attitude towards the product, a company can increase its marketing productivity. Market segments that are negative or hostile towards a product can be avoided, saving valuable time and money. Attempts can be made to persuade those who are indifferent, while those who are enthusiastic or positive can merely be encouraged to support the product in future. For example, the well-publicised battle between smartphone users depicts iPhone advocates as being 'snobby' and 'cult-like', and mocked by Samsung, which is run on the Android operating system.[12] It would be easier for either brand to focus their marketing campaigns on those who are indifferent rather than loyal to competing brands.

Developing segment profiles

Every segment considered by the enterprise must be described fully with respect to its size, demographic and psychographic details, lifestyle, behaviour patterns and product usage. Such a profile enables marketing management to develop products that will provide the need satisfaction utilities desired by customers, and to design marketing communication messages that will appeal to them. In a later section, we provide practical hints on how to accomplish this.

Bases for segmenting industrial markets

Traditionally, industrial firms were reluctant to accept marketing segmentation as a marketing tool.[13] This can be attributed to the fact that industrial firms tend to be more engineering oriented, often focusing on product specifications rather than customer requirements. At the other extreme, one may find many industrial firms producing products or services customised to their customers' needs. Consequently, they have no reason to segment their market as they are producing for individual customers. Currently, the importance of market segmentation is increasingly being realised by business-to-business marketers.

Table 5.3 shows the most popular bases for segmenting industrial markets, and it is clear from this that the marketer will consider totally different variables when segmenting the industrial market.

Table 5.3 Bases for segmenting industrial markets[14]

Demographic
• On which industries should we focus?
• What size company must we target?
• How many employees are in the company?
• Which geographical areas must we target?
• How long has the company been in business?
• Does the company have one/multiple establishment(s)?
• Is it a local/national/international company?
Operating variables
• On what technologies should we focus?
• On what user types should we focus (heavy, medium, light, non-users)?
• On what product types must we focus?
• How frequently does the customer require delivery?
• Should we focus on customers requiring many/few services?
Purchasing approaches
• How centralised/decentralised is the purchasing function?
• Should we focus on companies that seek quality/service/lower price?
• Should we focus on companies that demand quick delivery/convenience/reputation/ economy?
• Should we focus on the companies with which we have strong links, or should we go after the most desirable ones?
• Should we concentrate on organisations that prefer leasing/service contracts/systems purchases/sealed bidding?
• Should we focus on businesses that are financial/marketing/production/engineering dominated?
Situational factors
• Should we focus on customers who require periodic quick delivery or on those that require regular steady delivery?
• Should we focus on a special application of our product or on all applications?
• Should we be focusing on small/medium/large orders?
Personal characteristics
• Should we focus on companies that have values similar to ours?
• Should we concentrate on organisations that are risk takers or risk avoiders?
• Should we focus on companies that show high loyalty towards their suppliers?

Demographic dimensions

Any demographic dimensions – such as company size, as reflected in the sales volume, number of employees or other criteria; geographic area; number of outlets; or scope of operation (local/national/international) – may be used to classify companies into market segments.

Operational variables

Companies can also be classified according to their operational characteristics such as technology, user types, product types or frequency of delivery.

Purchasing approaches

Marketers of industrial products often have to negotiate with the purchasing departments of other businesses. It would therefore make sense to segment the market along these dimensions. Among the most important variables to be used are the degree of centralisation or decentralisation of the purchasing function, the power structure of the company, the nature of the existing relationship with the customer, the purchasing criteria employed by the company, and so on. In a *centralised* purchasing department, for example, the buyer is more likely to consider all transactions with suppliers on a global basis to emphasise cost savings and to minimise risks. A *decentralised* purchasing department will, however, be more concerned with the user's need, tend to emphasise product quality and prompt delivery, and is likely to be less cost conscious.[15]

Situational factors

Criteria such as the delivery requirements of customers, the product application or the order size are regarded as situational factors. Often, the marketer will find that about 80% of sales will be to customers who order in large quantities, while only about 20% will be to those who buy in smaller quantities. The needs and demands of these segments often vary greatly, justifying segmentation along these lines.

Personal characteristics

Marketers may also choose to segment the industrial market on the basis of the organisational values, risk profile or loyalty towards suppliers. Customers who are loyal to their suppliers can, for example, be treated with less aggression by salespeople, while the salesperson will have to be more aggressive in an attempt to retain the less-loyal market segments. It is also advisable to spread one's risk between risk takers and risk avoiders, which decreases the likelihood of a disaster.

As in the case of the consumer market, the industrial marketer must compile a comprehensive description of the characteristics, needs and demands of the various market segments, based on the criteria provided in this section. Figure 5.1 provides guidelines in this regard.

First, it is necessary to identify the various market segments in the particular market. Second, the manager must list the characteristics of each of these segments. Third, the marketer must derive the needs and preferences of each segment by studying their characteristics. Once this process has been done, the product or service can be developed around the needs of the identified market segments.

This process allows the marketing manager to adapt his or her marketing strategy to the unique requirements of the targeted market segments.

In an increasingly competitive business environment, this can only enhance the competitiveness of the enterprise.

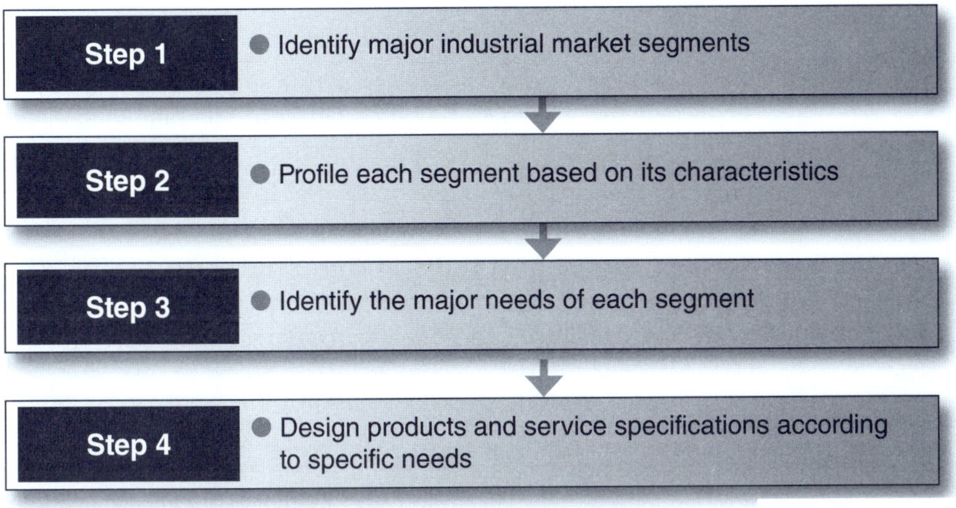

Figure 5.1 Compiling a profile of the industrial market[16]

Market targeting

After developing a comprehensive profile of the market segments based on the criteria indicated above, the next step is to decide to target only one segment or a few, or even the whole market. This is referred to as *market targeting*. In this section, the focus is, first, on the *criteria to be used to evaluate market segments*, and, second, on the *approaches available to the enterprise*.

'In this section, the focus is, first, on the criteria to be used to evaluate market segments and, second, on the approaches available to the enterprise.'

Criteria for selecting potential target markets

Before a specific market segment is selected as a target market, it must first be evaluated according to five important evaluation criteria:

Segment size and growth possibilities

The size of a target market is not relative to its profitability. A small segment may be more profitable than one in which a large sales volume can be realised. Marketing management should be convinced that there are further growth possibilities, thus making the segment sustainable. The market for Rolex watches or Ferraris may be small, but the profit potential is huge. This makes it a very attractive segment.

Attractiveness and potential profitability

The attractiveness of a target market depends not only on its size and growth potential, but also its promise of long-term profitability. Attractive segments can draw intense competition which may have a negative effect on future profits. Aggressive competitors who can launch price wars, intensive advertising campaigns, or develop new substitute products are serious threats that need to be considered. The growing power of buyers and suppliers also threatens attractive target markets.

If the threat is very serious, an enterprise that does have the necessary resources and skills can decide not to take the opportunity to select the segment as a target market.

A target market is generally attractive if it has some degree of interrelationship with other segments. Instead of serving a number of small segments, it would be much better to combine interrelated segments. Interrelationships exist among segments that use the same raw materials, similar production methods or joint distribution channels.

The resources and skills of the enterprise

Even if a segment has great potential, if it doesn't fit in with management's long-term objectives, it cannot be used. The same applies if the resources and skills are not available to take full advantage of the opportunity. A segment can only be chosen as a target market if marketing management is fully committed to serving it better than any other competitor does. This implies that the market offering must have an undoubted differential advantage to target market members. If not, it would be advisable to commit the cost and energy to an alternative option.

Compatibility with the enterprise's objectives

Besides the resources and skills of the enterprise, the target market's compatibility with the enterprise's objectives must be considered. If the enterprise's objectives cannot be enhanced, the market segment in question should be disregarded.

Cost of reaching the target market

When a potential target market is inaccessible to an enterprise's marketing strategies, or the cost to reach it is too high, it should not be considered.[17]

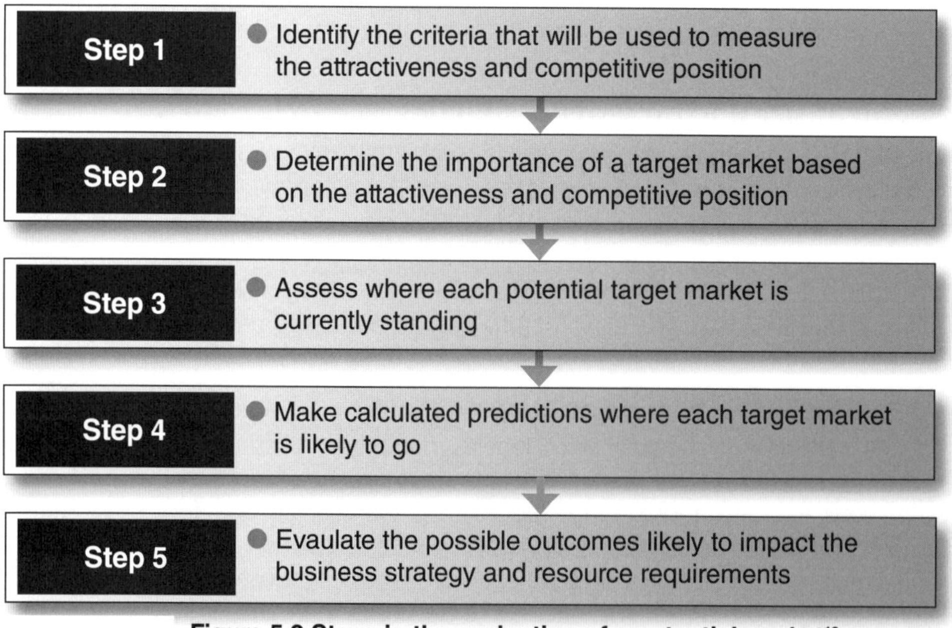

Figure 5.2 Steps in the evaluation of a potential market[18]

Steps in the evaluation of a potential market

To assess the potential of each of the market segments identified during the segmentation process, Walker, Boyd and Larréché[19] propose five steps, as shown in Figure 5.2. The evaluation of potential market segments starts with the selection of a set of criteria which can be used to assess, firstly, the *attractiveness of the particular target market* and, secondly, the *competitive position of the enterprise* with regard to a specific market segment. Because not all evaluation criteria are of equal importance, these factors are then weighed to reflect the relative importance of each.

The enterprise then rates every market segment it is considering. Scores that reflect the market attractiveness and competitive position of the enterprise are posted on a market attractiveness/competitive position graph. Such a graph is shown in Figure 5.3 below. Once this has been done, the marketing manager considers likely future changes that might manifest themselves. The segment near the area illustrated with a star in Figure 5.3 shows that this segment is expected to become less attractive in the future, while the organisation also believes that its competitive position will deteriorate. It is critically important to consider likely future changes since the choice of a particular target market commits the enterprise to it. Should changes occur in the future, the competitive position of the enterprise may be adversely affected. Area A would therefore represent the most attractive target markets in terms of both market attractiveness and competitive position. Target markets that lie on the equilibrium (line) would indicate those of only moderate attractiveness, while area B (bottom right) would indicate unattractive target markets.

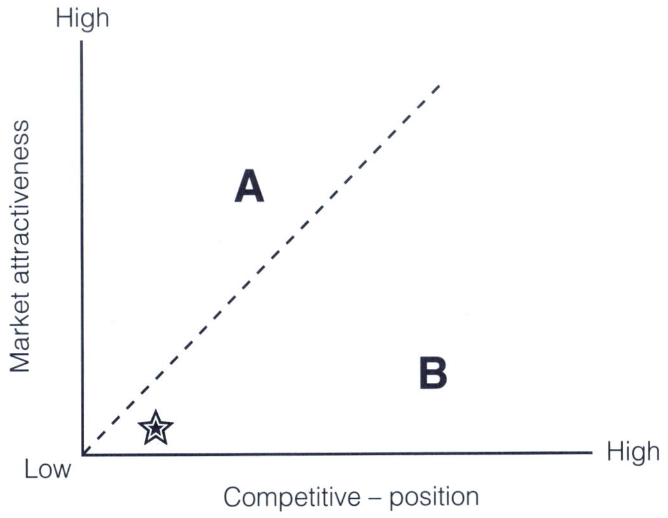

Figure 5.3 Market attractiveness/competitive position graph[20]

Given these possible changes, the marketing manager will lastly evaluate the implications of possible future changes with regard to their impact on company strategies and resource requirements. Only once this has been completed will the marketing manager finally choose a market segment or segments to target.

Targeting market segments

Marketers may choose one, two or multiple market segments to target. In essence, marketers can choose between three broad segmentation approaches to the market: *undifferentiated targeting, differentiated targeting* and *concentrated targeting*. Figure 5.4 reflects these approaches.

Figure 5.4 Approaches to market targeting[21]

Undifferentiated marketing

An undifferentiated marketing strategy is used (also known as the *aggregation strategy*) when the company chooses to ignore the differences that are found in the market. Instead, it pursues the total market with one basic market offering. In practice, the enterprise would concentrate on the commonalities of the market segment rather than on the differences. One of the major advantages of such a strategy is the economies of scale that can be achieved with a standardised product and marketing strategy. This strategy has lost ground in recent years as consumers have become more discriminating.

Differentiated marketing

In differentiated market segmentation, the enterprise elects to target two or more market segments, developing a unique marketing strategy for each one. This strategy allows the organisation to cater for the diverse needs of the different segments. It is, however, a costly strategy. To cater for the diverse needs, the enterprise incurs extra production costs as production runs become smaller, advertising costs rise because communication strategies must be adapted for the different market segments, administrative costs increase as separate marketing plans have to be developed, and inventory costs go up as a greater variety of products must be maintained.

Concentrated marketing

Concentrating the market offering on one specific segment can lead to greater expertise in production, distribution and marketing communications. Because the product offering is aimed at one market segment only, it would be fair to argue that the enterprise will also be able to achieve greater customer satisfaction in this singular market segment. A big disadvantage, however, is that all efforts are then concentrated on one source. The risk of product failure and non-acceptance of the product is thus concentrated in a single target market. Should the preferences of the target market change, or should competitors enter the market with an improved offering, the enterprise may find itself without any business.

Product positioning

The ultimate aim of the marketing actions of marketers is to position their products or services in the minds of their customers in a way that they want the customers to perceive them – that is, the company as a reliable supplier, a value-for-money product, a quality product, etc. Product positioning therefore refers to the way in which customers perceive a product in terms of its characteristics and advantages, and its competitive positioning. It thus involves the creation, in the minds of the targeted buyers, of a distinctive position with regard to the organisation's product relative to those of competing organisations. For positioning to be effective, it is important that the marketer understands customer-buying criteria, and recognises the performance of each competitor on each of the evaluative criteria.

DEFINITION

Positioning
Positioning is the way customers perceive a product in terms of its characteristics and advantages, and its competitive positioning relative to products of competing organisations.

Product positioning maps to aid decision making

Marketers often use positioning or perceptual maps to portray market positions visually. A perceptual map is a multidimensional graphic image

'The ultimate aim of the marketing actions of marketers is to position their products or services in the minds of their customers in a way that they want the customers to perceive them.'

depicting consumer perceptions. These maps assist marketers in developing focused marketing mixes or strategies. They also help the manager to assess the advantages of an organisation's marketing programme.[22]

Many variables or determinants, such as those listed later in this chapter, can be used to compile similar positioning maps. However, marketing information and sophisticated statistical testing is necessary for the development of positioning maps.

The positioning process

A seven-step approach can be adopted when positioning brands. (The term 'brands' is preferred here since it is individual producers' brands and not products that compete against each other in a market. Positioning maps can, however, also be developed for product categories.) These steps are shown in Figure 5.5.[23]

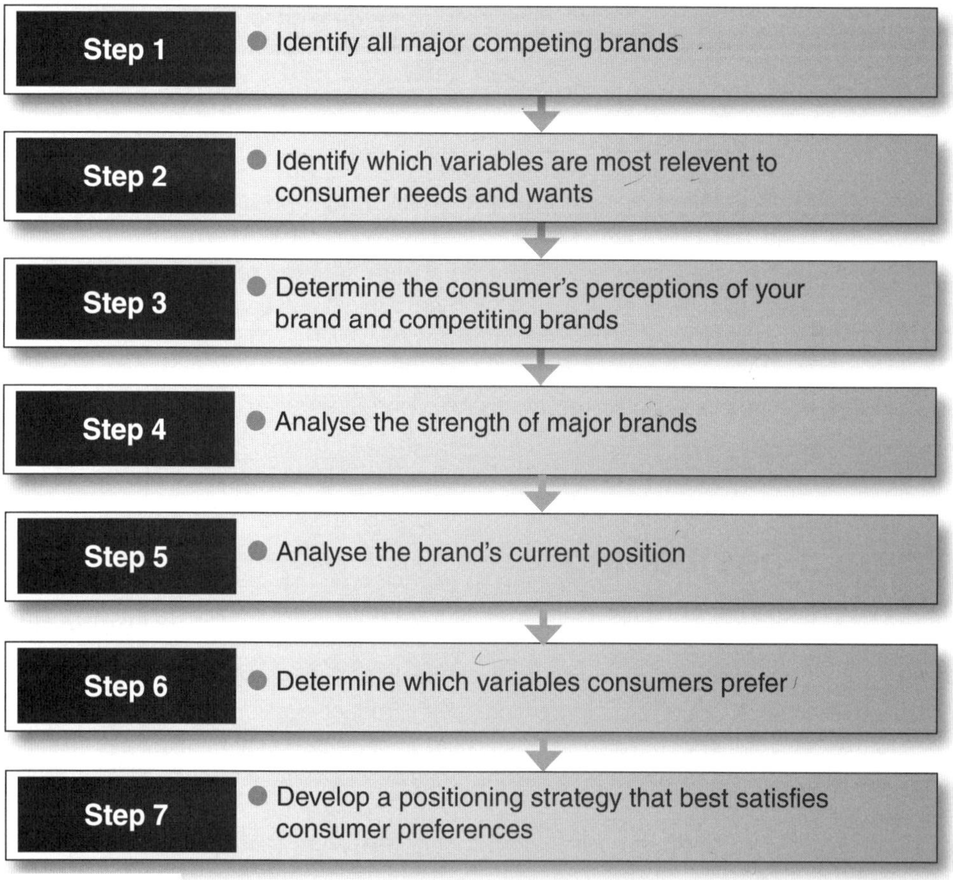

Figure 5.5 The positioning process[24]

Identify all major competing brands

The positioning process starts with the identification of a relevant set of competitive brands to which a particular producer's brand will be compared. It is essential that all relevant competing brands be identified to make the positioning effort worthwhile. This enables marketers to identify the strengths and weaknesses of their own brand against a competing one. It also helps them to decide whether to reposition the brand to strengthen its position in the market. Repositioning refers to the changing of a brand's (mostly undesirable) position in the market in the hope that the new positioning will improve the brand's appeal among consumers.

Identify which variables are most relevant to consumer needs and wants

In essence, product positioning has to do with competitive differentiation and the effective communication of this to customers. Kotler and Keller[25] suggest that an enterprise or market offering can be differentiated along four different dimensions: product, services, personnel or image. Table 5.5 summarises the main differentiation variables suggested by Kotler and Keller. These are not the only variables that can be used, but the most obvious ones have been discussed.

The marketer must decide which of the differentiation variables shown in Table 5.5 (or other variables) should be used in developing a positioning map. In this case, Walker et al.[26] refer to determinant variables. They suggest that marketers select those variables that play a major role in helping customers to differentiate among alternative brands in the market.

The example on the right entitled 'Using determinant variables' serves to illustrate the importance of using such variables.

Table 5.5 Differentiation variables[27]

Differentiation item	Differentiation variable
Product	Features Quality Durability Reliability Style Design
Service	Delivery Installation Repair Training After-sales service
Personnel	Competence Knowledge Credibility Reliability Responsiveness
Image	Symbol Media Events Atmosphere

Example E

Using determinant variables

Although safety is a major concern for all airline passengers, it is not regarded as a determinant variable as most customers use other features such as price, convenient flying times, service or frequent flyer programmes to differentiate between competing airlines. Appropriate marketing research can aid the marketer in identifying determinant variables.

Determine consumers' perceptions of your brand and of competing brands

The marketer must establish how consumers perceive the various brands in terms of the determinant variables selected in the previous step. This step involves the collection of primary data from a sample of consumers. Using a structured questionnaire, these consumers (named respondents) are questioned about their perceptions of the various brands. The collected data is then analysed, using several statistical techniques. These include factor analysis, discriminant analysis, multidimensional scaling, and so on.

Analyse the strength of major brands

When a consumer is unaware of a brand, such a brand clearly cannot occupy a position in the mind of the consumer. In such instances, brand awareness must first be established. However, when a consumer is aware of a brand, the intensity of awareness may vary. In many markets, the awareness set for a particular product class may be as little as three or fewer brands, when there are more than 20 brands in the product class. In such markets, the marketer of the lesser-known brand must attempt to increase the intensity of awareness by developing a strong relationship between the brand and a limited number of variables.

Competing directly with dominant brands is not advised. Instead, the marketer must identify as a target a position within a market segment that is not dominated by a leading brand. Alternatively, the marketer must concentrate on a variable that is highly prized by a particular market segment.

Analyse the brand's current position

From the data collected from consumers about their perceptions of the various brands in the market, the marketer can establish how strongly a particular brand is associated with a variety of determinant variables. To do this, a positioning map, similar to the one shown in Figure 5.6, is developed. Brands that are close to each other on the map can be expected to be close rivals, while those that are far apart are considered very different from each other, thus competitive rivalry between them is expected to be limited.

Develop a positioning strategy that best satisfies consumer preferences

The discussion thus far has focused on consumers' perceptions of existing brands and has given no insight into the positions that would appeal most to consumers. This can be achieved by asking survey respondents to think of the ideal product or brand in a particular product category. Respondents would be asked to rate their ideal product and existing products on a number of determinant variables. The result of such an analysis of electronic gadgets is shown in Figure 5.6. The determinant variables that are closest to the ideal point are more important to consumers, while those that are further apart from each other are considered less important.

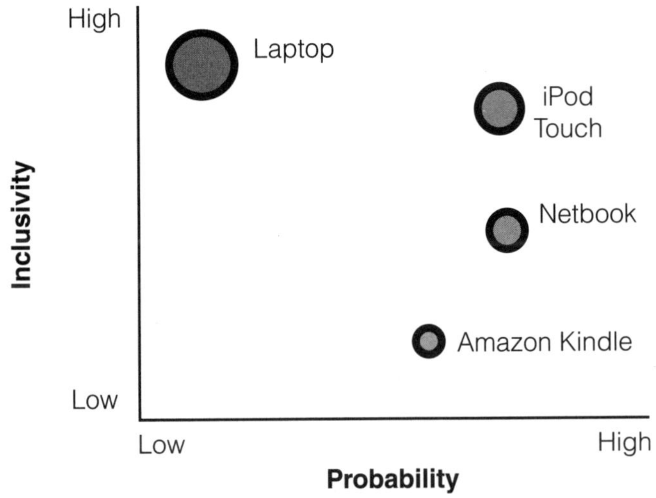

Figure 5.6 Perceptual map of electronic gadgets based on ideal points[28]

Select positioning strategies

Deciding where to position a new brand or where to reposition an existing one depends on the market targeting analysis discussed earlier, as well as the market positioning analysis. The position chosen must reflect customer preferences and the positions of competitive brands. The decision must also reflect the expected future attractiveness of the target market and the relative strengths and weaknesses of competitors as well as the organisation's own capabilities. Specific positioning methods are discussed in the next section.

Positioning methods

In general, seven positioning methods can be distinguished:[29]

- **Attribute positioning**. The enterprise positions itself in terms of one or more outstanding attributes. Castle Lite has chosen to position its beer as the leading premium light beer and 'cold'.
- **Benefit positioning**. This positioning method emphasises the unique benefits that the enterprise or product offering offers its customers. For example, Vanish promises effective stain removal.
- **Use application positioning**. An enterprise can position itself or its products in terms of the product use or application possibility. Graça, for example, is positioned as a wine to be enjoyed at all kinds of fun occasions.
- **User positioning**. The enterprise may position its products with its users in mind. Marketers of skydiving can position their market offering to appeal to thrill-seekers.

'When a consumer is unaware of a brand, such a brand cannot clearly occupy a position in the mind of the consumer. In such instances, brand awareness must first be established.'

Example *E*

Benefit positioning[30]

After conducting research to understand why Southern Sun's brand equity had decreased, the company decided to launch the 'Project Magic' campaign. The campaign decided that the following three pillars were crucial to customers:

- **The welcome**. The first impression is the most important thing.
- **The bedroom**. This is a private space and therefore guests should not be bombarded with advertisements there.
- **Dining**. This is an integral part of guests' experience at a hotel, and the company wanted to ensure that it could cater for individual diners' needs.

Southern Sun's purpose is to create great memories for customers by promising the above-mentioned attributes and satisfying them.

- **Competitor positioning**. Some products can best be positioned against competitive offerings. BMW finds it useful to position its cars directly against those of Mercedes-Benz, its closest rival in South Africa.
- **Product category positioning**. An enterprise can position itself in a product category not traditionally associated with it, thereby expanding business opportunities. A museum or planetarium, traditionally regarded as an educational institution (such as the Apartheid Museum) may elect to position itself as a tourist attraction.
- **Quality/price positioning**. The enterprise may claim its product is of exceptional quality or the lowest price. While Woolworths is known for high-quality garments, Mr Price is known for unbeatable prices.

After the marketer has decided on a particular positioning method, it must be communicated to the target market.

Summary

Market segmentation remains one of the cornerstones of modern marketing. In this chapter, we defined the main theoretical concepts associated with market segmentation, targeting and positioning, and explained how marketers can apply them. It is imperative for those in marketing management to realise that they cannot hope to satisfy all markets. Instead, they must divide the heterogeneous market into more homogeneous groups of customers; choose one or more to target with their product offering(s); and position themselves relative to their competitors. Ultimately, the success of marketing management will depend on their ability to select profitable target markets in an ever-changing marketing environment, as well as their ability to satisfy the needs of the chosen segment(s).

References

1. Business Express. 2008. *Business Express*. [Online] Available from: http://www.sarcc. co.za/be.asp [Accessed: 2009-01-26].
2. Kotler, P. & Keller, K.L. 2006. Segmenting consumer markets. In Cant, M.C., Strydom, J.W., Jooste, C.J. & Du Plessis, P.J. 2006. *Marketing management*. 5th ed. Cape Town, South Africa: Juta & Co., p. 108; Examstutor. n.d. *Market segmentation*. [Online] Available from: http://www.examstutor.com/business/resources/studyroom/marketing/market_analysis/5_market_segmentation.php [Accessed: 2013-07-16].
3. Hashim, A. 2009. *Does consumers' demographic profile influence online shopping?* [Online] Available from: https://www.google.co.za/url?sa=t&rct=j&q=&esrc=s&source=web&cd=1&cad=rja&ved=0CDgQFjAA&url=http%3A%2F%2Fwww.cscanada.net%2Findex.php%2Fcss%2Farticle%2Fdownload%2Fj.css.1923669720090506.003%2F58&ei=tSldUaSMI42whAephoDoAQ&usg=AFQjCNFTkmr2Q0bd7Ek3-O2SKm8H4vegw&sig2=6HhiCok8h1VXv90PfTz2tA&bvm=bv.44770516,d.ZG4 [Accessed: 2013-07-13].

4. Cant, M.C., Van Heerden C.H. & Ngambi, H.C. 2010. *Marketing management: A South African perspective*. 1st ed. Cape Town, South Africa: Juta & Co., p. 78.
5. South African Advertising Research Foundation. 2008. *The South African Advertising Research Foundation's living standards measure* (LSM). November.
6. South African Advertising Research Foundation. 2012. *LSM descriptions*. [Online] Available from: http://www.saarf.co.za/lsm-descriptions/2012/SAARF%20LSM%20Descriptions%20AMPS%20Dec%202011.pptx [Accessed: 2013-07-13].
7. Businessdictionary.com. n.d. *Psychographics*. [Online] Available from: http://www.businessdictionary.com/definition/psychographics.html. [Accessed: 2013-07-04].
8. Businessdictionary.com. n.d. *Lifestyle*. [Online] Available from: http://www.businessdictionary.com/definition/lifestyle.html. [Accessed: 2013-07-05].
9. UKessays.com. 2013. *Analysing value and consumption behaviour*. [Online] Available from: http://www.ukessays.com/essays/marketing/analysing-value-and-consumption-behaviour-marketing-essay.php [Accessed: 2013-07-05].
10. Davis, K. 2013. *Secrets of dynamic communications: prepare with focus, deliver with clarity, speak with power*. West Bow: Thomas Nelson Inc, p. 65.
11. Based on Joubert, P. (ed). 2010. *Introduction to consumer behaviour*. Cape Town, South Africa: Juta & Co., p. 74.
12. Fried, I. 2011. *Samsung mocks 'Cult of Apple' in ad for Galaxy SII*. [Online] Available from: http://allthingsd.com/20111123/samsung-mocks-the-cult-of-apple-in-ad-for-galaxy-s-ii/ [Accessed: 2013-06-07].
13. *Nielsen Sociomonitor*. 1997, 1999.
14. Cant et al., 2010, op cit., p. 90.
15. Ibid.
16. Adapted from Cant et al., 2010, op. cit., p. 92.
17. No author. 2013. *Marketing target market selection*. [Online] Available from: http://www.slideshare.net/helpwithassignment/target-market-selection-9219822 [Accessed: 2013-07-19].
18. Cant et al., 2010, op cit., p. 95.
19. Adapted from Cant et al., 2010, op. cit., p. 92.
20. Cant et al., 2010, op. cit., p. 97.
21. Ibid. p. 99.
22. Walker, O.C., Boyd, H.W. & Larréché, J.C. *Positioning decisions*. In Cant et al. 2006, op. cit., p. 126.
23. Walker et al. In Cant et al., 2010, op cit., p. 105.
24. Walker, O.C., Boyd, H.W. & Larréché, J.C. In Cant et al., 2006, p. 105.
25. Kotler, P. & Keller, K.L. In Cant et al. 2006, op. cit., p. 132.
26. Walker et al. In Cant et al., 2006, op. cit., p. 166.
27. Cant et al., 2010, op. cit., p. 106.
28. Violante, M. 2010. *Marketing examples. Product positioning/positioning map*. [Online] Available from: http://uwmktg301.blogspot.com/2010/01/product-positioningpositioning-map.html [Accessed: 2013-06-06].

29. Marketing Segmentation Study Guide. 2012. *Positioning categories*. [Online] Available from: http://www.segmentationstudyguide.com/all-about-positioning/positioning-approaches/ [Accessed: 2013-06-06].
30. Van Heerden, C.H. 2013. *Contemporary retail and marketing case studies*. 1st ed. Cape Town, South Africa: Juta & Co., p. 202.

Product decisions

CHAPTER 6

✓ Learning objectives

After studying this chapter, you should be able to:

- identify the basic concept of a product;
- explain the different product classifications;
- explain the terms 'product line' and 'product mix decisions';
- identify the different types of new products;
- describe the consumer adoption process and the different categories of adopters; and
- describe the characteristics of the different phases of the product life cycle.

Introduction

The product or service that a company offers is usually based on intensive research that has taken place to determine the needs of the market – that is, what consumers want, the features of the product, the characteristics they want, and so forth. You may have heard the expression 'sell the sizzle, not the steak', and this is true in most cases. In many instances, customers buy a product based on what they see and feel (or smell!), rather than on the technical aspects. Someone wanting to buy fast food will be attracted by the appearance of the venue, the brand name, or even the price when making a decision. Most people are unlikely to purchase fast food from an unknown restaurant that is dirty with cockroaches running around. The immediate reaction would be one of scepticism and mistrust. Is this quality? Will it not give me food poisoning? Is it hygienic? However, on the other hand, a restaurant that is clean and radiates great ambience will elicit a completely different emotion from the customer.

It should be clear that marketers must know their customers and ensure that the product offering meets their needs in such a way that sales will be generated and that both parties benefit from the purchase of the item.

Products and product preferences change. Marketers must stay abreast of these changes and ensure that they adapt to them within the constraints of their own resources and abilities. Consumers are now more demanding than ever with higher expectations of companies. For example, consumers are becoming increasingly concerned with the wellbeing of the environment and therefore want products that are 'green' and produce a smaller carbon footprint. Over the last decade, more products have been made from recycled materials and are more environmentally friendly. Cars, for example, are designed to consume less petrol, or powered by alternative fuels and advanced technologies such as biodiesel or hybrid electric cars.

In this chapter the core aspects of product decisions are discussed.

DEFINITION

Product
A product is an item, idea or service, or a combination of all three, that is marketed or sold to a customer to serve a need or satisfy a want.

What is a product?

People tend to associate a **product** only with the physical item that they can see and feel. If asked what a product is, the answer would normally refer to the physical item. With some prodding, other elements may emerge, such as the warranty, the fact that it is available in different shapes and sizes, that there is a seven-day money-back guarantee, and so forth.

From a marketing viewpoint, the key element of a product is that it satisfies consumer or business needs – that is, products provide benefits. Indeed, successful marketers focus on the benefits products supply to consumers, be it the final consumer or an intermediary such as a retailer.

Example

Product from a customer's viewpoint[1]
The fact that a company like Checkers offers different payment options to clients, such as cash, credit card, debit card and lay-bys, is based on the payment options customers want in order to be able to purchase the store's products. Checkers customers can also pay their telephone, water and electricity bills, book at Computicket, buy air tickets, and more. Moreover, Checkers has MediRite pharmacies, and also Liquor Shop, which stocks extensive ranges of top alcohol brands, all of which benefit the customer as they are able to do one-stop shopping.

From a customer's point of view, a product will mean something different and the marketer must be aware of this. Why do you think a mother buys a specific type of clothing for her child from a specific store? The generally accepted reason is that the consumer wants the benefits from buying the product. In this case it may be to buy warm clothes for her child and to be able to return them if they do not fit, as well as being able to buy them on account. The specific features of each product are important only in so far as they are translated into the specific benefits that the consumer wants.

It is always helpful to think about products from a customer's viewpoint. Customers purchase products for their benefits, which astute marketers will emphasise in their marketing efforts.

The product concept

Whenever a person wants to buy someone a gift, a number of things come to mind: What will I buy? How much will I spend? Where will I buy it? Will the recipient be able to exchange it if it is not right? Does it carry a warranty? Will it be gift-wrapped and delivered?

Like a gift, a product is more than what it seems. A product includes everything that a customer receives in an exchange. There are five layers that represent the product concept. This is shown in Figure 6.1, and includes the *core product, the tangible (actual) product*, the *augmented product*, the *potential product* and the *product image*. These five layers are explained briefly below.

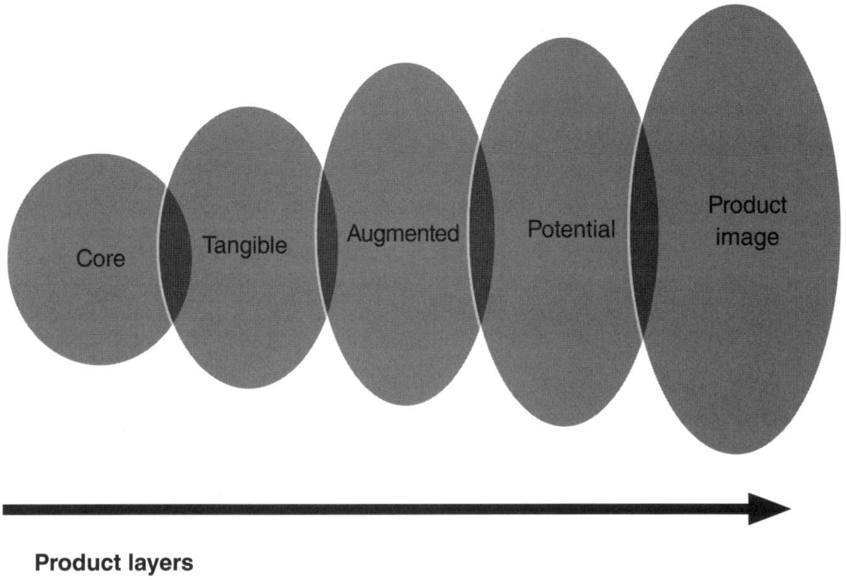

Figure 6.1 Layers of the product concept[2]

'There are five layers of the product concept:
- Core product
- Tangible product
- Augmented product
- Potential product
- Product image.'

The core product

The first layer of the product is the core product, which is essentially what the customer is buying. When buying a car, the customer is buying transport from point A to point B. It is the essential benefit or need satisfaction that the consumer expects to obtain from the product.

'The core product is essentially what the customer is buying.'

Marketers do not sell transport so their focus should not be on what the customers are looking for – a means of transport – but rather on the benefits they are looking for. They should therefore be selling product benefits. A *product benefit* is what the customer receives from owning, using or experiencing a product. The core product consists of the benefits that the product will provide for consumers or business customers. The customer purchasing a Mercedes-Benz does not buy it because it is made of metal and has a steering wheel with an engine. The customer buys it because it is safe, of high quality and provides status (and the envy of friends), and it has a maintenance plan and other attributes such as central locking, air bags, etc. Similarly, a person buying a camera does not buy camera components but rather memories that can be captured with the device.

Typically, a product provides a number of different benefits with varying degrees of importance. For example, the primary benefit provided by a cell phone is communication – that is, allowing customers to call whomever, whenever they wish. Having the latest smartphone adds various other communication mediums such as access to e-mail, social networking sites and instant messaging. An expensive smartphone may be a statement about the status or prestige desired by the buyer.

When designing products, marketers must first define the core benefits the product will provide to consumers. In many instances, the marketer will add something extra to make it more specific to the customers' needs.

'The tangible product includes the unique features of the product, such as aesthetics, appearance or packaging.'

The tangible or actual (physical) product

The second layer of the product is the physical object (product) or service offered to the consumers. The tangible product includes not only the commodity or service, but also the unique features of the product, such as the appearance or styling, the packaging and the brand name. Take, for example, a cell phone. Cell phones come with different features to meet the needs and wants of various customer segments. Sony, for example, has a range that is the most durable and water resistant, whereas Samsung has 'human activity recognition' and the iPhone has an extensive app store and simple user-friendly interface.

Two important components of the tangible product are its *brand name* and its *packaging*. The brand name can be a potential advantage that can sell the product. For example, the ingredients in a product such as baby shampoo are fairly standardised across brands but many parents prefer Johnson & Johnson because they regard it as a known and dependable brand, and they do not want to risk using anything else on their baby. In this case, brand name is more important than the content. The packaging can also be critical. One of the reasons that Campbell's Juice Works failed was because competitive brands were in aseptic packaging, while Juice Works was not. Product design is another important attribute. Cars, for example, require good design of the visible components of the product. Luxury was a key element in Toyota's design of its Lexus LS400 cars. As a result, the expensive model became a dominant player in the South African prestige market segment, making serious inroads into the market share of competitors such as Mercedes-Benz and BMW.

Example (E)

Augmented service
First National Bank (FNB) not only offers the standard services as other banks but also introduced PayPal, eBucks and fuel rewards, and gives customers the choice to purchase tablets or smartphones at a reduced rate. These features have differentiated FNB from the other banks, and benefited customers.

The augmented product

The third layer is the augmented product – that is, the tangible product plus additional consumer services and benefits (also called *features*). These features can include a *warranty, credit, delivery, installation, product repair and maintenance service after the sale*, and *instructions for customers on use of the product*. A sound-system manufacturer may offer installation, user training and after-sales service, for instance, to enhance the attractiveness of the product package. None of this affects the actual sound system itself, but will affect the satisfaction and benefits the buyer receives from the exchange. Going that extra mile for customers by offering an augmented product typically is an effective way for a company to stand out from the crowd in a way that buyers appreciate. Successful companies add value to their products that will not only satisfy but also delight the customer.

The potential product

The potential product is the absolute reason as to why consumers are purchasing it, and therefore a significant aspect in the product concept.

The potential product can be defined in terms of its possible evolution, for example new ways of differentiating itself from the competition. Consider the example of the Sony Xperia.

We can say that the potential product reflects such high levels of added value and is so different that it is better protected against competitors and substitutes. Achieving this kind of potential has been one of the foundations of success for organisations such as Kellogg's and Levi's jeans over many years. Potential simply reflects what is possible or what remains to be done with the product in the future, thus providing a strategic focus and long-term profitability for the company.

The ultimate aim of most companies is to establish and sustain market leadership. This can be achieved by providing value to the customer while simultaneously obtaining a profit. One way of establishing market leadership is through *product differentiation*.

Product differentiation occurs when a company attempts to distinguish its products physically or psychologically from other basically identical competing products, so that the consumer considers them to be totally different from those of competitors. This can be achieved by way of *shape, colour, dimensions, quality, packaging, brand name, image, status or other need-satisfying attributes*. When a company has succeeded in differentiating its product from competing products, we can say that it has created a *competitive* or *differential* advantage.

In order to be competitive, to survive and to grow in the market, a company must have a competitive or differential advantage over competitors, and this advantage must be sustainable over a certain period. Differential advantages are necessary to outperform the competition. A differential advantage is thus the ability to deliver superior value to the market for a protracted period of time.

> **Example** (E)
>
> **Product differentiation**
>
> The new Sony Xperia cell phone range is able to compete with other smartphone brands however, it has a unique feature in that it is waterproof. This feature has differentiated the Sony Xperia range from competitors such as iPhone, Nokia and Samsung, which are not waterproof.

The product image

The last layer of the product concept is the product image, which encompasses all the previous layers and refers to how the product is perceived by consumers. In other words, it is the total product concept, as perceived by consumers, created by all the product attributes and the effect of the other marketing instruments – that is, *distribution, price* and *marketing communication*. Symbolic and psychological value can, for example, be enhanced through packaging, while marketing communication can also support the product image.

Classifying products

The marketplace is full of products being offered, and every day more and more new ones are added to the market. The main reason for this is that customers always want more choice, and many companies survive only because they cater for specific needs of customers. Some try to be everything to all people, while others try to be the best in certain areas. Some products have to be more easily available to

Example

Product differentiation[4]

Harley-Davidson is a well-known classic brand, and the world's leading designer and manufacturer of heavy weight motorcycles. By adopting a focused differentiation strategy based on its distinctive design and heavy customisation, the brand was able to command a premium for its products. In South Africa, the Harley-Davidson dealership is founded on years of excellent service and dedication to the customers and iconic brand. With the slogan: 'Live to ride, ride to live', the brand has managed to satisfy a niche market of motorcycle fanatics.

customers, while for others, customers will go to extra trouble to obtain them. Many products are primarily for use by other companies or in the production of other products. Because customer purchase behaviour differs depending on the type of product being purchased, marketing strategies must also differ.

Marketers therefore have to come up with product classification systems that separate products according to certain criteria.[3] In doing so, they can take decisions that are more closely attuned to specific customer wants and needs, or that can even change any preconceived ideas that customers may have about certain products. We will now examine these systems and characteristics.

Classifying products according to their durability

Products may first of all be classified by means of their durability. The three categories in this dimension, depicted in Figure 6.2, are *durable products, non-durable products and services.*

Consumer products can be classified as durable or non-durable, depending on how long the product will normally last. For example, it is expected that durable products like a car or a washing machine will last for a reasonably long time, while items such as fruit and milk will keep for only a short period before starting to go off.

Durable products

Durable products are consumer products that are used or consumed over a long period of time, usually at least three years. However, technology-driven improvements can shorten this timespan considerably, for example in the case of cell phones and computers. These items are, however, still technically usable even if they have been surpassed by newer models. Products that typically have a relatively high value are classified as durable products and include items such as major home appliances, video cameras, furniture and building materials.

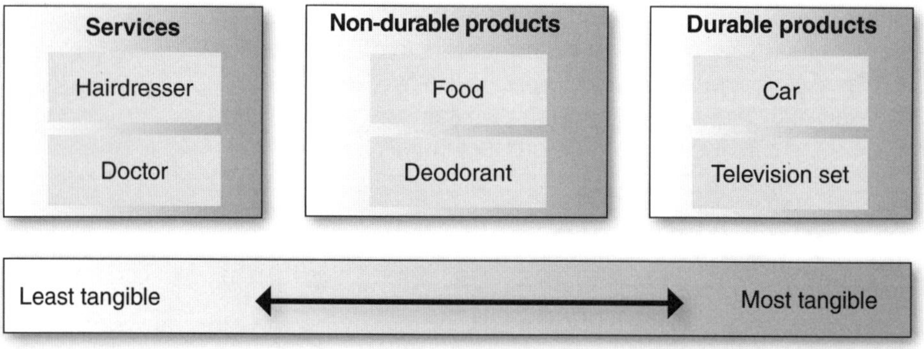

Figure 6.2 Classifying products by durability[5]

Non-durable products

Non-durable products are used or consumed over a short period of time, or after one or a few uses. They provide benefits for a shorter time, and include products such as grocery items, food and clothing. These products are divided into packaged products (for example toothpaste, detergents and sweets) and non-packaged products (for example petrol). Typically, the unit value of these items will be not as high as in the case of durable goods.

Services

Services are *intangible* benefits that are purchased by consumers, but do not involve ownership. When we pay to use the Gautrain, we are buying the services offered (getting from Pretoria to the OR Tambo airport, for example) by occupying a seat on the Gautrain that belongs to somebody else. In the same way, if we take our car to a panel beater, we do not have him for our exclusive use but rather for a limited period where his skills are applied to fix a problem such as a dent in the bumper from an accident. There are major differences in marketing decisions for durables, non-durables and services. For example, customers are likely to deliberate more when buying *durables* and consult a wider range of information sources. This means that when a consumer buys a refrigerator, a computer or a house, he or she will spend more time and energy on the decision-making process, often gathering lots of information and evaluating the various alternatives. As a result, personal selling will be a more important element in the buying process, while advertising is more likely to provide consumers with information. Durables are also distributed selectively rather than on a widespread basis. Product decisions for durable products must address the relative importance of various product benefits, the desire for different product features, and the greater importance of warranties, service, customer support, and so on.

In the case of *non-durables*, the purchase is not generally considered particularly important. The purchase of non-durable products is typically classified as habitual decision making. In these situations, price and availability are often more important than product attributes. Branding is especially important in developing product decisions for non-durables as consumers often rely on brand reputation and/or are more likely to be brand loyal. Advertising is more likely to be used to convey images and symbols than to provide information. Distribution is fairly extensive, while sales promotions such as free samples and price-cutting are used frequently to encourage consumers to switch to a company's brand. Take a look at your local supermarket to see the use of sales promotions in practice.

Services represent intangible products comprising activities, benefits or satisfactions that are not embodied in physical products. Items such as financial services, holidays, travel and personal services create problems for marketers because of the intangibility and inherent perishability. Because services are intangible, advertising is used to try to make their benefits more tangible. Most services are delivered on a person-to-person basis, and are often variable, so an important

Example E

Differential advantages – King Price insurance[6]

King Price insurance entered the short-term insurance industry in 2012 with unique differentiated advantages that are likely to disrupt the South African market with an aggressively discounted pricing strategy. The company makes the following promises:

- Their low insurance premiums decrease every month.
- They are the cheapest 71 % of the time.
- Customers can choose the excess amount that they prefer.
- They firmly believe in customer service.

element in the marketing mix is to ensure that they are offered at a standard level of quality. Ways have to be found of either bringing the service to the consumer or persuading the consumer to come to the service delivery point. Communication has to develop both functional and psychological benefit themes, as well as reassuring the potential customer of the quality and consistency of the service offered.

Classification of consumer products

Consumer products can be loosely defined as those products bought by individual consumers for their personal or family use. It is practical for marketers dealing in the consumer sector to classify products and services based on the time, money and risk incurred by the consumer during the purchase decision.[7]

The *time* referred to has a direct correlation to the effort the consumer has to put in to buy the product – that is, effort in terms of time. Does it take long to do? Are there many things to consider? Are price comparisons needed? Is it something that you can pop into a store and buy? The *money* aspect naturally includes the purchase price, but it also includes the cost of searching for and evaluating alternatives, as well as the cost of owning and disposing of a product. The *risk* involved in making a purchase includes social risk (the consumer's peer group might not approve of the purchase), functional risk (the product might not perform adequately), and financial risk (the consumer may end up wasting money on a bad purchase).

Classifying products in this way makes the development of strategies by the marketer much more effective as consumer behaviour during the purchase can guide marketing actions. Once you know how consumers buy a given product, you will have a basic idea of how it should be marketed. Using the variables of time, effort and risk produces three common categories for consumer products: *convenience products, shopping products* and *specialty products*.

Table 6.1 Classification of consumer products[8]

Convenience products	
• Staple	Products that are regularly and routinely purchased
• Impulse	Products that are purchased on the spur of the moment where exposure to them plays a crucial role
• Emergency	Products whose prices and quality comparison are the least important factors
Shopping products	
• Uniform	Price comparison of products play a crucial role
• Non-uniform	Quality comparison of producers play a crucial role
Specialty products	
	The branding and style of a product are important Exposure is not very important Shopping is focused on locating the product There is maximum brand loyalty

These three classification methods shown in Table 6.1 are briefly discussed below.

Convenience products

The name 'convenience' says it all. Convenience products are those products the customer wants to purchase with the least amount of effort. They do not want to go to a lot of trouble to buy or look for them, and want to spend as little time as possible on buying them. These products are relatively inexpensive ones such as milk, sweets and cigarettes, which are purchased frequently with a minimum of comparison and effort. For example, you would buy convenience products such as a bar of chocolate, a tube of toothpastes or a taxi ride with very little comparison and effort. Convenience products are usually low priced and widely available. Look at the number of shops at filling stations – these shops are there for the convenience of customers to purchase things anytime and anywhere.

Consumers generally know all they need to know about a convenience product, devote little effort to purchases, and willingly accept alternative brands if their preferred one is not available in a convenient location. This is especially true of supermarket-based shopping. If the desired brand of a particular product (for example a cream soda soft drink) cannot be found on the shelf in the store, the shopper is visiting, he or she will probably buy an alternative brand or do without rather than take the trouble to go to another shop.

Convenience products can be further classified as *staple products, impulse products* and *emergency products*.[10] This classification is based on the pattern or way they are bought.

Staple products

Staple products are bought on a regular basis and include items such as milk, bread and petrol. They are available almost everywhere, are considered by most consumers to be basic necessities, and there are few, if any, perceived differences among brands. While certain brands of milk, bread and even petrol attempt to differentiate their products through advertising, many consumers are not convinced that big differences exist.

Impulse products

Impulse products are normally bought without much preplanning and effort. It invariably happens when you enter a café with the aim of buying bread and milk that you walk out with more than these items. Many stores encourage this shopping behaviour by having typical impulse-buying products at the checkout points. Low-priced items such as magazines, soft drinks and sweets are displayed there to encourage impulse buying. Because consumers seldom plan to purchase these items, it is essential that they be available and highly visible.

Marketing mix considerations – convenience products

The following marketing mix considerations apply to convenience products in general:[9]

- **Distribution is wide and intensive** since convenience products have to be made readily available to consumers at as many retail stores as possible.
- **Communication needs to be aimed directly at consumers** so that they are involved in the creation of the brand image and brand loyalty, which will decrease the likelihood of brand switching.
- **The manufacturer is usually responsible for the marketing campaign** as convenience products are mostly marketed on a self-service basis.
- **The manufacturer has to advertise extensively to develop brand recognition and preference for his or her product** as self-service requires effective packaging, shelf space and point-of-sale advertising, especially since many convenience items are bought on impulse.

Continue to next page

Emergency products

To a large extent, these are products customers would prefer not to buy, but only do so because an 'emergency' situation has arisen. Bandages, umbrellas and something to unblock the drain are examples of emergency products – typical products or services consumers would rather not buy but have to because of some type of emergency. In many cases people will be prepared to pay more for these products or services. Because of the emergency character of the purchase, price is usually irrelevant. Furthermore, these products are needed when they are needed, not the next day, therefore marketers make sure that they are widely available.

Shopping products

Shopping products are exactly what the name says. The consumer is prepared to shop around for these products and compare prices and other features before making a decision. The prices of shopping products are higher than convenience products and more risk is involved for the customer, who will therefore spend more time on the total buying process. Shopping products typically include clothes, appliances and furniture.

Shopping products can be divided into *uniform* and *non-uniform* products.[12] Uniform shopping products are those products seen as being similar in quality by the customer, but different enough in price to justify shopping comparisons. A person who, for example, sees kettles as very similar will limit the shopping effort to making price comparisons, thus price competition is usually extensive for these products – the seller has to 'talk price' to the buyer.

However, when a consumer is shopping for clothing, furniture and other non-uniform products, product features are often more important than price. If the buyer wants a new dress, the cut, fit and look are likely to be more important than small price differences. The seller of non-uniform shopping products must therefore carry a wide assortment to satisfy individual tastes and must have well-trained salespeople to give information and advice to customers.

Specialty products

Specialty products are products which are perceived by the customer as being unique with specific characteristics and for which the consumer will make a special effort to search and buy.[13] The level of consumer involvement in these purchases is high, and the purchase is often the result of brand loyalty. This means that a buyer insists on a particular brand and will accept only that one. Substitute products are therefore avoided, even if the acquisition of the preferred brand requires considerable time and effort. Typical products that are regarded as specialty products are, for example, a Porsche sports car and a Rolex watch, or any brand that has a reputation for high performance, such as Canon cameras. Buyers do not usually compare specialty products.

Continued from previous page

- **Packaging and brand image need to be as attention grabbing and as memorable as possible** to facilitate recognition and positive brand choice at the point of sale (this is usually done by using bright colours, and unusual shapes and sizes). Retailers usually stock several brands of specific convenience products (for example toothpaste), and are not keen to advertise individual products.
- **The quality and prices of competing convenience products are reasonably uniform** as these products do not call for much explanation to the consumer, and the retailer does not receive much incentive to promote one brand over another.

Marketing mix considerations – shopping products

The marketing mix considerations for a shopping product are very different from those for a convenience product:[11]

- **Prices are higher for shopping products and distribution is likely to be selective** because products are not purchased as frequently, and consumers are prepared to shop around for them.

Continue to next page

It is important to recognise that the same item could be a convenience, shopping or specialty product. This is because the classification of products is based on how consumers view them, rather than on any inherent physical characteristics, as the example overleaf entitled 'In the eye of the beholder' shows.

Another point is that many consumers view certain product categories differently as they lose their distinctiveness. When CD players were first introduced, they were a specialty item, a new way to play music with little distortion. As they became more widespread, they were viewed as shopping products, with consumers comparing many alternative brands more closely.

Industrial products

Sales to organisations account for much more than sales to final consumers. This means that industrial products represent more sales in our economy than consumer goods do. Industrial products are those products bought by individuals and organisations for further processing or for supporting the manufacturing of other products directly or indirectly, and in reselling, thus the distinction between a consumer product and an industrial product is based on the purpose for which the product is purchased. If a consumer buys a lawnmower for use around the home garden, the lawnmower is a consumer item. If the same consumer buys the same lawnmower for use in a landscaping business, the lawnmower is classified as an industrial product.

Industrial products can be classified in three ways: *production goods, installations and accessories*, and *supplies and services*, as reflected in Table 6.2.

Table 6.2 Classification of industrial products[14]

Type of industrial products	
Production goods	• Raw materials • Manufactured materials
Installations and accessories	• Buildings • Fixed equipment • Factory equipment • Office equipment
Supplies and services	• Operating supplies • Repair items • Advisory services

Production goods

Production goods are products used to manufacture a final product. They enter the manufacturer's product completely, either through further processing or as components. They fall into two classes: *raw materials* and *manufactured materials or parts*. Raw materials include farm products (for example wheat, cotton, livestock, fruits and vegetables) and natural products (for example fish, crude petroleum and iron ore).

Continued from previous page

- **The consumer is more likely to seek out certain specialist retailers** and see what they have available rather than purchase impulsively from a supermarket shelf because of the nature of the product and the buying behaviour it invokes.
- **Product characteristics are likely to be more distinct** as the characteristics of, for example, clothing or cars can differ markedly, whereas the ingredients in toothpaste or detergent brands are similar.
- **Product differences are likely to be focused on in advertising**, for example Pantene's focus on its range of hair product which has a formula that claims to prevent breakage and split-ends.
- **Personal selling is likely to be important** because consumers seek information about alternative brands.
- **The name of the retailer is often more important** because brand preference and insistence play a lesser role, and the name of the retailer rather than that of the manufacturer is often more important to the buyer of shopping products.

Marketing mix considerations – specialty products

Some marketing mix considerations for specialty products are highlighted below:

- **Strategies for specialty products are characterised by high prices** because consumers in this case are insensitive to low-price appeals.
- **Distribution is on an exclusive basis to ensure a status image** as normally only one outlet in a specific area is used and the manufacturer markets directly to selected retailers.
- **Products must have an element of uniqueness** for consumers to view them as specialty items.
- **The uniqueness of the product is usually advertised.**
- **Personal selling is particularly important** in guaranteeing continued loyalty and good service.

Farm products are supplied by many small producers who turn them over to marketing intermediaries to process and sell them. Natural products usually have great bulk and low unit value, and also require transportation to move them from producer to user. There are fewer and larger producers, who tend to market them directly to industrial users.

Manufactured materials or parts include component materials (for example iron, yarn, cement and wires) and component parts (for example small motors, tyres and castings). Component materials are usually processed further – for example, pig iron is made into steel and yarn is woven into cloth. Component parts enter the finished product completely with no further change in form, for instance when small motors are put into vacuum cleaners, and tyres are added to motor cars. Most manufactured materials and parts are sold directly to industrial users. Personal selling, price and service are the major marketing factors, while branding and advertising tend to be less important.

Installations and accessories

Installations and accessories are industrial products that support the manufacturing process. *Installations* consist of buildings (factories, offices) and fixed equipment (generators, large computers, elevators). Because installations are major purchases, they are usually bought directly from the producer after a long decision-making period. Consequently, salespeople must have the technical expertise necessary to describe product performance. Buyers also tend to be price insensitive, and base their purchases on product performance.

Accessories include portable factory equipment and tools (hand tools, lift trucks) and office equipment (fax machines, desks). These products do not become part of the finished product. They have a shorter life than installations and simply aid in the manufacturing process. Most accessory equipment sellers use middlemen because the market is spread out geographically, the buyers are numerous and the orders are small.

Supplies and services

Supplies and services are products that support the manufacturing process but are not part of it – they do not enter the finished product at all. Supplies include operating supplies (lubricants, coal, fax paper, pencils) and maintenance and repair items (paint, nails, brooms). *Supplies* are the convenience products of the industrial field because they are usually purchased with a minimum of effort or comparison.

Business services include maintenance and repair services (window cleaning, fax machine repair) and business advisory services (legal, management consulting, advertising). These services are usually supplied under contract. Maintenance services are often provided by small producers, and repair services are often available from the manufacturers of the original equipment.

The product's characteristics therefore have a major effect on marketing strategy. Marketing strategy will also depend on factors such as the number of competitors and the state of the economy.

Product line decisions

When deciding on the product line or combination of products to offer to the market, it is important that these decisions should be reflected in the total product strategy of the company.

The company must plan product line growth carefully. The line is too short if the manager can increase profits by adding items, and too long if the manager can increase profits by dropping items. Product lines tend to lengthen over time. The length of the product line can be increased by stretching the line. *Product line stretching* occurs when a company lengthens its product line beyond its current range, *by trading down, trading up*, or *trading both ways* (that is, up and down), as shown in Figure 6.3.

Trading down

Many companies initially locate at the high end of the market (that is, offering more expensive and more prestigious products) and later stretch their lines downward (that is, offering less-expensive and less-prestigious products). A company may, for example, find faster growth taking place at the low end, or it may have first entered the high end to establish a quality, upmarket image, intending to roll downward later. The company may add a low-end product to plug a market hole that would otherwise attract a new competitor, or it may be attacked at the high end and respond by invading the low end (see Figure 6.3).

Trading up

Companies at the lower end of the market may want to enter the higher end. They may be attracted by a faster growth rate or higher margins at the higher end, or they may simply want to position themselves as full-line manufacturers (see Figure 6.3).

Trading both ways

Companies in the middle range of the market may decide to stretch their lines in both directions by offering lower priced as well as higher priced items to cover a broader spectrum of offerings to the wider market[15] (see Figure 6.3).

Example *E*

In the eye of the beholder

Shower gel is a convenience product for the consumer who thinks that all shower gels are alike and buys the cheapest one. Shower gel is a shopping product for the consumer who sees distinct differences between brands and goes through a process of extensive decision making in comparing them. For example, if a customer prefers one with germ protection he or she is likely to opt for one within the Dettol range. For the consumer who seeks out one particular shower gel brand that can be purchased only from exclusive cosmetics retailers, the shower gel is a specialty product, for example if a customer chooses to buy shower get only from the Body Shop.

Marketers might therefore position their brand (shower gel) as:

- a convenience product – as the lowest-priced shower gel on the market;
- a shopping product – as the product that has the best and safest ingredients to cleanse the skin; or
- a specialty product – as the most distinctive and highest-quality product on the market, available only from certain exclusive sources.

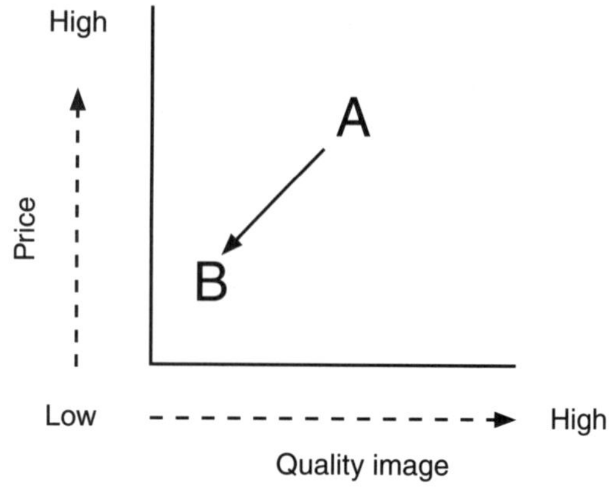

Trading down occurs when current products (A) decrease in both quality and price for new products (B)

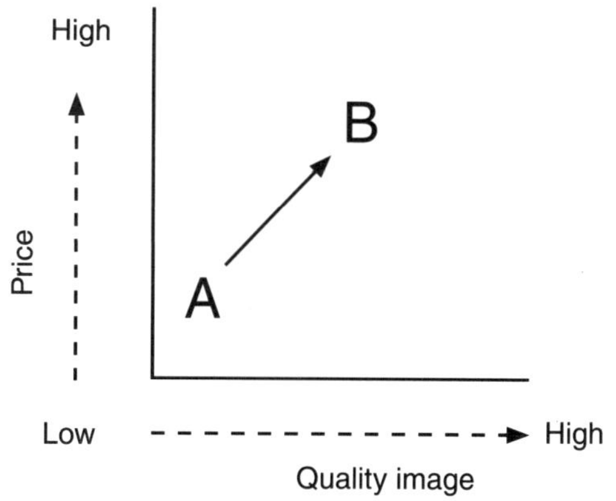

Trading up occurs when current products (A) increase in both quality and price for new products (B)

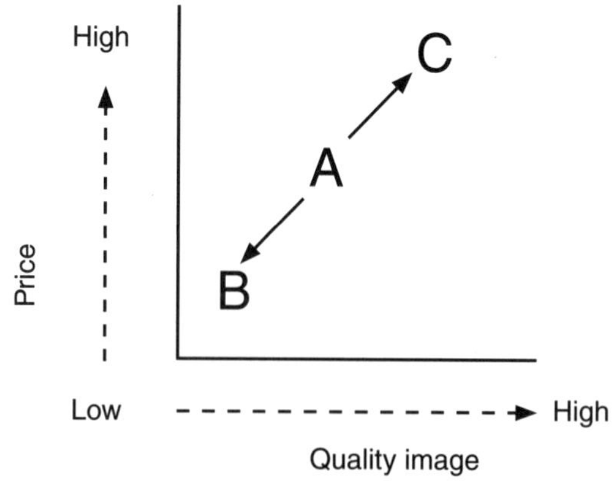

Trading down and up is when current products (A) decrease in both quality and price for new products (B), as well as increase in both quality and price for new products (C).

Figure 6.3 Product line stretching[16]

DEFINITION

Product line
A product line is a group of products manufactured by one company that are similar in nature as they have the same functions and the same target market, and are marketed through similar outlets or fall within the same price range.

Example

Product line
The Coca-Cola Company has a few product lines, for example:
- Soft drinks line which consists of Coca-Cola, Coca-Cola Light, Coca-Cola Zero, Fanta Orange, Sprite, Creme Soda, Iron Brew, etc.
- Bottled water line, which consists of Valpre, Bonaqua, Pump.
- Energy drink line, which consists of Powerade and Play.
- Juice line, which consists of Minute Maid, Just Juice, 5 Alive and Mazoe.

In each of these categories there are a number of alternatives to satisfy customer preferences.

DEFINITION

Product mix
The product mix is the range of all the products that a company sells.

Product mix decisions

A business that has a number of product lines has what is called a **product mix**. Product lines consist of several sub-lines, while each sub-line consists of various product items. The product mix of Edgars is provided as an example on page 134. Also see definition in side column of page 132.

A company's product mix can be described as having a certain *breadth, depth* and *consistency*.[17]

Breadth of product mix

The *breadth* of a product mix refers to how many different product lines the company carries. Defy, for example, carries a number of product lines, including stoves, extractor fans, dishwashers, fridges and microwaves. By increasing the breadth of a product mix, the enterprise diversifies in an endeavour to benefit from its good reputation and skills in existing markets, thus more product lines or items are added.

Gillette has a number of product lines, including small electric appliances, toiletries, dental products, and razors and blades. Even with the breadth of this product mix, Gillette's profits are concentrated in one line, the razors and blades, which accounts for a large portion of its sales and profits. Many other companies may be in a similar situation.

Depth of product mix

The *depth* of a product mix refers to the number of versions offered of each product in the line. Thus if, for example, Colgate toothpaste comes in three sizes and two formulations (paste and gel), Colgate has a depth of six. By increasing the depth of the mix (specialising) and adding more items to lines, the company tries to attract the patronage of consumers with widely differing tastes and needs. Another example is the case of a jeans manufacturer, whose individual products may include denim shorts, denim jackets, stovepipe jeans, bootleg jeans, etc, with or without different brand names.

Consistency

The consistency of the product mix refers to how closely related the various product lines are in end use, production requirements, distribution channels, or in some other way.

It is the task of marketing management to adapt its product mix in the light of environmental changes so as to strive constantly for the realisation of company objectives. Management has to continually evaluate the various product lines and items in terms of their contribution to the realisation of these objectives. Consumer needs and preferences are continually changing, competitors alter their marketing strategies, and even business objectives can change. Also, if the company does not continually develop new products or eliminate obsolete ones, it can eventually end up with an extremely unbalanced product mix. Each product line should therefore be evaluated in terms of *sales growth, market share, cash flow* and *profitability*.

Example (E)

Trading down

iPhone smartphones are relatively expensive, so in order to gain more market share the company is looking into creating a generic iPhone which is less expensive and thus more affordable for price-conscious consumers.

Example (E)

Trading up

When Chrysler purchased Lamborghini, the maker of exotic, handcrafted sports cars, it added prestige to its current products. The Rover Company started off with Land Rover and later introduced a more prestigious Range Rover line.

Example (E)

Trading both ways

- A computer company may, for example, offer a tablet for R8 999, but also decide to expand this to offer models in the price range of R4 999 and R10 999. By doing this, the company offers a broader spectrum to the market where some models offer fewer specifications and others offer more to the market. In this way a company with a strong product may even dominate the market.

Example (E)

Product mix

Edgars' product mix consists of product lines, sub-lines and items:

- Edgars' product mix consists of accessories, active wear, home ware, cell phones, cosmetics, footwear, fragrances, handbags, children's wear, ladies' wear, lingerie and men's wear.
- Each product line consists of several sub-lines; for example, cosmetics include lipstick, rouge and powder.
- Each sub-line has many individual items; for example, lipsticks have different colours such as pink, red and bronze.

Product diversification

The various decisions that need to be made on the existing product mix revolve around a concept called product diversification.[18] Product diversification *means the expansion of the product mix by adding new product lines or items*. Diversification can also result in expanding into new products and markets. This type of diversification involves the development or acquisition of products and services new to the organisation, and the introduction of these products to markets not previously served by it.

There is a distinction between *related* and *unrelated diversification*. Related diversification occurs when a company develops internally or acquires another enterprise that has products and customers in common with its current business. This process can contribute to internal synergy through the sharing of operation facilities, brand names, research and development skills, or marketing and distribution skills.

Unrelated diversification means expansion into unrelated fields (that is, unrelated products and markets) where the company finds itself in a totally unfamiliar field and can easily fail. It cannot rely on loyal consumers, existing distribution channels or a familiar brand name. However, successful unrelated diversification offers the possibility of large profits. South African Breweries (SAB) (now known as SABMiller), for example, successfully effected unrelated diversification in the 1980s and 1990s, but has since reversed this trend to some extent due to its strategic realignment with its core business.

Brand decisions

The meaning of brands

For centuries, marketers have been devising ways to identify their products and distinguish them from those of competitors. This has been accomplished by using *branding*.

Consumers view a brand as an important part of the product, and branding can add value to the product. For example, most consumers perceive Mercedes-Benz as a high-quality, expensive product, but another brand with similar features as Mercedes-Benz may not be as highly regarded.

Branding has become a major issue in marketing strategy. On the one hand, developing a branded product requires a great deal of long-term marketing investment, especially for advertising and packaging. On the other hand, most manufacturers eventually learn that the power lies with the companies that control the brand names. Japanese and South Korean companies, for example, have spent heavily to build up brand names such as Sony, Panasonic and Samsung for their products. Even when these companies can no longer afford to manufacture their products in their homelands, their brand names continue to command customer loyalty. The lesson is that consumers are loyal to the brands, not to the producers.

We should first become familiar with the language of branding with the following key definitions:[19]

- A **brand** is a name, term, sign, symbol, design or a combination of these intended to identify the goods or services of one seller and to differentiate them from those of competitors.
- A **brand name** is that part of a brand which can be vocalised, for example Nike and McDonald's.
- A **brand mark** is that part of a brand which can be recognised but is not utterable, such as a symbol, design or distinctive colouring or lettering. For example, Nike has the swoosh (or tick) logo and McDonald's has the yellow 'M'.
- A **trademark** is a brand or part of a brand that is given legal protection in that it protects the seller's exclusive rights to use the brand name or brand mark.
- Finally, a **copyright** is the exclusive legal right to reproduce, publish and sell the matter and form of a literary, musical or artistic work.

Example (E)

Consistency of the product mix

With end use as a basis, a very close relationship and consistency exists between the different product lines of Dove:

- Women's – skincare products for different skin types.
- Men's – a range of grooming products, which includes shaving cream, scrubs, deodorants and aftershave.
- Body wash.
- Beauty bars.
- Shampoos and conditioners for different hair types.

The benefits of branding

Branding carries benefits for all parties involved in the exchange process which, in theory at least, makes it easier to buy or sell products. We will now look at the benefits of branding from the perspective of the consumer, the manufacturer and the retailer. These benefits are summarised in Table 6.3.

Table 6.3 The benefits of branding[20]

Benefits of branding		
For the manufacturer	**For the retailer**	**For the consumer**
• Helps create loyalty • Creates differential advantage • Allows for premium pricing • Facilitates product diversification	• Benefits from brand-marketing support by the manufacturer • Attracts customers	• Makes product identification easier • Communicates features and benefits • Helps with product evaluation • Reduces risk in purchasing • Creates interest/character for product

Consumers' perspective

Branding holds various benefits for consumers:

- Branding facilitates product identification.
- It communicates the product features and benefits.
- It helps with product evaluation.
- It reduces risk in purchasing.
- It creates interest and character for the product image.

The manufacturer's perspective

The manufacturer benefits from the relationship the buyer has with the brand. The following are the benefits of branding for the manufacturer:

- Branding helps create brand loyalty.
- It creates differential advantage.
- It allows premium pricing.
- It facilitates product diversification.

The retailer's perspective

The retailer also benefits from branding to a certain extent; however, the retailer often does not want the consumer to be too brand loyal.[21]

Branded products are well supported by advertising and other marketing activities, and so the retailer has some assurance that they will sell.

Branded products do draw customers into the store, but the disadvantage is that if a brand is unavailable in one store, then the shopper is likely to go elsewhere. The retailer may prefer the shopper to be less brand loyal and more store loyal. Supermarkets have always recognised the value and necessity of manufacturer-branded goods, but they have also looked for ways of reducing the power that this gives the brand owner. This is done through promoting store brands (also called retailer brands). In some of the supermarkets there is a price differential in favour of store brands.

Retailers are under pressure to stock increasing numbers of lines within a product area, which means in turn either that less shelf space is devoted to each brand or retailers will refuse to stock some brands. The consumer may also begin to see too much choice, and at some point there is a risk that the differences between brands may become imperceptible to the consumer, resulting in confusion.

Types of brands

So far we have focused on the brands created and marketed by manufacturers and sold through retail outlets. An area of growing importance, however, is the brand created by a wholesaler or retailer for that organisation's sole use. This development has taken place partly because of conflicts and power struggles between manufacturers and retailers, and partly because the retailers also need to generate store loyalty in a highly competitive retail sector. This section therefore distinguishes between the brands emanating from different types of organisations.

Manufacturer (national) brands and private (dealer) brands

Two types of brands may be identified:

- A **manufacturer brand** is designated, owned and used by the manufacturer or producer of the product.[23] Examples of manufacturer brands include Nestlé, Panasonic, Adidas and Asus. Because they are usually marketed nationwide, manufacturer brands are often referred to as national brands.

Example (E)

Related product diversification

If Dove decided to expand and start selling skin-care products for babies, this would be a related diversification as the brand operates in the skin-care market. However, launching a range of chocolates would not be related at all.

DEFINITION

Brand

A brand is a product, service or concept used by a company to differentiate itself from others by creating an image based on the perceptions of consumers.

Example (E)

Related product diversification[22]

McDonald's starting McCafé is an example of related product diversification. McCafé offers new products that are not available in traditional McDonald's stores. McCafé specialises in serving coffee, which attracts a different target market from that which usually goes to McDonald's for fast food. McCafé has its own section of the store which is clearly distinguished from the traditional McDonald's store, and is modern with a relaxed mood.

Continue to next page

- A **private brand** is designated, owned and used by a wholesaler or retailer; it is sometimes called a *dealer* or *store brand*. Many large South African supermarket chains such as Pick n Pay have their own private 'no name' brands for many popular products ranging from dog food to baked beans. Private brands are promoted to a limited extent by the wholesaler or retailer, but they do not achieve the national recognition that manufacturer (or national) brands do.

The relationship between national and private brands has been changing in recent years. Stop and think about why a national brand would be attractive in the first place – it supposedly offers the consumer the security of a recognised, high-quality supplier, rather than some obscure local supplier. However, in many product categories, the perceived difference between national and private brands has narrowed, prompting more and more consumers to make the switch to often cheaper, private brands. There has also been a significant shift to private brands because retailers or wholesalers guarantee the private labels sold in their stores. This has prompted national marketers to work hard to reduce their manufacturing and marketing costs in order to get on a more competitive pricing ground with private brands.

The attack of private labels has not been universally successful. In product categories such as toothpaste, canned tuna, baby food and shaving cream, private labels have either failed to make much headway or are falling back from earlier gains. In other product categories, however, private brands have been very successful. Consider the example of 'Manufacturer versus private brand' in the margin.

Generic brands

A generic brand is a non-branded product that is identified only by its product category such as 'paper towels' or 'tea'. Generic brands have a plain look. They are unbranded, plainly packaged and less-expensive versions of common products such as spaghetti, paper towels and canned fruit. The lower price is often made possible by lower-quality ingredients, lower-cost packaging and lower advertising costs.

The price savings of generics appeal strongly to consumers, but product quality remains an important factor in their buying decisions. Generics sell better in the product categories where consumers are not concerned with quality or see little quality difference between generics and national brands. However, generics have had less success in such areas as health and beauty aids, where consumers are less willing to trade quality for price, and usually buy a branded product.

Individual or family brands

Marketers preferring national brands have at least three branding options, namely *individual brands, family brands* and *company names with a brand*.

Example E

Continued from previous page

This is important as it attracts new market segments of customers who go to the café not because they are hungry but rather to drink coffee and chat in a relaxing environment. McDonald's McCafé is an example of performing diversification by developing new products for new markets.

Example E

Manufacturer versus private brand

For products such as paper towels and bread, private brands have been successful because consumers say: 'They all work. Why pay for a name?' However, when it comes to a product such as baby products, manufacturers' brands are preferred. The response is: 'For something like that, you want to make sure you get the good stuff. I don't know anything about this baby food or products, but I know Purity and Johnson & Johnson.'

'A generic brand is a non-branded product that is identified only by its product category such as "paper towels" or "tea".'

CASE STUDY

Brand extension – Discovery[24]

The vision of Discovery founders in 1992 was to create a different company that would tap into the spirit of consumerism, and that would deliver innovative health insurance products that would appeal to all, including the young and healthy. Two decades later, Discovery is a very different company. It has grown from being a small, specialist risk insurer to a large, integrated financial services company offering a range of innovative and best-of-breed financial services solutions on four continents. Discovery is a proudly South African company, but has expanded its operations to the UK, the USA and China. The company brand has now been extended to include various products such as health insurance,

Continue to next page

Individual brands

This is a separate brand assigned to an individual product item within a product line. This approach is followed by Brandhouse for its beer products, for example Amstel Lager, Heineken, Strongbow and Windhoek Lager. Using an individual branding strategy has one important advantage: if one product fails, the negative impact is unlikely to affect the company's other products. In addition, individual branding allows companies to expand into new, unrelated product areas without confusing customers.

Family brands

This brand is assigned to an entire line or mix of product items. KOO makes KOO baked beans, KOO concentrated wet stock, KOO pasta meals, and KOO canned vegetables, for example. This approach is followed by Apple Inc., which produces items such as computers, phones, accessories, music players and tablets. A powerful name, however, is no guarantee that family branding will succeed. Xerox tried unsuccessfully to extend its powerful brand name to computers and printers.

Company names with a brand

Some manufacturers use their company name along with an individual brand name for each product. The company name adds the firm's reputation to the product, while the individual name sets it apart from other company products. Colgate South Africa follows this branding approach for its toothpastes, for example Colgate Total, Colgate Max White and Colgate Prevident.

Other branding issues

We will now look at three other important branding issues, namely *brand extension, brand equity* and, in the next section, *selecting a brand name*.

Brand extension

A brand-extension strategy is any effort to use a successful brand name to launch new or modified products.[25] Virgin, for example, is a strong, established brand that has extended across airlines, bank accounts and cellular networks to gyms, and the list goes on. Brand extension saves the manufacturer the high cost of promoting a new name, and creates instant brand recognition of the new product. At the same time, however, if the new product fails, this may hurt consumer attitudes towards the other products carrying the same brand name.[26]

Brand equity

Many marketers nowadays talk about *brand equity* when they refer to the *value* of a brand name.[27] Companies such as Coca-Cola, Allan Gray and Gillette invest heavily in advertising in an attempt to re-emphasise their brands instead of using price-oriented promotions. Brand equity is therefore seen as the added value that a brand name brings to a product beyond the product's functional value.

Selecting a brand name

A good name can add greatly to a product's success and should thus be carefully chosen[28]. Choosing an effective brand name is an important decision for both the manufacturer and the distributor of brands.[29] The brand name communicates a great deal, affecting both brand awareness and brand image. In general, an effective brand name suggests something about the product's benefits; it is easy to pronounce, recognise and remember; it is distinctive in some way; and it may be translated into other languages. The following guidelines may be used in the selection of a 'good' brand name:

- It must say something about the *product's benefits*. Ideally, a brand name should help to communicate to consumers the major benefits of the company's product. If this is achieved, the brand name will help to link brand awareness with brand image. As consumers become aware of the brand name, they will begin to associate it with specific product benefits (for example Canderel, FedEx and SureSlim).
- It must be *easy to pronounce, recognise and remember* by the target market, to help in establishing brand awareness (for example Omo, Jik, BMW, Spar).
- It must be *original and distinctive* (for example Pajero, Nintendo, Nike, Garmin).
- It must create a *unique image of exclusivity*, even if it is sometimes difficult to pronounce (for example D&G, Aca Joe, Cape Union Mart).
- It must indicate *high quality* (for example Elite choice butter, Golden Crown margarine).
- It must be *versatile and applicable to a product line* or even the entire product mix (for example Pfizer, Toyota, Defy).
- It must *translate into foreign languages* if it is possible that it will be marketed internationally.

Packaging

Initially, the main aim of **packaging** was to protect the product. This has, however, changed over the years, and packaging has taken on a more meaningful role. (Also see the definition of packaging on your right.)

One of the functions of packaging is to serve as a tool in promotion strategy. Amid the plethora of different products held in stock by retailers, packaging is evidently an indispensable means of attracting consumers' attention, conveying the necessary information, and eliciting positive action from the consumer (buying the product). As the average packaging on the shelves of supermarkets is observed only for a fraction of a second by the scanning eye of a consumer, it is essential that every

CASE STUDY

Continued from previous page

life insurance, long-term savings and investment products, short-term insurance, credit card protection and wellness benefits.

Example

Brand names

What is your opinion of these brand names? Are they effective or not?

- Coca-Cola
- Vodacom
- Mitsubishi Pajero
- Absa
- FIFA
- Jamaica Blue
- Spar
- Ricoffy
- Black Label
- Seiko
- Johnny Walker

DEFINITION

Packaging

Packaging involves decisions related to the design, manufacture and materials used for containing, protecting, handling, preserving and delivering a product that will be easily recognised and successfully marketed.

aspect of it – the *name, shape, colour, label* and *copy* – provides sufficient stimulation to attract the consumer's attention and become fixed in his or her memory. The packaging is usually depicted in the advertisement because the consumer must know what the container looks like in order to recognise it on the supermarket shelves.

The tasks of packaging

From a marketing point of view, packaging has at least seven functions, which are listed below. Innovative packaging can give a company an advantage over competitors. The first companies to put their fruit drinks in airtight foil and paper cartons, and toothpaste in pump dispensers attracted many new customers. In contrast, poorly designed packaging can cause headaches for consumers and lose sales for the company. For example, many consumers found it difficult to open a box of Weetbix cereal after the packaging format changed. Another example is a dishwashing liquid brand that changed its packaging design. Even though the new packaging looked better, its new design was not easy to grip, and the container would become slippery when wet during the washing of dishes. Needless to say, such products remained on the shelf.

Functions of packaging[30]

Packaging serves a variety of functions:

- **Enclosure and protection**. Packaging facilitates the safe and easy dispatch, storage and handling of the product, for example cigarettes in a crush-proof box.
- **Reusability**. Packaging makes the product reusable and easy to store. The packaging can even be used after the contents have been consumed, for example Nestlé ice-cream tubs.
- **Communication**. Packaging communicates a specific product image through its design, labelling, colour, brand name and display. It is an important instrument of communication.
- **Market segmentation**. The selection of a package design, colour, shape, size and material enables the organisation to direct its products at specific market segments.
- **Distribution**. Packaging must satisfy the needs of the wholesaler, retailer and consumer; for example it should be stackable to enable optimal use of space.
- **Product development**. A new package can be an important innovation for the enterprise, for example toothpaste in a pump dispenser.
- **Differentiation**. The packaging differentiates a product from virtually identical competing products – it makes the product unique in the eyes of the consumer.

Many companies can testify as to how packaging alone, or as part of a new marketing strategy, has improved the sales of products.

WWW:

- http://www.tis-gdv.de/tis_e/verpack/funktion/funktion.htmcom/

Types of packaging

There are a number of choices which can be made with regard to the type of packaging chosen.[31]

Family or individual packaging

Marketing management has to decide whether family packaging will be used for all the company's products, or whether separate and unique packaging is to be used for each product item. Family packaging denotes either a general uniformity, or uniformity with regard to one or several principal features of the packaging used for a line of products. Pantene shampoo, for example, is packaged in identical bottles, the only difference being the colour of the bottles for dry, oily and delicate hair. Individual packaging is used for certain types of liquor, with each item in a different type of packaging.

Special packaging

The purpose of this type of packaging is to give a product an exclusive image. Some expensive liquor is placed in uniquely shaped bottles, and perfume is sold in crystal flasks. Specialty packaging is particularly popular for gifts. This strategy is a good example of a case where packaging stimulates the demand for a product. For example, during Easter, Lindt releases a special edition of a chocolate bunny.

Reusable packaging

An enterprise may market its products in containers that are designed to be used for something else once the original contents have been consumed. This practice, which is followed with products such as ice-cream tubs and coffee containers, helps to induce decisions to purchase, particularly if it does not excessively increase the price of the relevant product. This packaging may also lead to repeat purchases if the consumer wishes to collect a full set of containers, but reluctance to discard the 'nice' containers may prompt a consumer to stop buying the product once enough containers have been collected. A new packaging line could be designed to stimulate the collector's urge anew.

Multiple packaging

This strategy entails the packaging of related products in a single container, as in the case of deodorants, aftershave lotions, shaving cream and hairspray for men; various types of sweets; toothbrushes and toothpaste; and razors and razor blades. Multiple packaging is particularly useful as a means of introducing a new product and to win brand recognition. It is also frequently used for special price offers, for example packaging containing aftershave lotion, shaving cream and soap, especially over the Christmas season.

Kaleidoscopic packaging

This packaging strategy is implemented by regularly altering certain details on the packaging. Examples are the reproduction of photographs of a series of personalities (for example Soccer World Cup personalities) on the inside of soft drink bottle tops or on tins, or series of pictures of different kinds of animals on cereal packaging. The intention is to create a demand for the product by creating a demand for the packaging.

Labelling

The label is the printed material that appears on a product package. Labelling is a particular area in the packaging field which represents the outermost layer of the product. Labels have a strong functional dimension in that they include warnings and instructions, as well as information required by law or best-industry practices. Labels state, at the very least, the weight or volume, a barcode and the name and contact address of the producer. Consumer demand has also led to the inclusion of far more product information such as ingredients, nutritional information and environmental friendliness. Information about the extent to which the packaging is made of recycled materials or can be recycled is also much more common now. It is used to project the image of a manufacturer who is concerned about the environment.

WWW:
The Institute of Packaging (SA)
- http://www.ipsa.org.za

'Consumer demand has also led to the inclusion of far more product information such as ingredients, nutritional information and environmental friendliness.'

The prominence and details of health and safety instructions are also becoming increasingly important, as organisations seek to protect themselves against prosecution or civil liability should the product be misused. These instructions range from general warnings to keep a product out of reach of children, to prohibitions on inhaling solvent-based products, through to detailed instructions about wearing protective clothing while bathing a dog with shampoo that also contains tick and flea repellent agents.

Product support services

'Customer service, a major component of relationship marketing, applies to both products and services.'

An important product component is customer service which describes the assistance provided to help a customer with the purchase or use of a product – a service that augments the actual product.[32] Customer service, a major component of relationship marketing, applies to both products and services. For example, a consumer installing Internet on their Telkom line is buying the basic service of being able to have access to the Internet from specified locations within the home. Telkom has been castigated about its after-sales service. Subscribers often have to wait more than three weeks to have telephone lines repaired – poor customer service indeed.

For many products, customer service differentiates competitors. Providing exceptional customer service can give a firm a marketing advantage. For example, Sony's Vaio desktop and laptop range invests heavily in their customer service. The Vaio range is viewed as top of the line, but Sony still surveys customers immediately after their purchase and again after 30 days and 90 days, and monitors various aspects of its customers.

New product development[33]

Just think how many products are introduced in South Africa every year. Have you ever wondered if all of these products are really new? One way in which new products are distinguished is by determining from whose perspective they are to be viewed: the customers' or the marketers'. In this section we will discuss these two perspectives.

Types of new products

New products are categorised in terms of how they are perceived by businesses and the marketplace.

New-to-the-world products

These are product innovations that create entirely new product categories. Such products are truly new, and only 10% can be placed in this category. These products involve the most risk because they are new to both the firm and the market. Examples include Google Glass, mobile fuel cells and flying cars.

New-to-the-marketer products

In this case the product is new to the marketer but is already being offered in the marketplace by other competitors. The marketer may be following the market leader or may be diversifying the organisation's product range to include the particular product.

Line extensions

A line extension is a product that applies the marketer's brand to new products that supplement a firm's established product lines. This could be a new package size, a new flavour or a new application. A juice company, for example, could extend its line by adding tropical punch and grapefruit to its existing orange juice line. The majority of so-called new products are line extensions.

Repositioned products

Here a product is marketed in a new way to change its position in the marketplace. Existing products are targeted at new segments or markets, which could require a new market positioning. For example, Old Spice's outdated image was changed and given a fresher, more edgy voice through YouTube videos that went viral. Another example is Johnson & Johnson's baby powder, which was repositioned to attract adult users as well.

Improved products

An improved product is an improved version of an existing product which provides better performance or greater perceived value. This is the least risky and least innovative category, yet a great deal of attention must still be paid to marketing such a product to achieve success. For example, BlackBerry made improvements to its operating system and functionality to ensure that its cell phones were more user friendly.

The new product development process

In this section we will explain the new product development process. The steps in the process (shown in Figure 6.4) follow a logical sequence, beginning with a broad spread of possible ideas and narrowing down to the commercialisation of the product. The implementation of this process depends on the type of organisation and its markets. In a very complex, high-tech market, the process may be formal and take a number of years (for example pharmaceuticals, motor cars). In a fast-moving consumer goods market or in the fashion business, the process could be much shorter and could take place a number of times each year.

The steps in the new product development process are as follows:

1. Idea generation
2. Idea screening
3. Concept testing
4. Business analysis
5. Product development
6. Test marketing
7. Commercialisation

CASE STUDY

Idea generation – Aqua Salveo[34]

How do marketers find promising new product ideas? First, they view every customer contact as an opportunity to identify unmet or changing needs, spark new ways to solve old problems, or innovatively apply old technology and techniques to new problems. A company can observe how customers use its products and competing products; ask customers what they would like the company's product to do (even if it sounds impossible);

Continue to next page

- **Step 1** — Come up with innovative ideas for products
- **Step 2** — Screen the ideas to determine which ones are viable
- **Step 3** — Test the different concepts to determine whether consumers will accept them
- **Step 4** — Analyse the business to determine whether it has the capability, skills or resources to develop the idea
- **Step 5** — Develop the actual product to be sold to consumers
- **Step 6** — Test different marketing strategies to determine which one will be the most effective
- **Step 7** — Commercialise the product into the market

Figure 6.4 The new product development process[35]

Step 1: Idea generation

Since the new product development process requires a great deal of investment and commitment, it is necessary to generate as many ideas as possible so that no potential opportunity is overlooked. If the enterprise is properly organised for new products, it should have a constant flow of new ideas. The objective at this stage is to generate as many ideas as possible, as many will be eliminated at the next stage if they are inappropriate. Most ideas arise from recognising a market need or gaps in the marketplace, or exploring a technical opportunity. There are many sources of ideas, which include customers, competitors, employees, research and development, channel members, and even top management. These sources will now be discussed in more detail.

Customers

This is the logical place to start looking for ideas. This is done by identifying customers' needs and wants through techniques such as surveys, focus groups and letters of suggestion or complaint from customers. Many good ideas come from having customers describe the problems they have with current products.

Competitors

Many organisations keep a close eye on the research and development (R&D) activities of their competitors. Industrial espionage is a very real phenomenon, and many high-tech companies spend sizeable amounts in making sure that their R&D activities are kept secret. Many Japanese organisations actually started out by imitating and improving competitor products. An organisation often buys a competitor's product and then dismantles it to see what new improvements or developments have been made!

Employees and R&D staff

The use of suggestion boxes and competitions can help to generate new ideas through the workforce. Many forward-thinking organisations operate such schemes successfully, and fully use the knowledge of the workforce to help them become more competitive. This 'continuous improvement' is often a result of the effective processing of new ideas in the organisation.

Top management

Top management can be the catalyst for new product development, either driving new product development themselves or making it easier for others in the organisation to generate ideas and develop successful products. They provide the leadership role necessary to ensure that the new product development process remains a key result area for the business.

CASE STUDY

Continued from previous page
use websites to invite customer ideas and feedback; interact with brand enthusiasts; and tap into feedback gathered by customer-contact employees such as salespeople and technicians. Marketers should document and keep new product ideas in an 'idea vault' which may be easily accessed at any time.

For example, Aqua Salveo is a family owned-business, focusing on innovative products and aiming to acquire the necessary national and international accreditations to supply for a global need. While attending the World Summit for Sustainable Development, the company identified a need: solving the water problems evident in rural areas in South Africa. Aqua Salveo took the idea and developed it with the help of a team of scientists to create a point-of-use water disinfectant that did not contain chlorine and was safe for consumption. The product is now sold to various countries around the world such as Ghana, Brazil, Australia and the UK, just to name a few.

Example *E*

Product development: Five questions to answer first[36]

Product development is important to business. By bringing new products to the market, a business is opening up new opportunities for the growth of the company. New product development is one of the most important things that a marketing strategy can focus on; however, it is a complicated process that requires a lot of careful attention. Before starting new product development, companies should answer these five questions in order to be successful and get their new products and services to the market faster.

- Who should be involved in the product development process?
- Have the risks associated with new product development been carefully considered?
- What is the expected time for this new product to reach the market?
- What are the company's best practices that need to be adhered to in the product development process?
- Can the product development process be improved by analysing information from a past development?

Continue to next page

Step 2: Idea screening

Once the ideas have been generated, the next step is to filter out those that do not fit the organisation's goals, those that are unlikely to be appropriate, or those that are unlikely to be successful. This is the objective: to assess whether the idea fits with the organisation's strategic plans and whether it is technologically feasible. There are many ways of screening products. One way is to develop a list of the criteria the organisation is looking for with its new product development process. Examples of criteria could be the ease of operations and the differentiation possibilities. Many organisations set up a weighting system to assign points based on the relative importance of each screening criterion. This produces a score for each product idea, thus allowing the enterprise to compare new product ideas and choose those most likely to meet the enterprise's objectives. Note that management judgement is required here, especially for those new product ideas that are in the middle range of scoring.

Step 3: Concept testing

This step takes place when the idea, which has been approved internally by the organisation in the previous phase, is tested externally with potential consumers and the market. This is termed *concept testing*. There are two main types of concept statement: *core ideas* and *positioning statements*. The core idea consists of short, general statements explaining what the product can do. The aim is to test whether the basic idea is acceptable or attractive to prospective customers. The positioning statements focus on main and secondary benefits, and also outline aspects of the product's marketing mix. The aim here is to try to assess the full concept that the customer may find in the marketplace. If the response is negative, the marketer should reconsider the concept carefully before making a final decision. Many successful products and services did not do well initially because prospective customers could not see the benefits of the product. Examples include the CNN news channel, online shopping and cell phones.

Step 4: Business analysis

During the fourth stage, the operation, marketing and financial projections are made for the product concept. The enterprise seriously considers the feasibility of the product because after this stage the new product development process gets expensive. This is because of the costs of developing physical versions of the product. The marketer must fully analyse the potential market, and the internal strengths and weaknesses associated with the product. This also implies that the marketing programme should be outlined in some detail. Associated with this is the viability of producing the product and aspects such as materials management, factory space and storage, labour, and machinery requirements. All these have an impact on the costs, and therefore the profitability, of the concept. The objective is to determine the financial viability of the product. A serious problem to investigate is the issue of *cannibalisation*, where a new product cuts into the sales of the marketer's current product line.

Step 5: Product development

One or two ideas would have progressed past the previous stage. At this point all the theoretical work has been done and now the real product must be manufactured. This is easier to do if the product uses known technology. If not, there are sizeable time and human resource costs that will have to be expended to proceed. The product developers have to communicate both the functional and psychological characteristics. The product will go through two tests.

Functional tests

These are conducted to make sure that the product performs safely and effectively.

Consumer testing

This is performed by testing the actual product's different forms. In some cases, where the product is monitored during its in-house use, this can help to fine-tune the product. Consumer testing also implies that all the marketing elements can be tested, such as brand identity, packaging and labelling, as well as the broad marketing mix.

Step 6: Test marketing

Test marketing takes place when new products are offered for sale in a limited geographic area for a specified time, and sales and costs are measured. This is done to establish whether customers will actually buy the product. The results help the marketer to fine-tune the actual marketing campaign and indicate how the product will perform in reality against the competition. The organisation can conduct market research during the test phase to establish consumer and trade response to the marketing mix, pinpointing which elements of the mix were successful and which need further revision. The test market can also indicate how the target segment/s rate the product's various attributes and features, helping to pinpoint possible product improvements that may be made before the full launch.

Note that test marketing should not be considered as an extension of the product development stage, but rather as a trial run for the major launch. This is why it is important that the organisation carefully considers exactly when to conduct the test marketing; it must be sure that the test market chosen is representative of the overall target market.

An important consideration to be borne in mind when deciding whether or not to conduct test marketing is that it will *give the competition a good indication of what is planned*. This could give them enough lead time to bring their own plans forward and launch their version of the product. If the new product is based on packaging or branding changes

Example (E)

Continued from previous page

Answering these simple questions ensures that a company's product development process becomes stronger every time it sets out to develop a new product or service.

Example (E)

Reasons for product testing on the usability of a product[37]

- To ensure that the usability of the product is simple and intuitive for the target group.
- To ensure that consumers regard the significant modifications made to the product as value-adding improvements.
- To document consumer perceptions throughout the whole product life cycle.
- To clarify if all needs are met by the adaptations of the product for a specific target group.
- To ensure that usability of the product is regarded as good in all international marketplaces.

Advantages of test marketing[38]

- It is a real test in a real environment.
- It offers a last chance for fine-tuning.
- It gives an opportunity to vary some of the marketing mix variables.
- It allows the assessment of aspects that are difficult to predict on paper, such as awareness generated, inclination for repeat buying, etc.
- It allows adjustment of the overall business plan and launch strategy.
- It provides a forecast of future sales.

When to use test marketing[39]

- Test marketing is a useful option when the product is expensive to market. If the product needs extensive distribution and national television advertising, it may be beneficial to test it in a few local markets first to see if things go as planned.
- It should not be used if competitors could make quick modifications to their product and launch a superior competing one.

Continue to next page

rather than on innovative product developments, this could easily be matched and the competitor could beat the business to the market. Another risk is that any actions taken by the competition could influence or distort the results of the test marketing effort.

The *timing and duration* of the test marketing could also be problematic. The marketer must ensure that seasonal influences that could distort sales results are taken into account in the evaluation of the test market. The actual duration of the test marketing effort must also be carefully considered. If it goes on too long, the enterprise could end up not learning anything further, delaying the actual launch, and giving the competition extra time to react and respond. If the test marketing period is too short, then the risk is that important information could be missed. The time frame must allow potential customers enough time to settle into a regular purchasing pattern and give the marketing communication efforts enough time to work.

There are two options which could be followed in overcoming some of the considerations mentioned above. The firm could run a *simulated test market*, where a reduced version of the full test market is run in selected stores. Customers' responses to the product and marketing mix could then be investigated and tracked. A second option is a *controlled distribution mini-market*, where the test market technique is store-specific, and purchases of the product could be monitored electronically. The advantages of these two methods are that they lower costs, produce results more quickly, and make less of a public splash than a full test marketing effort.

Because of the risks associated with test marketing, it is generally used only in certain cases.

Step 7: Commercialisation

At this point the product is ready for launching, and the organisation is faced with two main alternatives.

Immediate national launch

An immediate national launch means making the product available in all target markets at all outlets at the same time. This option has greater impact and gives the marketing communication effort a single focus. It also makes it difficult for the competition to respond and for them to gain a bigger share of the attention at the launch. The risk of a national launch is that things could go wrong, especially if test marketing was not done. The test marketing effort is practice for the launch, but cannot guarantee success as the scale is much bigger in a national launch. Mistakes at the launch would take a lot of time and effort to eradicate as first impressions are difficult to change.

Rolling launch

A rolling launch means that the organisation builds towards national coverage by starting out at one or two recognised distribution areas, and then gradually adds new regions or outlets. This allows the enterprise to manage the launch so that things go right and also to fine-tune the marketing strategies as it gains experience in the rollout.

The factors that would influence which alternative to choose include the resources available to the organisation, the experience of the organisation with new products, and the relation of the new product to existing products or brands. If the organisation follows a family branding approach, it may be easier to launch nationally than if a totally new product and brand are launched. In the latter case, a rollout may be wiser.

Once the product is launched, it is in the introductory phase of its life cycle. Before we consider the product life cycle, however, let us investigate how a new product or service idea is adopted in the marketplace.

Continued from previous page

- If the product is truly innovative, it may be beneficial to run a test market to ensure that potential consumers see its true value.
- If the product is a staple product for which the brand name is the primary differentiating feature, test marketing could be beneficial.

Example E

The rollout launch[40]

- Frito-Lay first sold its new Doritos Tortilla Thins exclusively in two towns in the US before distributing nationally a few months later.
- Procter & Gamble launched disposable training diapers for babies in Holland and the UK, and then expanded internationally to Canada and the US.

The consumer adoption process[41]

Any innovation takes some time to spread through the marketplace in a process called innovation diffusion. Marketers must consider those factors that influence the adoption process and try to understand them in order to make the introduction of new products or services more effective.

Factors influencing the adoption process

A number of factors affect the adoption process to which marketers must give careful consideration before launching their products. These factors are discussed below.

Differences in people's readiness to try a new product

People differ noticeably in their readiness to try a new product, which has given rise to a categorisation of individuals. This categorisation is shown in Figure 6.5.

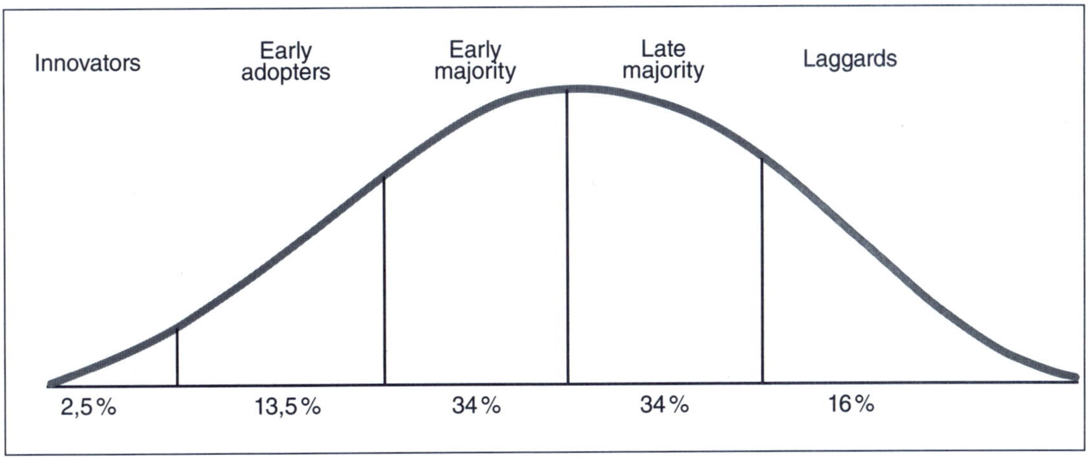

Figure 6.5 Categories of adopters[42]

> ### DEFINITION
> **Consumer adoption process**
> The consumer adoption process refers to the mental processes through which an individual moves from first hearing about an innovation through to the final adoption and becoming a regular user.

The different categories shown in Figure 6.5 are:

- **Innovators** – venturesome, willing to try new ideas at some risk (2,5 % of the population);
- **Early adopters** – guided by respect, opinion leaders in their communities; adopt new ideas early but carefully (13,5 % of the population);
- **Early majority** – very deliberate; adopt new ideas before the average person, although they are rarely the leaders (34 % of the population);
- **Late majority** – tend to be sceptical and adopt an innovation only after the majority of people have tried it (34 % of the population); and
- **Laggards** – tradition-bound and suspicious of change, and adopt an innovation only when it takes on a measure of tradition itself (16 % of the population).

A marketer should investigate the *demographic, psychographic* and *media characteristics* of the innovators and early adopters so that marketing efforts may be directed at them so as to influence the majorities (early and late) to adopt the product. This should speed up acceptance of the product in the marketplace. The early and late majorities form the mass market (68 % of the total population). The challenge in influencing these categories is to identify the characteristics of the early adopters for the respective product area and to market to both groups (early adopters and the majorities) so that diffusion of the product in the marketplace is quicker. Characteristics of early adopters are that they are younger, have higher social status, are in a more favourable financial position, and use more information sources than later adopters.

The product life cycle[43]

> ### EXPLANATIONS
> **Phases in the product life cycle**
> Phase 1: Introductory phase
> Phase 2: Growth phase
> Phase 3: Maturity phase
> Phase 4: Decline phase.

The aim of this section is to explain the general characteristics of a typical consumer product life cycle. A product has four phases in its life cycle, namely the *introductory phase* (when a new product is offered on the market for the first time), the *growth phase* (during which product sales gradually increase), the *maturity phase* (when product sales reach their peak), and the *declining phase* (when, unavoidably, stagnation and decreasing sales set in). Because consumer behaviour patterns and competition in the marketplace will inevitably change with time, the marketing strategy will often have to be adjusted during the product life cycle. When marketing management is threatened by competitors, it may be 'forced' to change or adapt the marketing strategy, depending on whether an attack or a strategic withdrawal is planned.

The course of the product life cycle

The different phases in the product life cycle

Products, just like biological beings, have specific life cycles. They are developed (prenatal phase), placed on the market for the first time (born), compete in the market and reach maturity (maturity phase), and are eventually withdrawn from the market (die). Product development ends with commercialisation. This is where the successfully developed and tested product is introduced to the target market on a large scale for the first time. The steps in the new product development process have already been discussed. In this section, the further course of a product's life is sketched.

During the product life cycle – that is, from its first introduction to its eventual withdrawal – the product finds itself time and time again in different competitive market environments, necessitating changes to the marketing strategy. Depending on the extent of and relative growth rate in product sales (which, measured over time, usually has an S-shaped development), an *introductory, growth, maturity* and *decline phase* can usually be identified in the life of the product in the target market.

Let us look at the four phases of the product life cycle in depth.

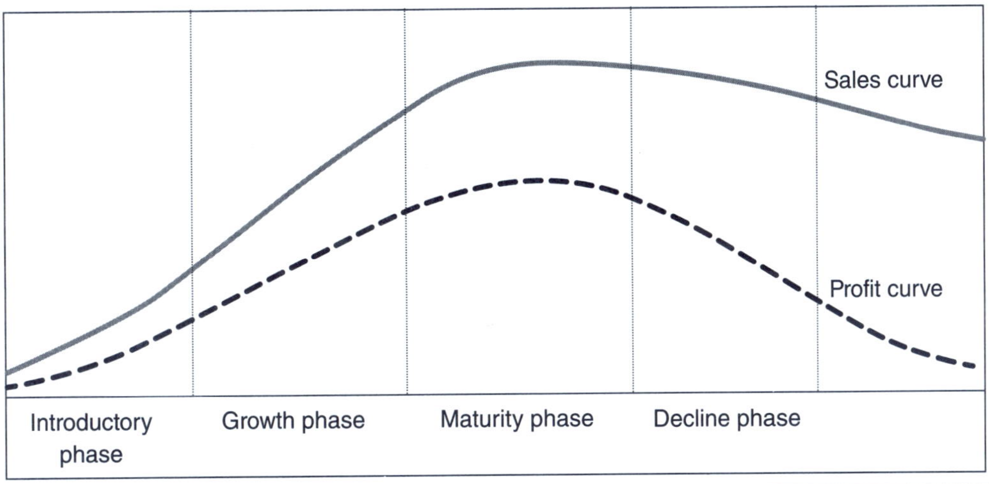

Figure 6.6 Phases in the product life cycle[44]

WWW:

- http://www.witiger.com/marketing/PLC.htm

Phase 1: Introductory phase

The introductory phase begins after preparations for entering the target market have been completed and the product is offered for sale. The initial sales are usually relatively small; however, after approval by the innovators, purchases by early adopters follow. Satisfaction, reinforced by marketing communication, leads to repurchasing and, as soon as sales increase further, the product exits this phase.

Phase 2: Growth phase

The growth phase is characterised by a strong growth in sales in the target market, especially because of the increase in repurchasing and purchases across a wide spectrum by the early majority of consumers. Competitors enter the target market with similar products (if they can), and the impact of their marketing communications gives further momentum to the demand for the product.

Phase 3: Maturity phase

As soon as the maturity phase is entered, sales growth and the demand for the product in the target market level off. The late majority is also already buying the product, and relatively few non-consumers remain in the target market. Few, if any, additional competitors enter the market with similar products. Improved products that satisfy the same needs are launched, attracting the innovators and early adopters. A stage of *market saturation* is eventually reached – sales of the product level off and start to decline. The laggards now start buying the product.

Phase 4: Decline phase

The decline phase is characterised by a rapid decline in sales in the target market. New uses for and consumers of the 'old' product are totally lacking, and all the new competing (and substitute) products enjoy increasing acceptance in the target market. Figure 6.6 shows the four phases in the product life cycle together with the sales and profit curves.

The sales curve increases during the introductory and growth phases, and reaches its peak in the maturity phase. During the decline phase, the sales curve starts declining. The profit curve has the same course, but starts to increase later in the introductory phase. The reason for this is the high costs of product development that have to be recovered before a profit is shown. The profit curve also starts to show a decline sooner than the sales curve. This results from intense competitive conditions, causing the price of the product – and thus also its profit – to drop. Together with the drop in price and profit, the costs of the product rise because of the need for increased marketing communication to stimulate demand. The marketing manager should strive to keep the product in the profitable phases of the product life cycle as long as possible.

When the product reaches the decline phase, management should consider withdrawing it. Alternatively, the product should be adapted physically and/or psychologically so that a new life cycle can be created for it before the profit curve starts showing its declining tendency. As soon as profit starts decreasing, the growing profit of a new model should make up for it.

For strategic planning purposes, it is necessary to take the investment recovery curve and the sales curve into account. Figure 6.7 on the next page shows the relationship between the product life cycle curve and the investment recovery curve. A new product penetrates the market as soon as sales of the 'old' product start declining.

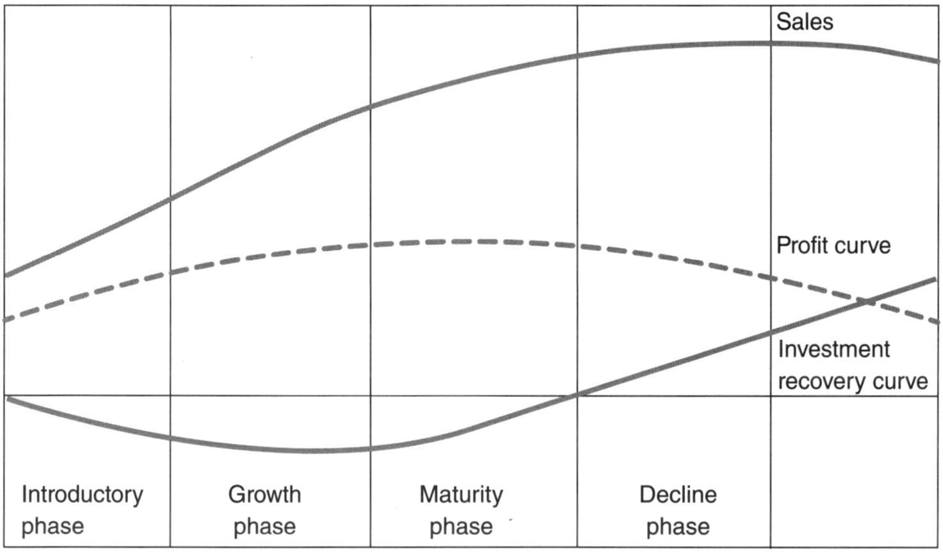

Figure 6.7 Product life cycle and investment recovery curve[45]

Different kinds of product life cycles

The sales and profit curves in Figure 6.6 show the traditional life cycle of a product. Note that not all products have this kind of life cycle. Product life cycles sometimes differ dramatically with regard to the period as well as the course of the curve. Figure 6.8 shows a few product life cycle patterns.

- The **traditional** product life cycle curve follows the clearly distinguishable periods of introduction, growth, maturity and decline.
- The **classic** product life cycle curve describes the surging sales growth and the reaching of a plateau phase where sales volumes stagnate as a result of a lack of new consumers or outlets.
- The **fashion fad** is a product which gains and loses popularity with the same rapidity. Examples of such products are fashion retail items that are only in for a season, and the sports jerseys of nations that participated in sporting events, for example the FIFA Soccer World Cup in 2010.
- The **extended fashion fad** follows a similar course, except that sales stabilise at a lower level after the initial success. An example of such a product is Zumba dance exercise classes – after an initial strong growth, the popularity of this fad has waned, but has not totally declined.
- The **seasonal or fashion** curve results when a product sells well in successive periods. Examples of such products are school clothes, sales of which are good at the beginning of the year and then decline, and subsequently show a sturdy growth again at the beginning of the winter season.

Example

Product life cycle – fashion fad and extended fashion fad[47]

- **The Pet Rock**. After hearing his friends complain about how expensive it was to care for their dogs, advertising copywriter Gary Dahl of the US joked about his pet rock and was soon writing a training manual for it. In no time Dahl had sold some 1,5 million ordinary beach pebbles at US$4 each. However, the fad, which began in October 1975, ended by the following February.
- **Trivial Pursuit**. In the mid-1980s the board game Trivial Pursuit was very popular. It was created by three Canadian friends, and it sold about 20 million copies in 1984 alone. Yet even with the fad long over, more than 1,5 million units of the game and its offshoots – travel packs,

Continue to next page

Example (E)

Continued from previous page

a children's version, and annual year-in-review editions – continue to be sold each year in 17 languages. The inventors have also been smart enough to revive the product with new technology, and have had a hand in developing a CD-ROM version of the game.

- The **revival** curve relates to a product that was regarded as old-fashioned and then is suddenly revived, regaining popularity. The Barbie doll is an example of a product that goes through revivals (new clothes, new versions of Barbie).
- The **fiasco** curve occurs when a product was a failure right from the outset.

The life cycle patherns are shown in Figure 6.8 below.

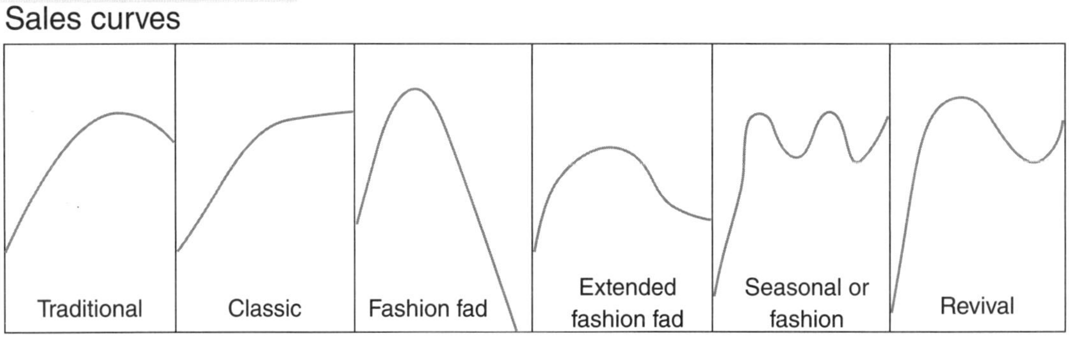

Figure 6.8 Different product life cycle patterns[46]

Summary

In this chapter, fundamental product concepts such as the *core product, tangible product, augmented product, potential product* and *product image* were introduced. The chapter further considered the classification of products by durability, focusing specifically on consumer and industrial products. Furthermore, product line and product mix decisions, as well as individual product decisions, were dealt with. Branding and packaging decisions were covered fairly comprehensively, and the importance of product-support services was emphasised.

The new product development process was examined, and the different types of new products developed by businesses were described. The steps to be followed in new product development were explained in detail, and the process by which new products are adopted, as well as the different types of adopters, was investigated. The four phases of the product life cycle, namely the *introductory, growth, maturity* and *decline phases*, were also identified and examined.

References

1. Checkers. 2011. *About us*. [Online] Available from: http://www.checkers.co.za/about/Pages/default.aspx [Accessed: 2013–03–06].
2. Adapted from Cant, M.C., Van Heerden, C.H. & Ngambi, H.C. 2010. *Marketing management: A South African perspective*. Cape Town, South Africa: Juta & Co., p. 156.
3. Ibid.
4. Harley-Davidson. 2012. *Our business*. [Online] Available from: http://www.hdavidson.co.za/profile/our-business [Accessed: 2013-03-06].
5. Based on Jooste, C.J. 2002. *Product management*. Claremont: New Africa Books, pp. 4–6.
6. King Price Insurance. 2012. *About us*. [Online] Available from: http://www.kingprice.co.za/About-Us.aspx [Accessed: 2013-03-06].
7. Adapted from Cant et al., op cit., pp. 159–169.
8. Ibid.
9. Van der Walt, A., Strydom, J.W., Marx, S. & Jooste, C.J. 1996. *Marketing management*. 3rd ed. Wetton: Juta & Co., p. 187.
10. Ibid.
11. Assael, H. 1998. *Marketing*. Fort Worth: Dryden Press, p. 3.7.
12. Cant et al., op. cit., p. 164.
13. Assael, op. cit., pp. 3.8–3.9.
14. Adapted from Cant et al., op. cit., p. 166.
15. Bovée, C.L., Houston, M.J. & Thill, J.V. 1995. *Marketing*. 2nd ed. New York: McGraw-Hill, pp. 241–243.
16. Adapted from Cant et al., op. cit., p. 166.
17. Bovée, C.L., Houston, M.J. & Thill, J.V. 1995. *Marketing*. 2nd ed. New York: McGraw-Hill, pp. 241–243.
18. Bearden, W.O., Ingram, T.N. & Laforge, R.W. 1995. *Marketing principles and perspectives*. Chicago: Irwin, p. 220.
19. Kotler, P. & Armstrong, G. 1993. *Marketing: An introduction*. Englewood Cliffs, NJ: Prentice Hall, p. 229.
20. Cant et al., op cit., pp. 173–178.
21. Ibid.
22. Marketing Examples. 2010. *Diversification*. [Online] Available from: http://uwmktg301.blogspot.com/2010/02/diversification.html [Accessed: 2013-03-06].
23. Cant et al., op cit., p. 173.
24. Van Heerden, C.H. 2013. *Contemporary retail and marketing case studies*. Cape Town, South Africa: Juta & Co., pp. 31–48.
25. Cant et al., op cit., pp. 176–181.
26. Ibid.
27. Ibid.
28. Bovée et al., op. cit., p. 251.
29. Bearden et al., op. cit., p. 225.
30. Cant et al., op. cit., p. 178.
31. Botha, J.A.R., Brink, A., Loubser, F.J., Machado, R. & Rudansky, S. 1994. *Consumer-oriented marketing communication study guide*. Pretoria, Department of Business Management, University of South Africa, p. 157.

32. Bearden et al., op. cit., p. 228.
33. Based on Strydom, J.W., Jooste, C.J. & Cant, M.C. 2000. *Marketing management*. Wetton: Juta & Co., Chapter 7.
34. Nieuwenhuizen, C. 2011. *Business and marketing cases*. Cape Town, South Africa: Juta & Co., pp. 8–11.
35. Adapted from Cant et al., op cit., p. 183.
36. Duncan, J. 2012. *Product development: 5 questions to answer first*. [Online] Available from: http://marketbold.com/product-development-5-questions-to-answer-first/ [Accessed: 2013-03-06].
37. Mystery Panel. 2013. *Product testing: Implementation examples*. [Online] Available from: http://www.mystery-panel.com/our-services/product-testing/examples.html [Accessed: 2013-03-06].
38. Brassington, F. & Pettitt, S. 1997. *Principles of marketing*. London: Pitman, p. 349.
39. Adapted from Churchill, G.A. & Peter, J.P. 1998. *Marketing: Creating value for customers*. New York: Irwin McGraw-Hill, p. 267.
40. Ibid.
41. Kotler & Armstrong, op. cit., pp. 250–260.
42. Cant et al., op cit., pp. 191–197.
43. Based on Strydom et al., op. cit., Chapter 7.
44. Taken from Cant, M.C., Strydom, J.W., Jooste, C.J. & Du Plessis, P.J. 2006. *Marketing management*. 5th ed. Cape Town, South Africa: Juta & Co., pp. 243; adapted from Neidell, L.A. 1983. 'Don't forget the product life cycle for strategic planning'. *Business*, April–June, p. 31.
45. Cant et al., op. cit., p. 196.
46. Ibid.
47. Adapted from Kotler, P. In Cant et al., op cit., p. 198.

Pricing decisions

CHAPTER 7

✓ Learning objectives

After studying this chapter, you should be able to:

- discuss the three categories of pricing objectives;
- analyse the factors that should be taken into consideration in pricing;
- calculate mark-ups, and analyse competitive and seller pricing methods;
- explain the methods of setting a price level; and
- suggest methods of adapting prices based on geographic and discount considerations.

Introduction

Sam and Pranesh are both looking for new cars. Both want the same features but will compromise on some of them for a good deal. Sam found a car package that totals R200 000 while Pranesh found a deal that totals R160 000. At first glance it looks as though Pranesh got the better deal, but what is included in each deal?

Sam's deal comes with financing from the dealership where he is going to purchase the car and a five-year motor plan with affordable insurance built into the price as part of the dealership's offer. While Pranesh has to look for his own financing and get quotes for insurance, the features that he wants for the car such as Bluetooth and a USB-compatible radio are extras that he needs to pay for.

So who paid the better price? Depending on the buyer's preferences, financial situation and values attached to time, effort and money, there really is no easy answer. Thus when marketers offer a product, not only is the monetary value considered, but also the core product and need-satisfying benefits.

Each car manufacturer needs to consider a number of factors. A manufacturer can look at the competitors' prices for the same-level car

> **Example**
>
> **Money offerings**
> Sandra is a married woman and the mother of two children. She works at an insurance company and earns commission plus a basic salary. Her husband, James, earns a substantial income as an engineer. They share the costs where possible and make sure that they have equal disposable income. Their expenses are divided as follows: Sandra pays for their daughter's school fees while James pays for their son's tertiary tuition. He is staying in a flat closer to university so James pays the rent, while Sandra pays for his bus fare to and from the campus. James also gives his son an allowance, with which he needs to purchase groceries and clothes. James has taken a mortgage out on the house and is responsible for the monthly payments. All other expenses are divided between Sandra and James as they see fit. Can you identify all the types of money offerings that are mentioned above as well as the need-satisfying goods or service? Some of the money offerings and need-satisfying goods or services are: commission for additional work; salary for employment; school fees and tuition for education; rent for accommodation; bus fare for transport; and an allowance for groceries and clothes. Can you identify the rest of the money offerings and need-satisfying goods or services?

and the probability of making a profit by offering that car to the market. Possible failure, such as the failure to make the forecast profits, will need a contingency plan, such as price promotions in the form of cash rebates or special financial arrangements for car buyers. Making the car attractive to car dealerships is also important, which can be achieved by providing cash discounts to retailers. The concept of price and issues pertaining to basic price determination are pertinent to this chapter, and pricing and all the considerations manufacturers and marketers and all parties involved need to consider will be discussed further on.

The meaning and role of price

Marketers in general want both a satisfactory *profit or return on their investments*, and the *highest possible sales volume*. These two areas are often in conflict. There are some instances when it makes sense to maximise profit margins, and others when it makes sense to maximise sales volume. A high sales volume (turnover) at a lower price may be more profitable in the long run than a lower sales volume at a higher price.

A price is the value given in exchange for something else, which in our modern economic system is paid in money.[1] We can also say that price is the value of something expressed in terms of rand and cents, or in the export market in other monetary units such as the US dollar, euro or British pound. It is simply the amount of money paid to purchase a product or a service. For marketers (sellers), price is essentially a means to achieve the objective of making a profit. For consumers and commercial users it is a means – a money offering – for acquiring need-satisfying goods or services. The money offerings can be seen in the example in the margin to the left.

When consumers are willing to pay to use the need-satisfying benefits of a product or service offering, the price at which the product or service is set at is known as the market price. In the car example in the Introduction, it is clear that the marketer considers a number of factors pertinent to the product or service such as the need-satisfying benefits provided, convenience, brand, quality and unique merchandise.

Price setting

The procedure for **setting prices** in a marketing-orientated manner consists of three stages. First, a *market price* is decided on. This is the price that most consumers of a particular product will be prepared to pay. This market price (in certain segments of a total market) is directed at a sales volume (turnover) that can be achieved. Second, a *target price* is calculated which will meet any price objective of the firm, taking into consideration the capital and other costs required to manufacture and market the product. Third, the market price and the target price can be compared, and decisions made on a *final selling* price.

The price-setting process is a step-by-step procedure, as shown in Figure 7.1

Figure 7.1 Steps in the price-setting process[2]

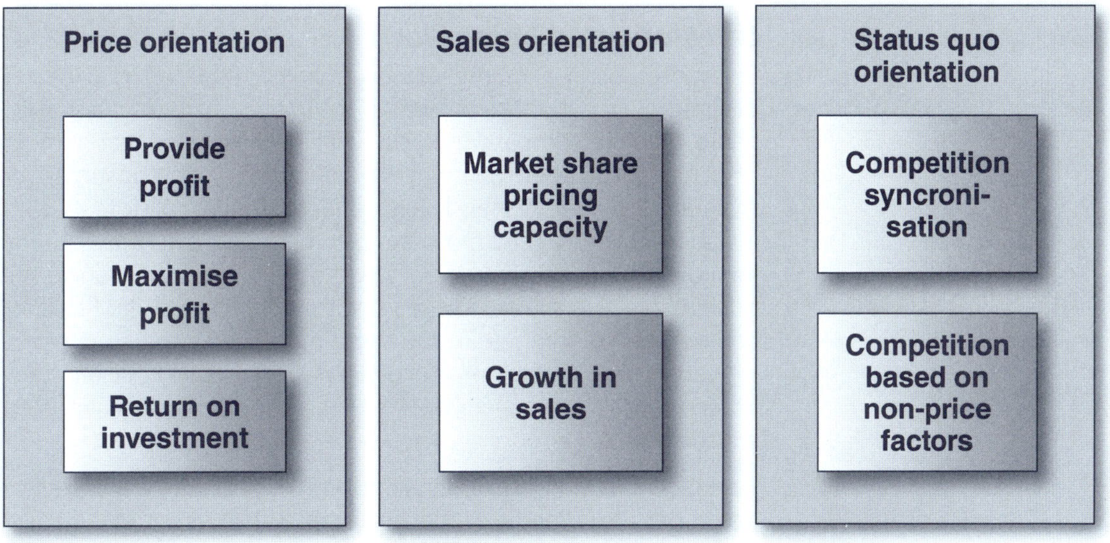

Figure 7.2 The three categories of pricing objectives

Let us now look at each stage in the price-setting process.

Step 1: Determine price objective[4]

Pricing objectives are goals that give direction to the whole pricing process. Before marketers can set selling prices for their merchandise, they must set specific, measurable price objectives that correspond to their marketing and enterprise objectives. Price objectives can be divided into three categories: *price-oriented objectives*, *sales-*

DEFINITION

Price setting

Price setting is the process of determining the cost to consumers of a company's product or service offering that they will be willing to pay under particular circumstances at a particular time.[3]

oriented objectives and *status quo-oriented objectives*. This is illustrated in Figure 7.2.

Price-oriented objectives

Enterprises usually utilise pricing objectives, profit maximisation, target profitability and return on investment for the guiding pricing decisions.

When profit maximisation is an objective, then the enterprise will set prices to obtain the best possible profit from sales. The profit is calculated by the level at which the price can be set to cover the production and distribution costs and generate a profit.

Return on investment is the net profit realised for every rand of capital invested in the enterprise. The return on investment is expressed as a percentage of the profit on invested capital. If the objective is to obtain an increase of 15 % in the profit, this means that the retailer wants to increase the profit earned by 15 %. If the objective is to earn a 15 % return on invested capital, this means that the retailer wishes to earn 15 % net profit for every rand of the capital invested in the enterprise. Return on net sales is the percentage calculated by dividing rand profit by net sales.

Sales-oriented objectives

Enterprises set sales volumes or market share to establish growth sales or to maintain current sales levels. If the market share is set a specific figure, then the company must do what it can to sell to that number of consumers. Either the company can attract new consumers or maintain the current sales levels. Attracting 'many' customers with initial low prices may also motivate customers to develop brand loyalty regarding the product involved. When obtaining a market share is a pricing objective, the enterprise's aim is usually to make it difficult for competitors to compete in the same market or market segments. However, when an enterprise experiences a decreased market share, lowering price(s) is frequently used to remedy the problem of maintaining a market share.

Sales growth as a pricing objective is concerned not with the competitive position or the immediate profit but rather with sales volumes that are on the increase. As this objective is not concerned with immediate profit, it is an indication that it does not have a long-term focus. Sales growth is a short-term objective concerned with a rapid increase in sales, which usually occurs when there is a surplus of inventory, especially at certain times like Christmas or seasonal departmental store sales.

Maintaining the status quo

Competitive objectives are objectives intended to either meet or prevent competition, or they consist of non-price objectives. When the objective is to meet the competition, then the aim is to imitate the price of the major competition. When the objective is to prevent competition, then the prices are set as low as possible to deter additional competitors from entering the market. When the objective is based on non-price, then the enterprise would rather compete on another basis, such as the quality of the product or services, location or merchandising strategy, than on price.

'Sales objectives are expressed in many different terms, though usually stated in quantitative terms to establish clear benchmarks. Most objectives are expressed in growth in sales, profit and especially in market share.[6]

Step 2: Demand determinant of price

Demand estimation is when the enterprise needs to estimate the amount of demand for a product or service, which is confined to a particular period of time. Often before offering a product to the market, the enterprise will have no idea what the price of the product will be, although once the demand for the product has been estimated, then the company can calculate an approximate price. By calculating according to the demand, the enterprise can avoid over- and under-pricing the product.[5] In most cases there is an *inverse relationship* between a product's price and the quantity demanded (the volume of sales). In some cases, as the price increases, the number of consumers willing to purchase the product or service decreases as there is a decrease in the number of consumers who consider the product or service as value for money. In other cases, consumers consider price as an indication of quality, and therefore are more likely to purchase it at the higher price.[7] A *demand curve*, like the simplified example in Figure 7.3, will indicate the reactions of many potential buyers to different prices for the same product. The curve's degree of slope reflects the quantities purchased (volume of sales) at different prices and the fact that different buyers have different sensitivities to a product's price. A *demand schedule* relates the quantity demanded at different prices.

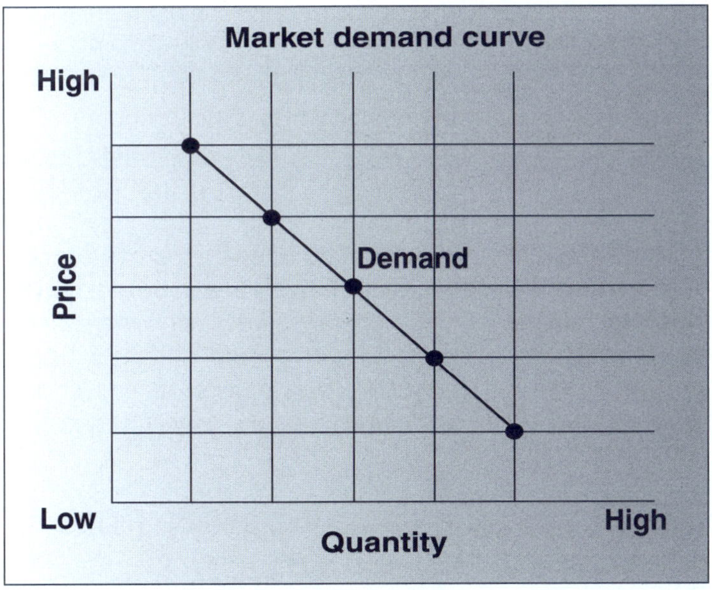

Figure 7.3 Demand curve for a product[8]

The following factors may affect customers' sensitivity to price changes:

- **Buyers' perceptions and preferences**. Customers are less price sensitive, and so less likely to be concerned about the price of a product if they perceive it to be special or have unique benefits, especially when there are poor-quality or no suitable substitutes. Buyers are also less price sensitive when they regard a product as one offering high quality, prestige or exclusiveness.

- **Buyers' awareness of alternatives or substitutes**. When buyers are unaware of substitute or alternative products, then they are less price sensitive. If they do not know that there is a cheaper brand of washing powder then they will be less likely to be too concerned about the price because they think there is no other washing powder available. Also, buyers are less price sensitive when it is difficult to compare the performance or quality of products. When comparing entry-level cars, there may not be a possibility of a benchmark because the performance and quality of both are more likely to be similar. Conversely, buyers will be more sensitive to price differences when they are well aware of and compare substitute product brands and other features. Knowing that there are different brands of herbal toothpaste, for example, will make a consumer more likely to compare the prices of the different brands, and thus become more price sensitive.
- **The buyer's ability to pay**. Purchasing power consists of the total personal income of an individual, a family or a group after deduction of certain compulsory expenses. This can be considered as the disposable income that an individual, family or group may have. If Sandy earns R10 000 per month more than her friend Phindi, yet their compulsory expenses are equal, Sandy has more purchasing power because she has more money to spend on what she wants.
- Closely related to the ability to buy is the concept of **discretionary purchasing power**, which is the amount of money a consumer unit has left over after its expenditure on necessities and which can be used for acquiring luxury goods and services of all sorts.
- Consumers are less sensitive to prices when their **expenditure for the products or services is relatively low in proportion to their total income**. As their income increases, consumers spend proportionally less on necessities such as food, clothing, housing, transport, and so on, and proportionally more on items such as household appliances, cars, garden furniture, recreation and travel.

'The exchange marketing activities are buying and selling. Ownership is transferred from one person to the other.'

'Estimating demand involves management practices and aids such as marketing research, market forecasting, as well as the use of a marketing information system.'

DEFINITION

Production concept
The production concept holds that consumers will favour products that are available and affordable.

Estimating demand involves management practices and aids such as marketing research, market forecasting, as well as the use of a marketing information system.

Step 3: Cost determinant of price

All income from the sales of products or services is achieved at a cost, and costs should therefore be analysed and controlled. Although all costs must be covered in the long term, products can sometimes be sold at or lower than cost to attract consumers to the shop. The total cost of a product item or a product line is a composite of all the costs of the activities performed by the various functions in the organisation, such as financing, staffing, purchasing, production, general administration and marketing. An understanding and analysis of product costs are basic to the selection of a price strategy.

Various types of costs

Fixed costs (FC)

Fixed costs are those expenses that remain constant despite the change in quantity of goods or services offered or sold. The expenses continue even when production comes to a halt. Fixed costs are costs such as rent for the factory/store, staff salaries, insurance, etc.

Variable costs (VC)

Variable costs differ from fixed costs. Variable costs fluctuate as the quantity of products and services offered and sold fluctuate. When there is an increase in the number of products manufactured, the costs increase as there may be a need to increase staff, and more raw materials are required.

Total cost (TC)

Total cost (TC) is the sum of the total fixed costs (FC) and the total variable costs (VC) for a specific quantity produced.

$$TC = FC + VC$$

Step 4: Selection of price

In the process of determining prices several, factors other than costs could influence the marketer's final decision.

Competition

Competition varies for each product life cycle, which may also affect the pricing decisions. An enterprise may decide to offer a product at a low price, which will discourage competitors from entering the market. Price wars could then ensue because of the intense competition, thus it is important to consider competitors' price strategies in order to be prepared for their reactions to their own pricing activities. There are also alternative measures to competing with other firms, such as on the basis of the quality of product, services and advertising.[9]

Characteristics of the merchandise

Characteristics of products may influence the pricing. An example is products, such as avocados, which are lower priced when in season. End-of-range summer clothes that are still on the shelves by the end of April are marked down because winter clothes are in season. The physical appearance of products is also important. If there is a large quantity of perishable products in stock, the prices be must set low enough so that they sell quickly before they perish and can no longer be sold. Unique products may be sold at higher prices because consumers of such products are usually not price sensitive. Product quality is also an important determinant that has to be considered when prices are being determined.

Other factors to consider

The basic price may also be influenced by the other elements of the marketing mix:

- **The product**. The end use of products is important. In some cases, whether a product can be leased, bought, returned or traded in is a consideration that consumers make. If a farmer has an old but reliable vehicle, but would like the option of exchanging it for a newer version with added features, a trade-in option would make buying a new vehicle more affordable and attractive for him.
- **Channels of distribution used**. The type of distribution chosen for a product influences the manufacturer's pricing strategy. Distribution channels include department stores, supermarkets, specialty stores, etc. By purchasing fresh produce from the farmers' market, consumers are ensured of lower prices as the produce comes directly from the farmers without going through a middleman, therefore the farmers can make use of a low price strategy to attract more consumers.
- **Promotional methods used**. The type of methods used to promote a product or service will influence the price strategy utilised. If a manufacturer is considering advertising a new perfume on television, then the high cost of such advertising needs to be take into consideration in the perfume's price.

'The price of seasonal products fluctuates according to output and sales related to the season of the year. Changes in seasons cause relevant peaks and troughs in production and sales.'[10]

We will now look at the *basic methods of price setting*. By combining all the available information on potential demand, costs and competition, managers can arrive at a price for a product or service by using one or more of the following pricing methods:

- Demand based
- Cost based
- Competition based.

Demand-based pricing

Demand as a basis for pricing is also referred to as *customer-based* or *value-based pricing*. In demand-based pricing, the perceived worth that consumers consider the product or service to be is used, as opposed to setting the price in terms of the actual cost of the product, the market price, competitors' prices or the historical price.[11] The goal is to align price with value delivered.

Skimming pricing

With this pricing strategy, the company sets a relatively high price for a product or service at first, and then lowers it over time. The idea is for the company literally to 'skim the cream off the market demand' and to recover its costs before competition steps in and lowers the market price.[12] A good example of skimming is the introduction of flat screen television sets. These have been on the market for some time now and were considered very expensive when first introduced.

'The objective of skimming pricing is to obtain maximum revenue for a new high-end product before substitute products enter the market. Once the substitute products have entered the market, the price for the high-end product is lowered to capture the low-end user and to spoil copycat competitors' revenue chances.'

Penetration pricing

Price policies that involve the setting of relatively low prices are called *penetration pricing*. The opposite considerations to skimming pricing apply here. This type of price policy can also be used to follow up skimming pricing as explained above. It is a widely used practice to start at a relatively low price during the initial stages so that the product life cycle can be extended, especially during the introduction and growth stages. *Flexible introductory price strategies* when entering the market can be used instead of penetration pricing if the marketer fears that penetration pricing will speed up reactions from the competition. In this case, 'price cuts' are only used for a limited period of time after which prices are raised to 'normal levels'. The idea is to attract attention and initial sales growth by means of an 'introductory sales offer', which can also be regarded as a type of promotional pricing. However, apart from this, it is often difficult to increase prices immediately afterwards.[13]

Price lines

A price line is a certain pricing zone or pricing point for merchandise which is normally sold at that price. This pricing policy eliminates the endless number of prices usually found in a store and replaces them with a series of prices that are set at certain intervals.

'The pricing lining policy objective is to direct retail selling prices at consumers in the target market.'

For example, instead of selling dresses at R70,23, R72,65, R78,30, and so on, all dresses in that pricing zone are priced at R79. Dresses in a higher pricing zone would all be sold at a price line of R99, and so on, therefore the number of prices at which merchandise is sold is limited. For example dresses are only sold for R79, R99 or R149. The advantage of this pricing policy is that it facilitates the buying process for consumers, and because certain prices are popular with consumers, the merchandise is sold more quickly. In addition, sales staff are more sure of prices. Advertising and sales promotion are more effective, and it is easier for the retailer to purchase merchandise. However, price lines may make it difficult for a store to adjust its prices to meet those of competitors. A limited number of price lines may also create the impression that the store offers only a small variety of merchandise.

The objective of a price lining policy is to aim retail selling prices at target market consumers. Retailers must first determine the most suitable pricing zone, which is the range of prices that appeals to a certain target market for certain demographic (income, occupation), psychographic (lifestyle, personality), product usage (heavy or light users) or product benefit (economic, social) reasons.

Odd-even pricing

Odd-even pricing is a manipulative method of pricing as items are priced in such a way as to make consumers believe that they cost less than they actually do.[14] Odd-even pricing is the strategy followed where prices are set so that they end on odd numbers. Prices have a psychological effect on consumers, and odd prices are used to encourage them to buy. Consumers take a price of 99c as being much lower than Rl since they pay more attention to the rand value than to the cent value. This pricing policy is especially prevalent in discount stores, but not in prestige stores since this could harm their image.

Multiple pricing

Retailers sometimes offer bulk items at a lower price than if the retailer had sold the same items separately. Consumers are conditioned to think that multiple prices are lower although this is not always the case, for example when four items are offered for R1,00 but each individual item is 25 cents. Items that are multiple priced are often regarded as a bargain. A multiple pricing policy is used especially for merchandise with a low unit value which is bought regularly or to clear stock at the end of a sales season.

Unit pricing

This is a pricing policy where prices are set per unit of measure. The price is therefore set per kilogram, metre, litre, and so forth, to enable consumers to make price comparisons between products of different sizes, shapes and quantities. Usually the price is not marked on the merchandise itself, but the price per unit of measure is marked on the shelf on which the merchandise is displayed.

Bundle pricing

Bundle pricing is the combination of products that are sold as one product. For buyers, the overall cost of the purchase shows a saving compared to purchasing each product individually. This method of pricing can be seen in combo deals such as a meal at KFC, or purchasing washing powder and softener as a bundle. A bundle of products is sometimes referred to as a package deal.[15]

Premium pricing

Premium pricing (also called prestige or image pricing) is the strategy of consistently pricing at, or near, the high end of the possible price range to help attract status-conscious consumers. Prestige pricing creates the perception that the product or service is of high quality or prestigious. High-end fashion labels such as Chanel or exclusive car manufacturers such as Ferrari make use of premium pricing. Consumers will buy a premium priced product because:

- they believe the high price is an indication of good quality;
- they believe it to be a sign of self-worth ('I'm worth it'), it authenticates the buyer's success and status, and also serves as a signal to others that the owner is a member of an exclusive group; and
- they require flawless performance in this application – the cost of product malfunction is too high to buy anything but the best, for example a cardiac pacemaker.[16]

Demand backward

Prices are established based on the consumers' willingness to pay for the items, subtracting the costs involved in order to determine whether the profit margin is adequate in meeting the company's profit objectives.

> **Special segment pricing**
>
> In certain industries, there is a special set of customers who are offered a product or service at a price that differs from other customers in the target market. Examples of this are when pensioners pay less for certain items at a supermarket on particular days, scholars pay a lower price for certain bus tickets, or children's meals are half price at a buffet. Other examples include paying a higher price for a better seat at a football game because the seating is closer to the field, or paying more for a golden ticket at a concert for a seat that is closer to the stage.
>
> The main reasons for offering special prices are to appeal to consumers' needs in order to build market share, brand image, and customer loyalty by being sensitive to these needs and rewarding loyal customers.

Cost-based pricing

Cost-plus pricing

This method involves the setting of a price of one unit of product equal to the unit's total cost (that is, fixed plus variable costs) plus a desired profit on the unit. Alternatively, we can say that the cost-plus approach to pricing is to add the cost of producing and marketing a product to the overheads of the product plus a desired profit margin (a percentage). Price would thus be calculated as follows:

Price = direct costs + overheads + percentage profit

The profit margin is normally a predetermined percentage. For example, if a target profit margin is 20 %, the price on a product item with a total cost of R50 would be calculated as follows:

Price = total cost (R50) + profit margin of 20 % = R60

> **Mark-up**
>
> The company sets the price by calculating costs per unit and then deciding the mark-up percentages required to cover selling costs and profits. The calculation for the selling price is the mark-up added to the cost price.[17] The calculation for the mark-up pricing follows:
>
> $$\text{Price} = \frac{\text{Cost of goods}}{(100 - \text{mark-up per cent}/100)}$$
>
> Continue to next page

Continued from previous page

To calculate the selling price, the mark-up is added to the cost price. For example, the mark-up on a dress purchased at R400 and sold at R600 is R200. An amount in rand is therefore added to the cost price, which is sufficient to cover the operating expenses and to realise a profit.

In the above example, the mark-up is expressed in rand, but mostly it is expressed as a percentage of the cost price or the selling price. Based on the example and the calculation above, the percentages may be calculated as follows:

50% mark-up on cost = (200/400)%

and

% mark-up on *retail selling price* = mark-up in rand ÷ retail selling price in rand

The example above:
33% mark-up on cost = (200 ÷ 600)%

Different types of mark-ups

- **Initial mark-up and initial retail selling price**. When the initial mark-up is added to the cost price, the initial selling price is obtained. For example, if the cost price is R20 and the initial mark-up is R10, then the initial selling price is R30. The initial mark-up is therefore the first mark-up that is placed on an item of merchandise.
- **Additional mark-up**. In certain cases the initial mark-up might not have been adequate to cover expenses nor to realise a satisfactory profit. An additional mark-up then has to be calculated. If, for example, the additional mark-up is R10, it is added to the initial mark-up and the cost price, and the new retail selling price is then R40.
- **Mark-up cancellations**. A mark-up cancellation is a reduction of the selling price long after an additional mark-up has already been done. This price reduction may take place as a result of a reduction of competitors' prices, too much stock or consumer resistance to high prices. If the cancellation is R5, the final retail selling price is therefore:

  R35 = R20 + R10 + R10 – R5.
- **Individual or cumulative mark-up**. Individual mark-up is the mark-up calculated for a single item, whereas cumulative mark-up is the mark-up calculated on more than one item, usually on a certain line of merchandise.
- **Maintained or net mark-up**. The maintained mark-up or net mark-up can be used to determine whether price objectives have actually been achieved. This mark-up is the difference between the cost of the merchandise and the price at which it is actually sold. This price may contain various mark-ups and mark-downs.

Break-even analysis

Break-even analysis calculates the number of sales in units of rand that are necessary for total income (price × units sold) to be the same as the total costs (fixed costs + variable costs) at a set price.[18] A useful tool in both cost- and demand-based pricing is the break-even analysis. A break-even point is the number of units of production at which the income from sales equals the total costs, assuming a certain selling price, thus there is a different break-even point for each selling price. Sales revenue of quantities of products above the break-even point results in a profit on each additional unit sold. The higher the sales are above the break-even point, the higher the profit per unit sold. Obviously, sales below the break-even point will result in a loss to the marketer.

A method of calculating the break-even point is illustrated below in Figure 7.4. At each of several prices, we wish to find out how many units must be sold to cover all costs. For example, at a unit price of R150, the sale of each unit contributes R120 to cover overheads, therefore we must sell about 2,1 units to cover the R250 at fixed cost.

Define unit	**3**
Step 1: Indicate the unit price	**R150**
Step 2: Indicate the variable cost per unit	**R30**
Step 3: Indicate the contribution to overheads (step 1 – step 2)	**R120**
Step 4: Indicate the total fixed cost	**R250**
Step 5: Calculate the break-even point (step 4/step 3)	**2,1 units**

Figure 7.4 Calculating the break-even point

In this hypothetical situation, the firm's fixed costs are R250 and its variable costs are constant at R30 a unit. (To simplify our break-even analysis, we assume that the variable costs per unit remain constant.) This is illustrated graphically in Figure 7.5. If the company sells five units, the total cost is R400 (variable costs $5 \times 30 = \text{R}150$ plus fixed cost R250). At a selling price of R80 per unit, the sale of five units will yield R400 revenue: cost and revenue will equal each other. At the same price, the sale of one unit above five will yield a profit.

Competition-based pricing

This occurs when the company bases its pricing on that of the competing products instead of on the costs involved in the production of the product or the customers' demand as a benchmark.[19] However, by setting the prices based on competing prices, the company can be sure that the competing price was set taking into consideration customers' expectations, production costs and overheads. The major pricing decision that the company must make can be set lower than, higher than or equal to competitors' prices, depending on the company's objectives.[20]

- **Setting prices lower than competitors' prices**. The aim is to effect a large turnover in rand as well as to have a high stock turnover rate. To be able to price lower than competitors, sellers must be able to buy merchandise at a lower cost than they can, their operating expenses must also be lower, and they will also need to offer the minimum of after-sales and other services. These sellers normally have a low-price image.

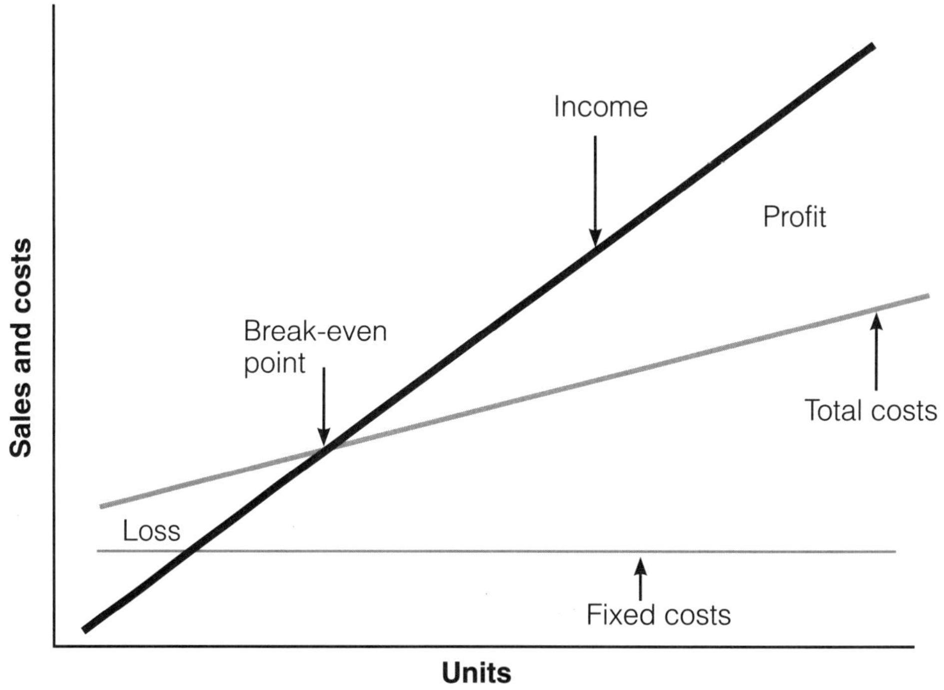

Figure 7.5 Break-even point[21]

- **Setting prices equal to competitors' prices**. Price is not used as the basis for competition, but the focus is on location, service, promotion, etc. Fixing prices equal to competitors' prices does not mean that sellers must follow every price change of competitors precisely, but that their prices must fall within the competitive range.
- **Setting prices higher than competitors' prices**. If prices are set higher than those of the competition, the higher prices must be justified in the mind of the customer by offering benefits such as better after-sales service, higher-quality products, exclusive products, personal attention to customers, a luxurious buying

atmosphere, a large sales staff, a prestigious image, a convenient location and longer business hours. Consumers must therefore believe that the extra service they receive is worth the higher prices, otherwise they will not buy from the store.

Leader pricing

Leader pricing is practised by intermediaries such as retailers who aim to attract customers to their stores by advertising and charging relatively low prices on specific items. The price cut is genuine in that the items concerned are freely available at the advertised price. However, the idea is to increase the sale of other products whose prices have not been specially reduced. In general, the so-called loss leaders are not sold at a loss, but below their normal price. Retailers must take care to rotate the products and brands selected so that certain items are not given a low-price image. The idea is to increase the price again after the campaign is over and to select other product items in their place for the next round.

Certain products are chosen for their promotion value and priced low, but above cost. In food stores, the leader prices are the 'specials' that are advertised regularly to give an image of low prices. Leader items are usually well-known, widely used items which are not stocked heavily (such as milk, butter, eggs, tea or coffee), but where customers will recognise a real price cut.

Step 5: Price adjustment considerations[22]

In this section we will discuss the various types of discount, namely *trade or functional discounts, quantity discounts, cash discounts, advanced purchase discounts and promotional allowances*.

Trade discounts

A trade discount, also known as functional discount, is offered by the seller to trade channel members who perform certain functions such as selling to and advising customers, storing goods and reducing bulk lots into smaller sellable quantities, delivering goods to customers, granting credit, and keeping records. These are not discounts available to the general public. Manufacturers may offer different functional discounts to different trade channels because of the different services they provide, but they must offer the same functional discounts within each trade channel. For example, a manufacturer may quote a retail list price as R400 with trade discounts of 40% and 10%. This means that the retailer pays the wholesaler R240 (R400 less 40%), and the wholesaler pays the manufacturer R216 (R240 less 10%). The wholesaler keeps the 10% to cover the costs of wholesaling functions, and passes on the 40% discount to the retailer. Trade discounts are generally offered to distribution channel members who, in exchange for the reduced price, undertake some of the responsibilities or functions for marketing the product. A retailer may, for example, undertake to display the product prominently on its shelves, display point-of-sale advertising

WWW:

- http://www.wisegeek.com/what-is-a-trade-discount.htm

material, talk to customers about the product, provide feedback to the manufacturer, and so on.

WWW:

- http://www.investopedia.com/terms/q/quantity-discount.asp

Quantity discounts[23]

A quantity discount is a price reduction offered to buyers who buy large volumes. A typical example for the channel members might be 'R10 per unit for fewer than 100 units, and R9 per unit for 100 units or more', while customers might get a 'two for the price of one' discount or a 'buy three and get the fourth free' discount. Discounts provide an incentive to the customer to buy more from one seller, rather than buy from a number of different sources. Generally speaking, quantity discounts are of three kinds: *non-cumulative, cumulative* and *minimum-order*.

- **Non-cumulative quantity discounts** are based on the size of an individual purchase order. They encourage large individual purchase orders, not a series of orders.
- **Cumulative quantity discounts** apply to the accumulation of purchases of a product over a given time period, usually a year. Cumulative quantity discounts encourage a single customer to repeat buy far more than non-cumulative quantity discounts.
- Finally, **minimum-order discounts** make it obligatory for wholesalers to purchase minimum quantities (usually measured in cases, truckloads, etc).

WWW:

- http://www.investopedia.com/terms/c/cash-discount.asp

Cash discounts

A cash discount is a price reduction to buyers or customers who pay their accounts promptly.

A typical example is '2/10, net 30', which means that although payment is due within 30 days, the buyer can deduct 2 % if the account is paid within 10 days, which is common in the business-to-business environment. The discount must be granted to all buyers meeting these terms.

Advance purchase discounts

These are discounts offered to consumers for buying products or services well in advance. Many hotels, for instance, offer a percentage savings (for example 20 %) on standard rates for booking accommodation in advance (for example 21 days).

WWW:

- http://www.investopedia.com/terms/p/promotion.asp

Promotional pricing[24]

Promotional pricing is the act of lowering a price below the normal one in order to enhance the effectiveness of the product sales efforts that the company is pursuing for cost-conscious customers. Department stores frequently have clothing sales in an attempt to attract shoppers to the store in the hope that they will purchase other clothing items that are not marked down. Promotional pricing is especially prevalent during holidays or around special days like Christmas, Mother's Day and Valentine's Day.

Geographic pricing[25]

This selling price is calculated based on the customer or market's distance from the distribution hub and includes transportation costs incurred.

If the geographic location of the buyer and the manufacturer or seller are far apart, the marketer has to decide on who will be responsible for transport costs. Prices may be higher to cover the higher shipping costs. The marketer can either charge all customers the same price regardless of location because customers pay their own transport costs (FOB), or the marketer can charge the same price plus freight to all customers, regardless of their location (that is, a uniform price – the freight charge is set at the average freight cost).

A number of terms are used in geographic pricing:

- **FOB (free-on-board)**. The seller pays for transportation of the goods to the port of shipment plus the loading costs. The buyer carries all costs and risks of loss of or damage to the goods from that point (that is, after the cargo has been loaded on board).
- **CIF (cost, insurance and freight)**. The seller pays the costs, freight and insurance to bring the goods to the port of destination.
- **Zone pricing**. Shipping costs are calculated according to shipping distance. If the buyer is close to the seller, shipping costs are cheaper, whereas if the buyer is further away, the shipping costs increase.
- **Basing-point pricing**. Certain cities or main centres are designated as basis points. All goods shipped from a given basis point are charged the same amount.
- **Freight-absorption pricing**. The seller pays all the shipping costs to obtain the desired business. This amounts to a price discount and is used as a promotional tactic.

CASE STUDY

KFC's pricing strategies[26]

Being number one isn't all it's cracked up to be, especially in an age where big isn't viewed as better, and consumers are inclined to support small, niche products and brands. The reality is that it's tough at the top. Just ask KFC. In 2004, KFC recognised that its position as market leader in South Africa was becoming the brand's Achilles heel. Amongst other factors that go with being at the top is pricing the products.

KFC is seen to be affordable. However, in comparison to other fast food retailers of chicken such as Chicken Licken and Hungry Lion, KFC is often at a premium. In fact KFC has always taken a hard line by never discounting or positioning on price, which is a tough stance to take in a category filled with price fighters.

In fact, many of KFC's competitors are all-out price fighters and seasoned discounters. Think of Roman's Pizza's blatant discount positioning, McDonald's small-change campaigns and Steers 2-for-1 Wacky Wednesday specials.

Continue to next page

Continued from previous page

Yet KFC consumers are not concerned about price as confirmed by a TNS price elasticity study. As discussed previously, in a survey of 1 698 respondents, the KFC brand had the lowest absolute price elasticity of any brand for which TNS Research Surveys has calculated price elasticity in South Africa. This demonstrates that consumers are loyal to KFC despite pricing.

As market leader, KFC has deep pockets. Therefore, it's easy to assume that they would be successful. Yet, KFC's marketing spend has remained at a constant 5 per cent of sales, which means the only increases in spend are as a result of previously successful campaigns that have increased turnover significantly. In other words, KFC's deep pockets are a result of successful communication that has led to business success.

KFC also believes that while it has a sizeable marketing budget, this pool of money needs to deliver returns that far outweigh the investment. So while KFC has big budgets and is one of the biggest spenders in South Africa, it is still able to consistently deliver a return on marketing investment of 5:1.

While KFC is mighty, it sees its biggest competitor as itself since it measures itself on the Beat Year Ago figure. So while the brand has significant budgets, it still manages to outperform its own targets year on year, let alone its competitors.

Questions

1. Name and discuss the most likely pricing strategy that KFC chose.
2. Provide a discussion on why KFC's price elasticity is the lowest compared to other brands in the TNS survey.
3. Name and discuss the likely pricing objectives that KFC has chosen.

Summary

The three categories of pricing objectives were discussed in this chapter, as well as the factors that should be taken into consideration in pricing. It is also necessary for sellers to understand and be able to apply the calculation of mark-ups and mark-downs, and develop a pricing policy (fixed or variable, odd-cent, multiple, and so on) to achieve price objectives. These price objectives must correspond to the firm's marketing and enterprise objectives, and include the general sales, profit and competitive objectives. Selling price can be adjusted by means of mark-downs, discounts and mark-ups.

References

1. Lamb, C.W., Hair, J.F. & McDaniel, C.D. 2012. *Essentials of marketing*. 7th ed. Mason, USA: South-Western Cengage Learning, p. 559.
2. Adapted from Rix, P. 2003. *Essential marketing skills*. Australia: McGraw-Hill.
3. BusinessDictionary.com. 2013. *Price setting*. [Online] Available from: http://www.businessdictionary.com/definition/price-setting.html [Accessed: 2013-04-08].

4. Lamb et al., op. cit., pp. 561–564.
5. Arthur, L. & Demand Media. n.d. *What is demand estimation?* [Online] Available from: http://smallbusiness.chron.com/demand-estimation-24651.html [Accessed: 2013-04-09].
6. eHow money. 2013. *Marketing objectives and strategy.* [Online] Available from: http://www.ehow.com/info_7959338_marketing-objectives-strategy.html [Accessed: 2013-04-09].
7. Blythe, J. 2012. *Essentials of marketing*. 5th ed. Essex, England: Pearson, p. 159.
8. Fysul Mirza. 2011. *The law of demand*. [Online] Available from: http://studypoints.blogspot.com/2011/05/what-is-law-of-demand-explain-it-with_4680.html [Accessed: 2013-04-10].
9. Lamb et al., op cit., p. 577.
10. Tutor2u. n.d. *Seasonality: Introduction.* [Online] Available from: http://www.tutor2u.net/business/strategy/seasonality-introduction.html [Accessed: 2013-04-08].
11. BusinessDictionary.com. 2013. *Demand-based pricing.* [Online] Available from: http://www.businessdictionary.com/definition/demand-based-pricing.html [Accessed: 2013-04-09].
12. BusinessDictionary.com. 2013. *Pricing objectives.* [Online] Available from: http://www.witiger.com/marketing/pricingobjectives.htm [Accessed: 2013-04-08].
13. Salmon, R. 2004. *The changing world of TV displays: CRTs challenged by flat-panel displays.* [Online] Available from: http://tech.ebu.ch/docs/techreview/trev_298-salmon.pdf [Accessed: 2013-04-08].
14. Author unknown. n.d. *Pricing objectives.* [Online] Available from: http://www.witiger.com/marketing/ pricingobjectives.htm [Accessed: 2013-04-08].
15. Kolb, R.W. 2008. *Encyclopedia of business ethics and society.* SAGE. [Online] Available from: http://0-knowledge.sagepub.com.oasis.unisa.ac.za/view/ethics/n645.xml?rskey=hptmZc& row=1 [Accessed: 2013-04-10].
16. KnowThis.com. n.d. *Promotional pricing product pricing.* [Online] Available from: http://www.knowthis.com/principles-of-marketing-tutorials/setting-price-part-2/promotional-pricing-product-bundling/ [Accessed: 2013-04-10].
17. Boundless. n.d. *Demand-based pricing.* [Online] Available from: https://www.boundless.com/business/product-and-pricing-strategies/pricing-methods/demand-based-pricing/ [Accessed: 2013-04-10].
18. Cant, M.C., Van Heerden, C.H. & Ngambi, H.C. 2010. *Marketing management: A South African perspective.* Cape Town, South Africa: Juta & Co., p. 250.
19. Ibid, p. 251.
20. Business Dictionary.com. 2013. *Competition-based pricing.* [Online] Available from: http://www.businessdictionary.com/definition/competition-based-pricing.html [Accessed: 2013-04-10].
21. CEO2go. 2011. *Finance & Admin: Break-even and cash-flow 101.* [Online] Available from: http://www.ceo2go.com.au/our-services/finance-admin/break-even-and-cash-flow-101 [Accessed: 2013-04-10].
22. Kerin, R.A., Hartley, S.W. & Rudelius, W. 2011. *Marketing: The core.* New York, NY: McGraw-Hill Irwin, pp. 278–279.
23. Cant et al., op. cit.
24. BusinessDictionary.com. 2013. *Promotional pricing.* [Online] Available from: http://www.businessdictionary.com/definition/promotional-pricing.html [Accessed: 2013-04-10].

25. BusinessDictionary.com. 2013. *Geographic pricing.* Available from: http://www.businessdictionary.com/definition/geographic-pricing.html [Accessed: 2013-04-10].

26. Van Heerden, C.H. 2013. *Contemporary retail and marketing case studies.* Claremont, South Africa: Juta & Co.; also adapted from Franching.com. 2013. KFC Business Overview. [Online] Available from http://www.franchising.com/kfc/overview.html [Accessed: 2013-04-10].

Promotion decisions

CHAPTER

8

✓ Learning objectives

After studying this chapter, you should be able to:

- understand the components of the marketing communication decision;
- understand the influence of marketing communications on the marketing mix; and
- evaluate the impact of advertising, personal selling, sales promotion, direct marketing, and public relations and sponsorships on the marketing communication mix.

Introduction

In our society, communication is of the utmost importance. In our daily lives we see the influence of the communication revolution – cell phones, computers, satellite linkups and social media are the most visible part of the communication revolution. An uprising and coup in Egypt, shooting incidents in Russia, a plane crash in San Francisco and a presidential election in the US can all be witnessed from our living rooms, and we can share in the tragedies and triumphs of the world.

The business world also communicates with its markets. This communication process aims to achieve three objectives:[1]

- **To inform**. The company must inform potential customers about the availability of the product or service. Most of us have read or viewed with interest the promotional material about the introduction of the new innovative Google Glass, which displays information in a smartphone-like hands-free format that connects to the Internet and works via voice commands. The information that is presented can be classified as an effort to inform us (the potential target market) about the availability of this technology.
- **To persuade**. The aim of marketing is to sell – that means in essence that the potential customer must be persuaded to buy the product. Even the most mundane advertisement includes an element of persuasion. When we see an advertisement for

'The communication process aims to achieve three objectives:

- To inform
- To persuade
- To remind.'

toothpaste and the message states: 'Buy XYZ toothpaste for the best cavity prevention', we are being persuaded by the manufacturer to buy XYZ toothpaste and no other brand.

- **To remind**. Consumers tend to forget communication messages, which is why manufacturers must remind them about their products or services. Eskom has inserts during prime time television warning consumers of high energy consumption, and reminding them which appliances around the house can be switched off in an effort to conserve energy.

The communication process is explained in Figure 8.1.

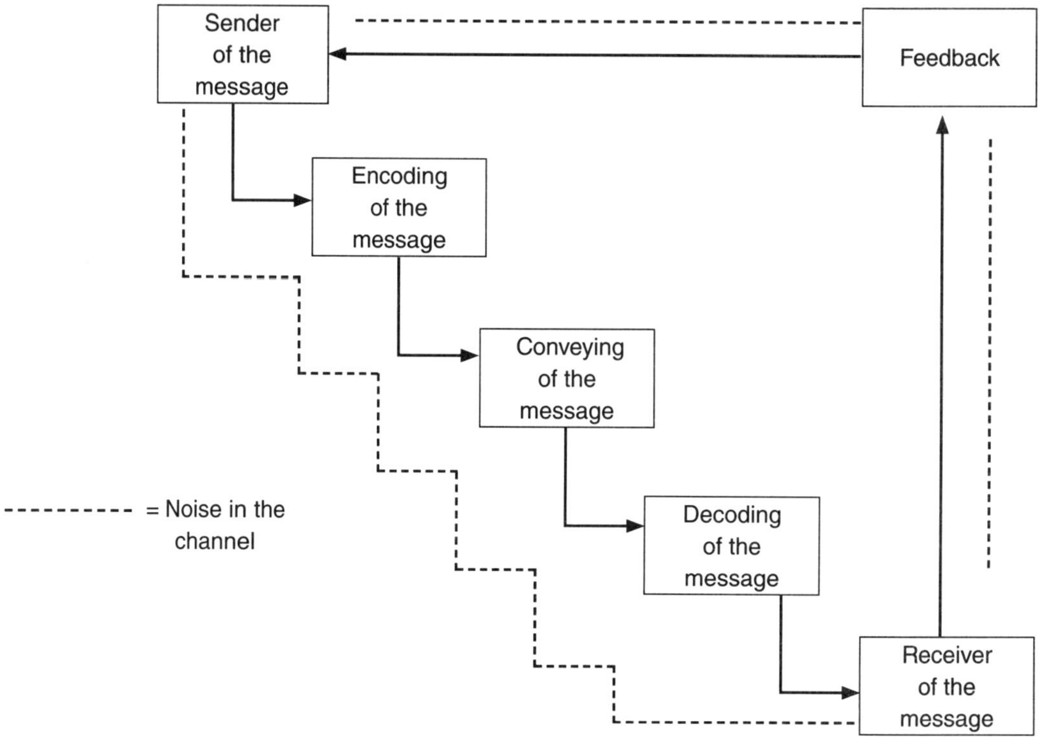

Figure 8.1 The communication model

As can be seen in Figure 8.1, there is a source that communicates the message to a target audience, which is called the receiver of the message. The *source* must be credible in the eyes of the consumer or the message will not have the intended effect.

The *message* that is encoded must meet the following requirements:

- It must attract and hold the attention of the target audience.
- It must convey a message that the audience will be able to understand.
- It must convince the audience about the benefits mentioned in the message.
- It must enable the audience to react positively, for example state where the product will be available.

The *transmission* that takes place can be through two basic communication channels, namely personal and non-personal. The personal channel is, for example, the salesperson who communicates in person with the consumer, while the non-personal communication channel is mass media such as newspapers, television and magazines. The *decoding* process is the way in which the *receiver* hears, reads or views the message. After the message has been received by the audience, the source or communicator will receive *feedback* to determine whether it has been correctly received by the audience. This is usually done by means of market research.

'The non-personal communication channel is made up of the mass media such as newspapers, television and magazines.'

During the whole process of communication, noise occurs. Noise means that a message has been distorted because of disturbances. The following three types of disturbances can occur:

- **Internal disturbances** occur when consumers disagree with the message. An advertisement promoting a certain restaurant can cause, for example, an internal disturbance for customers who had a bad service experience with this restaurant before.
- **External disturbances** happen when a physical disturbance prevents consumers from receiving the message correctly. Those with PVR decoders can fast-forward advertisements which create an external disturbance if they choose not to view them.
- **Competitive disturbances** occur when, for example, two competing services are advertised on the same page of a website. As a result of this disturbance, both competitors will lose some exposure to their target audience.

Integrated marketing communication

Integrated marketing communication (IMC) is necessary in a business so that synergy can be achieved in the communication with the consumer. The four basic instruments that can be used to communicate with the consumer are *advertising, personal selling, sales promotion and public relations and sponsorships*. In addition, *direct marketing* is also added as a communication instrument. These instruments will be discussed in the following sections. It is important that the marketer uses the optimal combination of the instruments to reach the target audience. To accomplish this, the marketer should follow an *integrated marketing communication approach.*

'The four basic instruments that can be used to communicate with the consumer are

- advertising;
- personal selling;
- sales promotion; and
- public relations and sponsorships.'

Marketing communication planning

Marketing communication with the consumer is not a random process. The large and successful organisations follow the basic principles of management, namely *planning, implementation* and *control*, with their marketing communications. This management of the marketing communication effort is divided into the following nine steps:

1. Determine the marketing communication opportunity or threat.
2. Determine the communication objectives.

Example *E*

Collect-a-Can[2]

At the core of this brand (Collect-a-Can) lies the issue of environmental responsibility, socioeconomic development and job creation. Through can collections and recovery projects, Collect-a-Can delivers on its promise to keep the environment clean.

Target market

Collect-a-Can speaks to a broad target market, which reaches across living standard measures (LSMs) 1–10. It includes collectors and recycling agents who fall into the lower LSMs, whilst also communicating with the corporate market in terms of sponsorships, as well as government and, of course, the general public.

Marketing strategies

All elements of the marketing mix have been used to communicate with these markets, from television commercials for launching various campaigns to radio and print. The brand also made use of outdoor advertising such as billboards and buses, as well as digital mobile campaigns. Collect-a-Can is active in Namibia and Botswana, where the same strategies are used. The brand is positioned in the market as the leader in can recovery, and is committed to retaining this position.

3. Organise the marketing communication effort.
4. Identify the target audience.
5. Determine the communication message.
6. Select the correct communications mix.
7. Calculate the budget required.
8. Implement the communications plan.
9. Measure the results (the control process).

Let us now look at the steps in the marketing communication plan in more detail.

Step 1: Determine the marketing communication opportunity or threat

Opportunities, such as a strong surge in the demand for a service or a new application of a product, may be the reason why a manufacturer or retailer decides to commence with a new marketing communications campaign. However, it is not always an opportunity that results in a business embarking on a marketing communications effort. In some cases, a negative issue must be addressed, and because it is done proactively, the business can reduce the damage to the image of the organisation.

Step 2: Determine the communication objectives

We saw earlier that the three basic objectives of a marketing communications campaign are to *inform*, to *persuade* and to *remind* the consumer. The following sub-objectives may be identified:

- To **create awareness** about the product. When tablets were first launched, the objective was to create awareness about this new product.
- To **create understanding** about the product. After the initial launch of tablets, potential customers needed to be educated on how to use the tablets.
- To **create changes or change perceptions about the product**. Consumers initially had negative perceptions about tablets with allegations that they may contribute to the formation of brain tumours. The manufacturers needed to change these negative perceptions.
- To **reward positive behaviour** (create positive enforcement) towards the product or store. Nowadays, many retail outlets use loyalty cards to reward customers if they make regular purchases from their stores. Customers earn loyalty points, which they may redeem for cash-back vouchers.

Step 3: Organise the marketing communication effort

Once objectives have been set, the organisation must determine whether it has the *resources* to achieve them. A recipe for certain disaster would be to set objectives for which 10 salespeople are required when the organisation does not have a sales force at all. This means realities such as the *current organisational structure* must be taken into account after the objectives have been set. The organisation should try to operate within the parameters of the organisational structure.

Step 4: Identify the target audience

The *target audience* is all the people in the marketplace that the organisation can reach by using a combination of communication instruments. Not all of these people will, however, buy the product for various reasons (for example the geographic location of the store). Using a billboard, for example, to reach all the people living in a certain area (the target audience) may be effective, but not all of them will become customers. Only those people who do will form part of the organisation's *target market*.

Step 5: Determine the communication message

Conveying the *right message* is the most important factor in the marketing communication campaign. Think about any memorable communication campaign (for example a television advertisement). It probably provided an entertaining, concise message about the range of services offered by the organisation.

'Once the objectives have been set, the organisation must determine whether it has the resources to achieve them.'

Step 6: Select the right communications mix

The right *communications mix* refers to the use of the communication instruments available. It was said previously that advertising, sales promotion, personal selling, and public relations and sponsorships are the four communications instruments. All four of these instruments may be needed to sell some products, for example perfume. It is possible to advertise in newspapers, on television and in magazines. This can be combined with personal selling by the manufacturer's own sales force. The manufacturer could promote the product by organising a contest, while a press release could be issued to obtain publicity.

'The right communications mix refers to the use of the communication instruments available.'

Step 7: Calculate the budget required

The *amount of money available for the communications campaign* will determine factors such as the duration of the campaign and what media instruments will be used. In most cases, a certain amount of money is set aside for promoting the product.

Step 8: Implement the communications plan

The *time frame* of the campaign must be determined. Will the campaign run for a week, a month or a year? The *responsibilities of the people involved* with the campaign must be determined.

Step 9: Measure the results (the control process)

This is one of the most difficult factors in the communication campaign. How does one *measure the results* of the campaign? One can do *market*

> **DEFINITION**
>
> **Advertising**
> Advertising is the activity of attracting public attention with non-personal presentation and promotion of ideas, products and services by an identified sponsor who paid for the communication of information, which is usually persuasive in nature.

research, but it is always difficult to determine the reliability of this as there are a number of other factors that could contribute to the increase in sales of a product. For example, a competitor may have ceased trading.

Advertising

Advertising is the most visible part of marketing and is perceived to be the one marketing communication instrument that will always deliver the message to the consumer.

If we examine the definition of advertising, we can see that there are certain key concepts to describe what advertising can do for the marketer:

- The first key concept is *non-personal*, which means that advertising is not person-to-person communication. Advertising takes place in the mass media, such as a radio advertisement during a show on 5FM which has many thousands of listeners.
- The second key concept is *ideas, products* and *services* which implies that advertising can be used to promote an idea (for example the 'Stop Koni' campaign that went viral, or the drink more milk with the 'Got milk?' campaign), or a service such as a cell phone provider, or a conventional product such as shoe polish.
- The third key concept is *identifiable sponsor*. Advertising is used as a means of promotion by a person, business or organisation. There is always a sponsor that can be identified in advertising.
- The last key concept is *paid*. There is always a sponsor in advertising that is prepared to pay (invest) money to promote his or her product, service or idea.

Different types of advertising

In this section we look at the different types of advertising that can be used.

Product advertising

Product advertising is the most straightforward type of advertising and is widely used in South Africa. Every time we see a television advertisement promoting Colgate toothpaste, we can say that it is an example of product advertising.

Institutional advertising

An institution such as the Cancer Association of South Africa (Cansa) or the Drive Dry campaign makes use of advertisements to promote awareness about cancer or to urge people to not drink and drive.

Pioneer advertising

This type of advertisement is used to promote a brand new concept or service for the first time. When PayPal was introduced into the South

African market, this kind of advertisement was used to inform the audience about the availability of the new concept of a widely used secure online payment system.

Comparative advertising

Comparative advertising is used when two products are physically compared in an advertisement with a message that one product is better than the other. This type of advertisement is used extensively in countries such as the US; however, it is in fact unlawful to use comparative advertising in South Africa.[3]

'Comparative advertising is done when two products are physically compared in an advertisement with a message that one product is better than the other.'

Competitive advertising

This kind of advertising is regularly used when one company advertises that its product is better than the rest of the products on offer. Advertisements stating that a company is the best or that it is number one can be categorised as competitive advertisements. The First National Bank (FNB) advertisements are an example of this – the 'Steve' advertisements compare the benefits of using FNB versus those of other banks.

Defensive advertising

Defensive advertising is used by companies when they realise that a new threat (for example a new competitor) has entered the market and that their sales or market share may be harmed. The message usually states that the company has been in the marketplace for a number of years and that it has built up a loyal client base. What this type of advertisement is saying is that customers should stay with the tried and tested company and not be lured away by a new competitor in the hope of saving money. When 8ta was introduced, the other cellular network companies were quick to lower their cost structure. This was promoted, for instance, on TV, and is an example of defensive advertising.

Reminder advertising

Companies use reminder advertising to remind consumers about a product that has been on the market for some time. For example, Coca-Cola launches various advertisements regularly to remind consumers of the product.

Reinforcement advertising

This type of advertisement is used after the sale has taken place, and is used to reinforce the positive attitude of the buyer. We usually see this kind of advertisement for cars. The Kia advertisement states that the Kia Picanto was the most fuel-efficient car in its class in the Total Savings Run. By doing this, Kia is telling Picanto owners that they made the right decision to buy this car.

'Reinforcement advertising is used after the sale has taken place to reinforce the positive attitude of the buyer.'

'Above-the-line communication refers to advertisements in the mass media such as the press, radio, television and cinema.'

'Below-the-line communication refers to the use of media such as direct mail, packaging, merchandising and, more recently, social networks, podcasting and event marketing.'

Above-the-line and below-the-line communication

It is important to explain these two concepts:

- **Above-the-line communication**. This refers to advertisements in the mass media such as the press, radio, television and cinema. Earnings for an advertising agency that executes the advertisement are above-the-line in the form of a commission.
- **Below-the-line communication**. This refers to the use of media such as direct mail, packaging, merchandising and, more recently, social networks, podcasting and event marketing. The advertising agency earns a fee for executing this activity. Most of the activities of below-the-line communication are classified as part of sales promotion (see the discussion later in this chapter).

Steps in managing the advertising campaign[4]

The nine steps in the advertising campaign will now be discussed in more detail.

Step 1: Analyse the present situation

The first step in the advertising campaign is to analyse the present situation. This must be done on a continuous basis, and forms part of the environmental scanning process. In this analysis, the market, the competitors and the product or service being sold must be analysed.

What is important to know about the consumers is who they are, what their preferences are, why are they buying the organisation's product or service, and what the factors are that affect the demand for the product. Competitors must also be evaluated by examining their range of products and services as well as their advertising campaigns, and how they are likely to respond to this particular campaign.

The organisation's own product or service must also be evaluated to determine where it can improve and what the competitive advantage is. It may be that the product is delivering superior value to that of competitors, or the opposite may be true where the organisation's product is perceived to be inferior. Either way, the organisation must determine whether it has the capability of producing sufficient volumes if sales increase due to the campaign.

Step 2: Set the advertising objectives

As is the case with any business decision, quantifiable objectives must be set, such as what basic message is to be delivered and to which target audience, the desired results of the campaign, and which criteria will be used to measure the success of the campaign. For example, the advertising objective may be to increase awareness of the product in the target market from the present 0% (nobody knows about it) to 20% by the end of December 2014.

Step 3: Determine the advertising budget

The key issue with most organisations is that they have a limited amount of money to spend on advertising. In most cases, the company will spend the amount of money it can afford. Some of the most frequently used methods to determine the amount of money to be used for advertising include the following:

- **Look at the previous advertising budget**. The rationale is to spend the same amount as for the previous year as sales may have increased during the past year and the amount is thus sufficient to increase sales for the current year.
- **Spend what the competitors are spending**. If an organisation knows the advertising budget of its main competitors, it may budget to spend the same amount.
- **Budget for a fixed percentage of the sales of the previous year**. Some companies will budget say 2% of the previous year's sales as a benchmark figure for the advertising campaign for the next year.

Step 4: Select the media

There are different types of advertising media that can be used:

- **Print media** are media such as newspapers, magazines, outdoor advertising in the form of billboards and direct mail that can be used to promote the product or service.
- **Audio-visual media** include television, which is widely used especially by the larger corporations. Radio and cinema are used more by small and medium enterprises (SMEs) as a means of promoting their products and services. Regional radio stations are mainly used to promote SME products and services. Another form of audio-visual media is the Internet and social media, which is of vital importance for any service organisation and increasingly becoming more relevant as more consumers shift towards the Internet.

Step 5: Create the message

Different approaches are used to create a message that will relate to the target market. Some of the approaches used include the following:

- **Rational approach**. The facts are stated so consumers obtain an objective and factual account of what the product or service can do for them. An advertisement stating that owning a Mercedes-Benz is an investment and the resale value is guaranteed to be the same over a three-year period is termed a rational approach.
- **Humorous approach**. This is a favourite of many advertisers. The Nando's advertisements are examples of this, from their 'Last dictators' to '#25 reasons to love South Africa' campaigns.
- **Fear-inducing approach**. This is used to illustrate the negative consequences of not using the advertised product. For example, an advertisement may show how to avoid a horrific accident by fitting the advertised brand of shock absorbers. Advertisements

for antibacterial soaps are another example. This approach is often used in public service advertisements. The Drive Dry 'Who's driving you home tonight?' campaign, which highlighted the severe consequences of drinking and driving, is one example. Another example is anti-smoking advertisements that show people who cannot speak as a result of throat cancer.

Step 6: Pre-test the advertising campaign

In most cases, the advertisement must be pre-tested to determine whether it will convey the intended message. A panel of consumers is selected from the target audience, and their reaction is evaluated. In some cases, the research with the consumer panel will indicate major problems that can be rectified prior to the launch of the advertisement.

Facts about social media for business[5]

General social media facts

- Social media is used by 62 % of the adult population.
- People spend more time on online social networks than they do e-mailing, searching or shopping.
- Social media is the most popular online activity.
- Of online time, 22 % is spent on social networks.
- Roughly 40 % of people use mobile devices to access their social media accounts.

Specific social networks

- Facebook is still the most popular social network.
- There are over 800 million profiles on Facebook.
- More than half of Facebook users access it every day.
- Of mobile users, 42 % share multimedia on Facebook.
- Of Facebook users, 51% are more likely to buy from brands they follow.
- Smartphone users now spend the same amount of time on social networking apps as they do playing games.
- Of Twitter users, 40 % search for products via Twitter on a regular basis.
- Of Twitter users, 64 % are more likely to buy from the brands they follow.
- Because of the information provided on Twitter, 12 % of people have bought a product.
- Pinterest is the third most popular social network, right behind Twitter and Facebook.
- Buyers referred from Pinterest are 10 % more likely to make a purchase.
- On mobile devices, Google+ is the second most used social network.

Demographic information

- Of 18- to 24-year-olds, 98 % use their social networking accounts every month.
- College towns have the highest Facebook logins.

Continue to next page

Continued from previous page

- Of Facebook users, 57% have completed some higher-institution qualification and 24% have degrees.
- Of Facebook users, 46% are 45 or older.
- Of Pinterest users, 60% are female.
- Of Pinterest users, 50% are in the US.
- Of Google+ users, 50% are 24 or younger.

Social media for business

- Of small businesses, 53% use social media.
- Of small businesses, 88% are using social media to get more exposure.
- Of small business decision makers, 60% spend less than R1 000 on social media.
- Of active social media users, 53% follow at least one brand.
- Of the world's top companies, 65% have active Twitter profiles.
- Of marketers, 90% use social media for business.
- Of marketers that use social media, 93% rate its tools as important.
- Of marketers, 43% have seen increased sales due to social campaigns.
- It only takes 20 people to build meaningful, many-to-many networking.

Social media for business-to-business (B2B)

- Of small to medium-sized business (SMEs) decision makers, 44% use social media.
- Of those SMEs decision makers, 86% use Facebook.
- Of SMEs decision makers, 41% use LinkedIn.
- Of SMEs, 33% use Twitter.

Social media and customer relations

- Of social media users, 20% are likely to purchase from a social media site.
- Of small business owners, 50% have gained new customers through various social media activities.
- Of consumers, 47% are fairly likely to buy from a brand they follow online.
- Active adult social media users are 75% more likely to spend more money on music.
- Active adult social media users are 47% more likely to spend more money on clothes, shoes and accessories.
- Social media users are willing to pay a premium of up to 21% for brands that deliver great service through social media.
- Social media users who have a great service experience tell an average of 42 people, compared to nine for those who are not using social channels.
- Of social media users, 60% are willing to post on Facebook about products or services if they receive a great deal or discount.
- Social media users who have a bad service experience will tell an average of 53 people, compared to 17 for those who are not using social channels.
- According to research from ComScore, brands that post at least once a day will reach 22% of their fans in a given week.

Step 7: Launch the advertising campaign

The advertising campaign is planned with a certain due date in mind. If a new product is to be launched, the manufacturing of the product and the launch of the advertising campaign must be synchronised to ensure that products are available at the right time, in the right place and in the right amount.

Step 8: Coordinate the advertising campaign

The advertising campaign must be coordinated with the other internal departments. This must be done so that if the advertisements elicit a reaction from the target audience, all the employees will be aware of the message and any undertakings that may have been made in it, and they will be able to communicate the correct information to customers.

Step 9: Revise the campaign

The question to be answered at the end of the campaign is whether it achieved its stated objectives. This is done with the aid of market research, and should be the input for the start of a new advertising campaign.

Personal selling

> **DEFINITION**
>
> **Personal selling**
> Personal selling is one-on-one communication between the customer and the business through its representative as a means of convincing the specifically targeted customer to purchase the product, service or idea.

The sales force forms an integral part of the marketing communication mix. It differs from the advertising component, which is the non-personal communication with the consumer, in the sense that in **personal selling**, there is one-on-one personal communication with the prospective consumer. Examples of personal selling include:

- delivery staff who sell (for example a newspaper delivery person);
- a teller in a bank;
- a travelling sales representatives (for example of skincare products from Israel); and
- point-of-sale merchandising.

Let us examine this definition in more detail:

- It is a personal (face-to-face) selling situation.
- The per capita costs involved are higher in reaching the customer.
- There can be a greater impact on consumers as they are directly confronted by the salesperson and the product, service or idea.
- The biggest advantage of personal selling is the fact that it is flexible communication. The salesperson can adjust his or her message to provide more information or to overcome objections.
- Certain products, such as expensive durable products (for example cars or appliances), actually require the services of a salesperson as a means of securing the sale.

Types of salespeople

Three basic types of salespeople can be identified:

- **Order getters** prospect for new customers. For example, sales representatives for a skincare range look out for new salons to call on. If they obtain new business from new customers, they are classified as order getters.
- **Order takers** call on existing customers who have already ordered their products before, and their objective is to make another sale. They are therefore interested in repeat sales from an existing customer base.
- **Support personnel** support the order getters and order takers, and execute the sales orders. An example is the technical assistant who provides an advisory service over the telephone to the customers.

Steps in the personal selling process

There are several steps in the personal selling process:[6]

- **Attaining knowledge**. A thorough knowledge of the customer's characteristics, motives, needs and behaviour is essential at the beginning of the selling process. The salesperson needs to be equipped not only with information about the clients and their industry, but also with detailed product information. The salespeople need to understand the motives and buying behaviour of prospective buyers.
- **Prospecting**. The focus is to seek new customers who can be identified in various ways, for example by following up on referrals from existing clients or by buying a database from companies that specialise in selling this kind of information.
- **The pre-approach to selling**. At this stage, the salesperson must obtain enough information about the prospective customer (the needs of the customer) to stand a reasonable chance of making a sale to the customer. This knowledge is important as it will assist in determining an appropriate sales method, and predict possible problem areas that can help avoid costly mistakes.
- **Making the approach**. With the initial approach it is all about first impressions. The saying: 'You don't have a second chance to make a first impression' is very true. It is important for salespeople to gain the attention of their prospects immediately and win their trust to make a good sales presentation.
- **Presentation**. The presentation is the cornerstone of the sale. Salespeople must stimulate interest and establish contact as a starting point. They may wish to present themselves as a problem solver for, say, the do-it-yourself painter. They would then present a way of cleaning rollers and brushes after the painting job is finished. They can also demonstrate the product in order to maintain interest and arouse desire of the customer.

The ultimate purpose of presentation is to show how the product can satisfy customers' needs and provide a solution to their problems.

- **Handling objections**. There are usually objections to a product or service, such as that the price is too high. The salesperson must anticipate this objection and must be ready with a sound reason why the price is high or why the product is superior by emphasising its distinctive qualities. Testimonials, money-back guarantees and warranties are a few examples that could be used to win over hesitant buyers.
- **Closing the sale**. It is important to reassure customers to get them to agree to the sale. A paint salesperson may close the sale by asking about a desired delivery date. (If the answer is that delivery is required by a certain date, the salesperson can rest assured that the sale has been closed.) The purchase must be packaged properly and handed over to the customer in a speedy and accurate manner.
- **Follow-up**. This is the step in the personal selling process that is the most neglected by salespeople. Regardless of how big the order was, it is important that a follow-up be done with all customers to find out if they are satisfied with their purchase. It is a proven fact that if the first order proceeds with no problems, it is likely that a long-term relationship will develop with the customer, which results in repeat orders and possible referrals.
- **Staying in close contact**. The salesperson should maintain a database of all clients' information. The function of an efficient database is to utilise client information for the purposes of gaining future sales and establishing a long-term relationship. Sustained long-term relationships acknowledge the importance of the Pareto principle, namely that 80% of an organisation's business comes from 20% of its customers.

Sales promotion

Sales promotion is used as a short-term communication instrument to promote the company's product, service or idea. It complements advertising, personal selling and public relations (the other three elements of the marketing communication mix), and is specifically aimed at ensuring that the customer buys with incentive-offering and interest-creating activities.

Sales promotions, in general, create a positive consumer attitude because of the perception that they might not have to pay for something. Examples of sales promotions include free samples or sales contests by manufacturers for their salespeople. The objective of this is to persuade them to sell more to intermediaries (wholesalers and retailers). A vacation and travel contest directed at the intermediaries could also be run to encourage them to stock more of the product.

Consumer sales promotions

Sales promotions are regarded as an aid to elicit a specific response from the consumer. A sales promotion deal stating: 'Buy one bar of soap and get a second one free' elicits a specific response from consumers – they will buy a bar of soap to take advantage of the offer. On the other hand, sales promotions can also achieve other objectives such as building brand loyalty and creating product awareness. Examples of consumer sales promotions include sampling and free trials of products, contests and sweepstakes, various price incentives and loyalty programmes.[7]

Sales promotions are also a flexible weapon in the hands of marketers to react to sudden actions by competitors. If their biggest competitor promotes heavily in the mass media, they can react quickly by introducing a sales promotion campaign, for example a contest for a family to visit Disney World. This will counteract the communications effort of the competitor to a large extent.

Trade promotions

Trade promotions are aimed at making intermediaries (the wholesalers and retailers) buy and sell large quantities of the company's products. In so doing, the company increases its sales volume to the intermediaries, which should increase sales to the final consumer. Trade shows are an example of promoting products, as intermediaries will attend them. A sales contest is another example that can be used. A company may launch a contest aimed at retailers, with the first prize being an overseas trip for the one who sells the most in the current financial year. Examples of trade promotions include handing out free products at trade shows, company calendars and offers of special prices.[8]

'Trade promotions are aimed at making intermediaries buy and sell large quantities of a company's products.'

Sales force promotions

Sales force promotions are aimed at the company's own sales force as a means of encouraging them to sell more of their product to intermediaries, increase distribution, promote new or seasonal products, and find prospects and build up morale within the company. Examples used to achieve this objective are sales conventions held for salespeople. This kind of convention is used to motivate the sales personnel to sell more, and is usually linked to a contest to determine the most successful salesperson. Prizes could be an overseas holiday, financial incentives and awards. Other activities that take place include sales meetings and manuals, training programmes and sales presentations. Examples of sales force promotions include contests for the sales force, bonuses, company-branded gifts and vacations.[9]

Direct marketing

Direct marketing has grown, and has become recognised as one of the more effective methods of marketing communications. Direct marketing combines the elements of advertising, sales promotion and personal selling, and it leads to a direct sales transaction without the presence and mediation of an intermediary. We can say that direct marketing is about acquiring and retaining customers. If we analyse the definition we see that the focus of direct marketing is as follows:

- **Response**. Direct marketing aims to make consumers send in order forms by mail or over the Internet, and to make telephone calls in response to invitations and offers.
- **Interaction**. Direct marketing is interactive in the sense that there are two parties involved, namely the supplier and the customer.
- **Relationship**. In some cases, the process is on-going so a relationship develops between the two parties.
- **Databases**. A database is constructed that focuses on weeding out unproductive activities so that cost-effective procedures can be determined.
- **Part of an overall strategy**. Direct marketing forms an integral part of the overall marketing communications strategy.

DEFINITION

Direct marketing
Direct marketing is when marketing materials are provided directly to the consumer on an individual basis, eliminating the middleman by communicating information about a product or service directly, which aims to elicit an action.

Direct marketing is therefore a method of *supplying a direct message* by using a variety of communication channels (for example direct mail, the Internet, and so on) and a choice of distribution channels (for example mail order and e-commerce). Apart from the advertising medium and the physical delivery of the ordered product, there are no further intermediaries involved. This means that the supplier cannot lose control of the distribution channel. Table 8.1 lists the benefits of direct marketing to customers and marketers.

Table 8.1 Benefits of direct marketing to customers and marketers

Benefits for the customer	Benefits for the marketer or supplier
• Direct marketing supports the trend of 'cocooning' (the trend to centre activities on the family and home) • It provides greater shopping convenience and service – there is no need to visit overcrowded stores and shopping malls • It allows the use of credit cards and other forms of electronic payment (the move towards a cashless society)	• Direct marketing provides the means to build a lasting relationship with the customer • It is aimed directly at an identified person or household • Results can be precisely measured • It provides the marketer with a database • The supplier retains control of the distribution channel

'Direct marketing is a method of supplying a direct message by using a variety of communication channels and a choice of distribution channels.'

Direct marketing methods

There are various direct marketing methods that can be used. The alternatives are shown in Figure 8.2, and will be discussed in more detail.

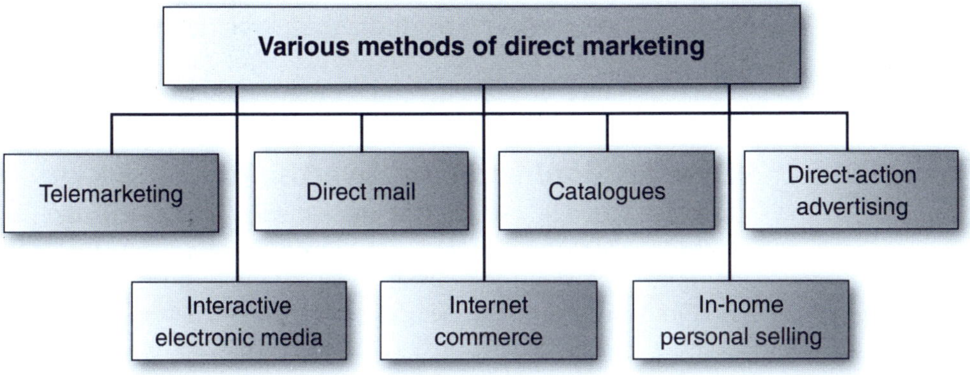

Figure 8.2 Direct marketing methods

Telemarketing

Telemarketing is marketing by means of the telephone where a salesperson sells, solicits or promotes a product or service to prospective customers. Two types of telemarketing are identified, namely inbound and outbound. *Inbound telemarketing* is when the telephone call originates from the customer. This is in response to a marketer's actions. It is important that the marketer allows enough time so that the customer can reach the number on the telephone to place an order. An example would be Verimark advertisements, which provide consumers with a contact number.

Outbound telemarketing originates from marketers and is aimed at opening new accounts, servicing clients, and acquainting themselves with their clients. A telephone call from a salesperson trying to sell a cell phone contract is an example of outbound telemarketing.

Direct mail

Direct mail uses the postal services or a private delivery organisation to deliver the product or the message to the customer. One of the advantages of direct mail is that it can capture the attention of the reader, and the message can be personalised. An example would be mail from a fashion retail outlet, which includes a personalised card, encouraging the consumer to sign up.

'Direct mail uses the postal services or a private delivery organisation to deliver the product or the message to the customer.'

The disadvantages of direct mail include that it is sometimes perceived as junk mail, there is a high cost per prospect involved, and the effectiveness is dependent on the quality of the mailing list (which can be outdated).

Two types of mailing lists may be used: the internal list is available from the marketer and consists of addresses of current and previous clients. External lists are collected and sold by outside sources.

Catalogues

Catalogues have been around for many years. In the past, one could buy a wide range of products from catalogues, including clothing and personal items. One of the most important factors is the perception of the company sending out the catalogue. If there is trust between the company and the consumers, the catalogue can be a very effective communication instrument.

Direct-action/response advertising

In direct-action advertising, the mass media (such as television and newspapers) are used to elicit a response from the customer. A toll-free number is provided to make it easier for the customer to respond. Methods of advertising include exhibits and direct mail. Note that telemarketing and direct-action advertising are closely linked.

> **DEFINITION**
>
> **Public relations**
> Public relations refers to the management task that aims to build good relations with the public. The internal public of the business includes the employees and the shareholders. The external public includes the government, suppliers and competitors. Public relations aims to enhance the reputation of a company by communicating with and through the media, which are key influencers in the hopes of obtaining favourable publicity, building social responsibility, or preventing and minimising negative publicity.

Interactive electronic media

When an individual television set is connected to a computer via a telephone line, a customer who wants to buy product seen on television may do so with a credit card using the computer. This type of technology has been replaced by Internet commerce.

Internet commerce (also called e-commerce)

E-commerce works just like interactive media, but is more sophisticated. Anyone who owns a computer and is linked to the World Wide Web can access e-commerce. Payment can be done by credit card or electronic transfer. It is now possible to do banking over the Internet, while books, music, computers, air tickets and a host of other products and services are traded on the Internet.

In-home personal selling

This type of direct marketing has reached the declining phase of its life cycle. It is still used by certain cosmetic houses, but has been side-lined by other direct marketing methods as a means of generating leads. This is partly due to the high cost of in-home selling and the fact that fewer people are at home during the day.

Public relations and sponsorships

Public relations is a separate part of management that attracts a great deal of attention. People tend to confuse public relations and marketing communications, thinking they are the same thing. We will, therefore, first define public relations and identify the place of marketing and public relations in the business.

Publicity is a marketing communication instrument used by public relations practitioners to fulfil the objectives of public relations. One method of publicity is *sponsorships*, which is used by marketing communications to achieve the communication objectives of the business.

From the definition in the margin, we can see that the public relations function includes a number of people and institutions inside and outside the organisation. Not all of these people are customers – in fact, most of them are not. This is where the marketing function comes into play. Marketing focuses on the consumer or potential consumer. Marketing seeks ways of satisfying the needs of the customer base while at the same time fulfilling the needs of the business, namely profitability maximisation.

Public relations activities

Following are examples of public relations activities:

- **Open-house policy and tours**. The value of a plant tour if the company is manufacturing a product cannot be discounted. These visits help to create a feeling of transparency and goodwill to the ultimate benefit of the company. An example of this is the guided tours by companies such as Toyota and BMW.
- **Exhibitions and shows**. The activities at exhibitions and shows also fall within the parameters of a public relations exercise.
- **Organised social activities**. The company golf day is an example of an organised social activity that is used to project a favourable image of the company. It is also a forum for networking with the company's external public.
- **Lobbying**. Lobbyists work with government representatives on behalf of the company. These lobbyists are used to inform and persuade the government on behalf of the company.

Publicity

Publicity is part of the marketing communications function and can be described as the non-personal influencing of consumers by means of the media. This is done by using the current news value of the company's products or services to obtain a favourable and free review of the products or services in the media. Some of the best-known forms of publicity include the following:

'Publicity is part of the marketing communications function and can be described as the non-personal influencing of consumers by means of the media.'

- **Press/news releases** contain newsworthy information provided to the press, and relate to the introduction of new products or the significant improvement of old ones. The securing of a large contract or the positive results obtained from an independent research body can be used in the press release.
- **Special events** can be organised by the business to gain attention and to create an opportunity for journalists to write about the business. A new holiday destination may result in, for example, inviting journalists for a free weekend in the hope that the resulting press reports will bring positive publicity.
- **Sponsorship** is gaining favour with companies as a marketing communication vehicle because it ties in with the greater realisation that companies should be seen to be socially responsible citizens. The investment in the broader community by means of sponsorships is an effective method of gaining favourable publicity. Sport sponsorships are a particularly effective way of obtaining publicity.

Although a company should always strive to obtain positive publicity, it sometimes happens that negative publicity occurs, which may have an immediate adverse effect on the company. The best approach for the business is to manage the crisis in an open and proactive way, and to try to rectify the problem(s) as soon as possible. Corrective action also has news value, and the media are sure to report on it. A company that manages negative publicity responsibly can turn the negative publicity into a positive action.

CASE STUDY

Standard Bank[10]

Introduction

For a bank to survive and prosper as a financial institution for well over a century, conventional wisdom would dictate a deep and unshakeable commitment to stability and dependability; and yet, since its birth when it rooted itself in a fledging South Africa, a defining characteristic of Standard Bank has been its readiness to explore uncharted territory.

Since its inception, Standard Bank has always felt that as an institution with considerable influence it could not stand apart from its communities; it must become a part of the fabric of society. Standard Bank recognises that the long-term sustainability of its business is closely linked to the societies in which it operates, and to realise this aspiration, it contributes 1% of its profit after tax to social relevance programmes. Standard Bank has a clear social strategy which focuses on supporting development initiatives in education, health and wellness, and enterprise development. It also focuses on certain 'green' issues that benefit the environment and on transformation. Another critical focus for the bank is its employees as in order for business to be sustainable, it believes it needs skilled, healthy staff working in thriving, growing economies.

Making internal connections – uniting 50 000 employees in 33 countries behind a new rallying cry

The executive team spent time fine-tuning the business strategy into specific goals that would work globally and across business units. In addition, the bank sought the views of all 50 000 employees across 33 countries through an employee engagement survey called 'Heartbeat' to provide insights into what employees thought of Standard Bank, its leaders and chosen direction. This feedback was used to build 'connections' with employees, further shaping Standard Bank's future. Standard Bank executives hosted 58 road shows in 26 countries at 33 locations around the world to connect with employees and to share insights into the group's history and plans for the future. Following a 'talk show' format, time was spent discussing the key focus areas and implications for each country, and employees were given opportunities to ask questions.

Continue to next page

Continued from previous page

At the same time, an internal social networking site called BlueConnection was launched. The site was a first for Standard Bank, and it enables employees around the world to connect with each other. Using features common to Facebook and Twitter, BlueConnection encourages employees to make connections, collaborate more easily and share ideas across borders and oceans.

Having laid the foundations for internal alignment, understanding and support for the business strategy and a clear brand promise, Standard Bank was ready to take the message externally, to start to prove that Standard Bank was moving with the times.

Connecting to 475 million consumers and stakeholders across 33 countries
What was essential was that the campaign was not developed out of a single market such as South Africa and that it had to be 'owned' by all the countries, ensuring a high degree of local relevance.

To ensure that all messaging had a locally relevant 'flavour', each market was encouraged to create its own campaigns, leveraging off the universal creative idea of 'making connections to move our customers forward' while tapping into local insights. For example, whereas the global campaign talks about 'connecting Africa to the world, and the world to Africa', the campaign in Jersey refers to 'connecting Jersey to emerging markets, and emerging markets to Jersey', and the campaign in Kenya talks about 'connecting Kenya to Africa and the rest of the world'.

A new creative look and feel was launched alongside the new positioning, utilising creative synergies through iconic design and audio mnemonics such as a uniform cadence and rhythm, which are easily applicable in each market, reinforcing the group's African roots.

This look and feel was extended across all campaigns to provide consistency and to achieve the desired breakthrough factor.

The campaign launched on 17 July 2009 across 33 markets simultaneously, comprising multiple levels of messages. At an international cross-border level, financial decision makers and cross-border travellers were targeted through broad reach elements of TV (for example CNN, CNBC Africa), print (for example *The Economist, Financial Times*) and outdoor (key international airports).

Additionally, for the first time substantial investment was put into digital marketing activities as well as launching their presence on digital platforms in the social media space. This was critical, given the bank's focus on Africa where the convergence of mobile and Internet platforms was beginning to dramatically change the classical marketing environment.

Standard Bank's step into social media platforms like Facebook, Twitter, YouTube and its blog also enabled it to tangibly reinforce 'making the right connections' by enabling real-time interactions and connecting its customers with the right country/department to help resolve their issues.

Continue to next page

Continued from previous page

From an in-country level, media were chosen that were specific to individual markets in order to further drive local relevance.

Results

Overall, the campaign was positively received in all markets of operation. While formal measurement and metrics are generally not available in most emerging markets, Standard Bank's home market of South Africa has been a good indicator of the success of the campaign.

Top-line results three weeks after launch indicated that the campaign was considered highly enjoyable, resonating on an emotional level with consumers as original, imaginative and informative. Liking levels exceeded norms at 8,13 out of 10, as did noting and main message takeout levels. In the digital environment, over 146 000 unique visitors to the global microsite were received, which was aimed at the corporate market. Over 120 enquiries were generated from this market via a microsite, which was a first for the bank. Similar success was seen in-country, with over 65 700 visitors accessing the South African microsite in a short period of time. Standard Bank's mobile marketing proved extremely effective, with over a 1,2% click-through rate to the new group and in-country mobile sites, the bulk of which came from their African markets. These social media platforms significantly improved Standard Bank's ability to manage its reputation in the informal social networking space as it could react in real-time.

Standard Bank has recently been independently evaluated and ranked as the most valuable banking brand in South Africa. It shot up the global rankings from position number 105 in 2010 to position 77 in 2011, with a brand value of $2,3 billion, 31 places and $400 million ahead of its nearest domestic competitor. Standard Bank was also awarded the top dealmaker in the African region by *The Banker*. This is an acknowledgement of the focus that it puts on its customers and clients, and its commitment to moving forward. *The Banker* also named Standard Bank as the best bank in Lesotho, Botswana, Malawi and Zimbabwe, while *Global Finance* awarded it the best bank in South Africa, Uganda, Namibia and the DRC. The Ask Afrika Trust Barometer rated Standard Bank as 'Most Trusted Company' and 'Most Sustainable Company', all demonstrating that Africa remains Standard Bank's calling card, and that Standard Bank is ideally positioned to capitalise on developments in the region.

Question

List, explain and discuss the various important promotional decisions that Standard Bank encountered.

Summary

In this chapter the components of the marketing communication decision as well as the influence of marketing communications on the marketing mix were discussed, and the impact of advertising, personal selling, sales promotion, direct marketing, and public relations and sponsorships on the marketing communications mix was evaluated.

References

1. Cant, M.C. 2011. *Marketing: An introduction*. Cape Town, South Africa: Juta & Co,. pp. 173–174.
2. Van Heerden, C.H. 2013. *Contemporary retail and marketing case studies*. Cape Town, South Africa: Juta & Co., pp. 14–17.
3. Rutherford, B.R. 2010. 'Trademarks and comparative advertising'. *Comparative and International Law Journal of Southern Africa*, 43(2), pp. 173–189.
4. Van Heerden, op. cit., pp. 60–87.
5. Mallon, S. 2012. *50 facts about social media for business*. [Online] Available from: http://blog.straightnorth.com/50-facts-about-social-media-for-business/ [Accessed: 2012-10-03].
6. Cant, op. cit., p. 183.
7. Du Plessis, F., Van Heerden, N. & Cook, G. 2010. *Integrated marketing communication*. 3rd ed. Pretoria, South Africa: Van Schaik, p. 179.
8. Ibid.
9. Ibid.
10. Van Heerden, op. cit., pp. 136–141.

CHAPTER 9

Distribution decisions (placement)

✓ Learning objectives

After studying this chapter, you should be able to:

- distinguish between the different types of distribution channel participants;
- discuss distribution channel design;
- identify and discuss various distribution channel activities;
- critically examine distribution channel management;
- appraise physical distribution (logistics);
- evaluate customer service;
- analyse the supply chain and the value chain;
- investigate distribution channels for services;
- explain import and export channels;
- discuss franchising; and
- understand vertical distribution systems or multilevel distribution.

Introduction

Distribution decision making starts with identifying characteristics of the product or service, and the target market to be served. The ultimate aim is to make the right products and services available in the right quantities at the right time in the right place – when and where customers want them.

A distribution channel usually consists of producers, consumers and any intermediaries that are aligned to provide a means of transferring title or possession of a product or service from a producer to a consumer. The participants are selected on their ability to satisfy customers in terms of product availability, convenience, price and after-sales service. The various participants are, in a sense, customers of each other. The chosen channel structure should enhance customer satisfaction, support the marketing objectives of each participant, and distribute the product efficiently by minimising total distribution costs. Finally, the nature of the product (such as its perishability, unit value, handling characteristics, technical complexity and standardisation) may lend itself to a particular type of distribution channel.

Distributing tea from tea plantations (the producer) situated in the Western Cape to retailers all over South Africa takes time and money, and forms a substantial part of the price of a box of tea. In effect, distribution contributes to the standard of living of a country. First of all, marketers use **distribution channels** to create exchanges with consumers. These exchanges facilitate the process of passing title or possession of a product from producer to consumer. Efficient and effective facilitation offers value to the consumer, and realises profits for the marketer. Effective distribution also complements the other elements of the marketing mix. Perishable products must be distributed quickly, expensive products must be sold in stores that are consistent with their image, and basic goods must be distributed to a large and geographically diverse market. Channel structure will then have an impact on costs and prices of products. Certain intermediaries take title to the product while others only perform certain functions and never own the goods. Service providers, such as hair stylists, deal directly with consumers but rely on distributors for supplies of hair care products. Transportation companies, financial institutions and other functional specialists also play specialised roles for channel members.

DEFINITION

Distribution channel

A distribution channel is the way in which a firm sells its products, including all the parties who play a part in the process, from production of the products to the final user.

Distribution channel participants

Before designing a channel of distribution, it is wise to find out whether the necessary intermediaries such as **wholesalers** and **retailers** exist, and are willing to carry the product. Intermediaries must be evaluated with respect to past sales, profits and clientele. Moreover, the entire marketing environment and its surroundings must be analysed – this includes competitors, political factors, economical factors, social factors, technological factors and legal factors. A company can eliminate intermediaries, but it cannot eliminate the functions they perform.

DEFINITION

Wholesaler

A wholesaler is a business that sells goods to other businesses such as retailers, and industrial, institutional or commercial users, who will then resell those goods to the final user.

The major channels of distribution used by marketers of consumer and organisational products are listed below. Channels may be distinguished by the number of intermediaries they include – the more intermediaries there are, the longer the channel is. The major *channels for consumer goods* are:

- producer ⟶ consumer;
- producer ⟶ retailer ⟶ consumer;
- service producer ⟶ agent ⟶ consumer;

- producer → wholesaler → retailer → consumer; and
- producer → wholesaler-agent → wholesaler → retailer → consumer.

Some examples are listed in the Definition box 'Distribution channels for consumer goods'.

The major channels for organisational products are:

- producer to user;
- producer to wholesaler to user; and
- producer to agent-wholesaler to user.

The direct channel in business-to-business marketing is the most commonly used one in the marketing of organisational goods. The names for the *manufacturer → wholesaler → organisational user* channel vary, and include jobbers or distributors who may deliver tools and/or equipment on the job. Business-to-business marketers also use agents. Brokers are used on an occasional basis, as needed. Manufacturers' agents operate on a commission in fixed geographic territories and tend to represent several small manufacturers who lack the financial resources to hire a sales force.

Wholesalers can also act as agents by buying merchandise on behalf of their customers. Wholesalers also add value to the distribution channel through storage and bulk breaking, and providing product ranges and assortments to retailers.

A retailer purchases products from suppliers that have the most suitable pricing, and then sell those products directly to consumers.[1]

DEFINITION

Retailer

A retailer is a business that conducts all the activities involved in selling goods and services directly to customers for their personal, non-business use.

Figure 9.1 illustrates the channel of distribution and intermediaries who participate in the process of distributing maize.

Importers, producers (farmers), manufacturers (plants and factories), suppliers (who resell on behalf of other importers, producers and manufacturers) and food processors provide food products to wholesalers and other intermediaries, who supply businesses and retailers who sell to consumers. In certain instances, a distribution system could involve manufacturers distributing directly to end consumers (for example roadside stalls). Marketers may also select direct distribution, which involves direct contact with customers. Suitable middlemen may not be available.

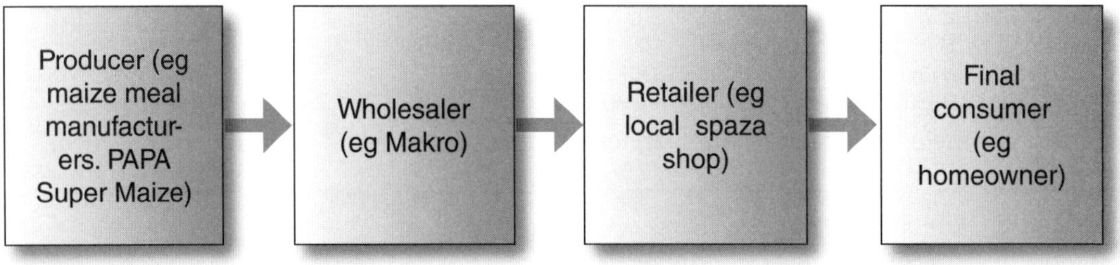

Figure 9.1 A basic distribution channel and the intermediaries involved in distribution of maize

A variety of distribution activities such as warehousing, bulk breaking and merchandising takes place between the different participants. It is important to note that retailers can also purchase products from other retailers, for example bakery shops that do not do their own baking but buy products in bulk from wholesalers. They then do bulk breaking and resell smaller product quantities to customers who do not have the means to shop at wholesalers themselves.

Industrial distribution channels (B2B: business-to-business)

There are two ways to analyse industrial distribution channels. The first focuses on the *basic flow of industrial materials between manufacturers and end users*. End users are not regarded in this instance as a final consumer purchasing a product for own or household use. End users may range from manufacturers, producers and processors to resellers. The goods distributed in such a channel may range from iron ore, limestone, cement and tools to others.

The second way focuses on the *network of intermediaries involved in the processing of raw materials into eventual consumer goods*. Figure 9.2 on the next page depicts such a network. It includes producers (farmers or cotton growers), processors (such as yarn spinners), wholesalers (clothing wholesalers), and retailers (clothing stores). The eventual outcome is that the consumer has a wider choice that can range from buying cotton for sewing purposes, or buying a shirt or other clothing item from a retail clothing outlet.

Every participant must, of course, add value and this is another measure of the effectiveness of the distribution channel.

Channel strategy

Distribution management consists of two major decision areas:

- The *formation of a sequence of intermediaries* who participate voluntarily or non-voluntarily in a distribution channel; and
- The *physical flow of products* through a distribution system.

Distribution strategy requires two major decisions concerning the structure and number of intermediaries that will be used. The first is *determining the structure of the channel*. Selection criteria are influenced by a number of elements in the marketing mix, by resources and by environmental factors. As the marketing mix strategy is formed, for example to target price-conscious or prestige-oriented consumers, the channel of distribution must match the intent. An example of organisational resources is Woolworths competing against other food retail chains by establishing upmarket food stores, even at roadside stops on national roads.

External environmental factors include issues such as market characteristics – the number and purchase influence of customers where shorter

DEFINITION

Distribution channels for consumer goods

- **The direct channel for consumer goods and services.** An arts and crafts shop that creates ornaments on the premises and sells them from there is an example of reaching consumers via a direct channel.
- **The manufacturer (producer) → retailer → consumer channel.** An example is when chocolate is produced at a factory, sold to a retailer such as Woolworths, and then sold by that retailer to its customers.
- **The manufacturer → wholesaler → retailer → consumer channel.** An example is when milk is produced on a farm (manufacturer), sold to Makro (wholesaler), who then sells it to a spaza shop owner (retailer), who in turn sells it to customers.
- **Channels that include agents.** Travel agents such as Flight Centre are the middlemen of these transactions, where a consumer books flights, accommodation, car rentals and activities through one organisation (the agent).

Direct distribution versus direct marketing

Do not confuse direct distribution with direct marketing. Direct marketing is a type of advertising campaign that seeks to elicit an action (such as an order, a visit to a store or website, or a request for further information) from a selected group of consumers in response to a communication from the marketer. The communication itself may be in any of a variety of formats including postal mail, telemarketing, direct e-mail marketing, and point-of-sale (POS) interactions. Customer response should be measurable. For example, a marketer should have measures in place to determine how many shoppers tasted an in-store promotion of juice.

channels are used to reach a small number of large clients. Consumer preferences and behaviours also shape preferences for selecting distribution channels. The nature and availability of intermediaries is seen as a difficulty when producers have to convince retailers to stock better-quality products such as a wool-blend line of clothes or to display them away from traditional, lower-priced clothing lines.

The second decision relates to the *extent of distribution* by, for example, determining the number of outlets. Selecting the number of wholesalers and/or retailers determines the number of outlets where potential customers can expect to find the product.

- **Intensive distribution** seeks to obtain maximum exposure for a product at the wholesale or retail levels.
- **Selective distribution** restricts the sale of a product to a limited number of outlets, for example Jeep clothing.
- **Exclusive distribution** carries with it the expectation of a maximum sales effort from the retailer or of a benefit from association with the prestige or efficiency of the retail outlet.

Distribution structure decisions

The best channel system should achieve ideal market exposure. Ideal exposure may be intensive, selective or exclusive.[2]

Intensive distribution

This is selling a product (usually convenience products) through as many suitable wholesalers or retailers as possible who will stock and/or sell the product – 'sell it where they buy it'. This involves the placement of products in as many locations as possible. It is generally an appropriate objective when a cost leadership strategy is employed as the firm's basic competitive position, and the emphasis of the target market segment is on purchasing convenience and low price, for example Pampers and Duracell.

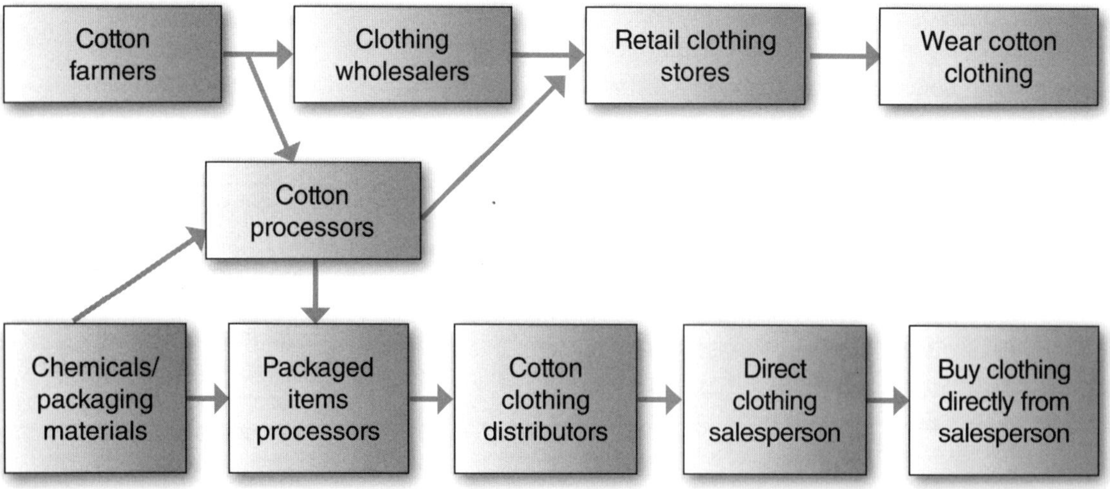

Figure 9.2 The flow of industrial products in the distribution of cotton

A *cost leadership strategy* involves producing and distributing products at a very low unit cost for price-sensitive customer segments. Low-cost production, technological improvements in production processes, and continued capital investment in production lead to cost leadership. However, when distribution costs in an industry are high, creative channel strategies can also lead to a low-cost position. An example is Vizio, an American consumer electronics company that designs flat-panel LCD and plasma TVs, which are manufactured in Thailand to reduce costs.

Selective distribution

This is selling through only those middlemen who will give the product special attention – 'sell it where it sells best'. Selective distribution involves the placement of products (usually consumer products) in a more limited number of locations. It may be an appropriate objective when a differentiation strategy is employed by the organisation. An example is Tie Stop, which specialises in neckwear, formal shirts and formal accessories.

A differentiation strategy emphasises uniqueness in a manner that is meaningful to non-price-sensitive customers. The uniqueness can be achieved through product design, performance and quality, or through meaningfully differentiated distribution networks and service offerings. An example is Apple's unique computer design and exclusive software, which make it the success it is today. Another is Jacob & Co., a high-end jeweller that has achieved differentiation through creating fine jewellery and timepieces that have gained significant recognition. Many celebrities such as David Beckham, Madonna and Beyoncé give the brand much exposure by wearing its jewellery and even speaking or singing about it.

Exclusive distribution

This is selling through only one middleman in a particular geographic area. An exclusive distribution objective limits availability of a product to a very small number of locations. This is generally an appropriate objective when a firm employs a focus strategy, and it is frequently employed when a firm desires to enhance a product's image or when considerable reseller support is desired.

A *focus strategy* involves concentration on a particular market segment in an industry. Focused strategies are designed to appeal to a unique segment (niche marketing). The focused competitor attempts to insulate itself from competition by serving a narrow market more efficiently or effectively than firms who are competing for the bulk of a market. For example, Honey Fashion Accessories sells through direct-sales consultants who travel with catalogues to show customers the range.

DEFINITION

Ideal market exposure
Ideal market exposure is when a product is available widely enough to satisfy target customers' needs but not exceed them, as this will increase the total cost of marketing.

'Intensive distribution is selling a product through as many suitable wholesalers or retailers as possible who will stock and/or sell the product.'

'Selective distribution is selling through only those middlemen who will give the product special attention.'

'Exclusive distribution is selling through only one middleman in a particular geographic area.'

www:

- http://www.jacobandco.com
- http://www.honeyacc.co.za
- http://www.tiestop.co.za
- http://www.vizio.com

Channel activities or functions

Channel intermediaries perform a variety of functions, including breaking bulk, accumulating bulk, sorting, creating assortments, reducing transactions, transporting, storing, communicating, financing, and providing management services and other facilitating functions. Broadly speaking, members of the marketing channel perform the following key functions:[3]

- They gather information about potential and current customers, competitors and other actors and forces in the marketing environment.
- They develop and disseminate persuasive communications to stimulate purchasing.
- They reach agreement on price and other terms so that transfer of ownership or possession can be effected.
- They place orders with manufacturers.
- They acquire the funds to finance inventories at different levels in the marketing channel.
- They assume risks connected with carrying out channel work.
- They provide for the successive storage and movement of physical products.
- They provide for buyers' payment of their bills through banks and other financial institutions.
- They oversee actual transfer of ownership from one organisation or person to another.

'All marketers, even not-for-profit and service organisations, engage in distribution because there is always some gap between the marketer and the customer that must be bridged.'

There are many variations of the traditional channel of distribution consisting of manufacturer → wholesaler → retailer → consumer. If the wholesaler is eliminated, then the manufacturer may have to hire a sales force, break bulk shipments into smaller sized lots, or finance sales. The key to setting the structure of a channel of distribution is to determine how the necessary activities or functions can be carried out most efficiently and effectively.

All marketers, even not-for-profit and service organisations, engage in distribution because there is always some gap between the marketer and the customer that must be bridged.

The functions and activities performed by intermediaries[4]

Intermediaries such as wholesalers and retailers assist with various kinds of transactional functions, such as contacting, promoting, negotiating and risk-taking. Some other functions performed by intermediaries include physical distribution, storing of inventory, sorting, researching and facilitating.

Intermediaries close gaps and provide utility

Channel activities, performed by intermediaries, fill gaps in form, time, place and possession, and provide form, time, place and possession utility between the manufacturer and the consumer.

Table 9.1 illustrates how channels of distribution create form, time, place and possession utility by closing the six gaps of quantity, assortment, time, spatial, knowledge and ownership between manufacturers and consumers.

Table 9.1 Providing utility and bridging gaps[5]

<table>
<tr><th>Form utility</th><th>Time and temporal utility</th><th>Place utility</th><th>Possession utility</th></tr>
<tr><td>Quantity gap
• Bulk breaking
• Storage
• Packaging</td><td>Time gap
• Storage and warehousing Inventories
• Financing
• Order taking
• Expediting</td><td>Spatial gap
• Transportation
• Materials handling
• Delivery</td><td>Information/ knowledge gap
• Sales promotion
• Advertising
• Personal selling
• Direct marketing</td></tr>
<tr><td>Assortment gap
• Accumulation or aggregation of an assortment
• Grading</td><td colspan="2">Intermediaries close gaps between manufacturers and consumers

Consumers receive value
... and utility
... and closure</td><td>Ownership gap
• Buying and selling
• Credit and financing
• Collection and delivery
• Servicing (eg product adjustments, technical service, warranty service)</td></tr>
<tr><td>Form utility
• Smaller assortment, graded and repackaged</td><td>Time utility
• In storage, paid for – waiting to be collected or is to be delivered</td><td>Place utility
• Delivered to consumer</td><td>Possession utility
• Product(s) received by consumer</td></tr>
<tr><td colspan="2">Temporal closure
• Supply = demand when they occur at different times, which is most frequently the case (eg agricultural mass production, etc)</td><td colspan="2">Spatial closure
• Transporting goods from production location to consumption location – provides 'place' convenience/utility</td></tr>
</table>

Retailers create utility advantages such as form, time, place and possession utility. The creation of utility adds value to products and enables consumers to pick and choose what they want. Form utility is created when a product is changed to fulfil the needs of the consumer. Butcheries provide form utility by offering different cuts and quality of meat products. Convenient locations and direct marketing methods create place utility for the consumer through catalogue purchasing, home delivery and the proximity of the convenience 'corner store'. Buying and selling transactions between retailers and consumers create ownership utility because ownership of products is transferred to the consumer. Retail trading hours and a wide product mix create time utility because

Example (E)

Closing the quantity gap

Channels are able to close the quantity gap. An example may explain this concept and make it more understandable. For instance, footwear manufacturers produce shoes by the thousands. Wholesalers and retailers buy them in batches of, say, 50 packs of each pair, and break them into smaller quantities – for example boxes containing only one pair each – so that customers can buy according to their needs. Wholesalers and retailers also sum up customers' desired variety of different types of shoes, socks, shoe-cleaning materials and other complementary products.

consumers can choose when, what and how much they want to purchase.

Intermediaries resolve discrepancies

Intermediaries are introduced into distribution channel structures when their specialisation facilitates the overall exchange process, and also to resolve certain discrepancies. Indirect channels are best when discrepancies and separations require channel specialists. These discrepancies are as follows:

- **Spatial discrepancy**. Supply sources are geographically dispersed throughout the country, and a basic need for physical transportation is created. The wine industry is predominantly located in the Western Cape, but certain raw materials and equipment are manufactured in other provinces and overseas. Wine consumers are also dispersed all over South Africa. The transportation problem is further aggravated by the fact that buyers distant from producers often require small product quantities resulting in the need for intermediaries who transport these smaller quantities to address spatial discrepancies. A channel that delivers inventory nearer to the customer can close the spatial distance between manufacturer and consumer, and add value to the product being sold.
- **Timing discrepancy**. Goods are manufactured in large quantities, but retailers order smaller ones thus creating a timing discrepancy. Emphasis is subsequently placed on the best timing of product flow through distribution channels via production scheduling, just-in-time ordering systems and inventory control procedures.
- **Temporal discrepancy**. In agricultural production and multi-manufacturing, goods are produced or grown at substantially different times than when they are demanded. The consumer wants the manufacturer's product immediately rather than whenever the manufacturer can supply it, thus there is a temporal discrepancy that a channel of distribution can solve by stocking the product. Intermediaries adjust and process products, and then store them until they are needed or in a form that allows for long-term storage, such as wine or cheese.
- **Discrepancy of quantity and assortment**. A discrepancy of quantity and assortment exists because manufacturers make large quantities of products, whereas consumers purchase in single units as part of an assortment. Intermediaries who categorise product offerings through sorting resolve this problem. *Sorting* is the ability of channel partners to create unique and need-satisfying product assortments through the following processes:
  - **Standardisation** – collecting uniform products from alternative suppliers and manufacturers. These products are subsequently graded according to aspects such as size, quality and weight.

- **Accumulation** – assembling standard products according to aspects such as size, quality and weight into large quantities for transport to other distribution channel intermediaries.
- **Allocation** – the general wholesale stage of providing adequate supply for numerous customers such as tools, hardware and building materials.
- **Assortment** – the assembly of specific goods into a customised order for specific customer groups such as department stores that offer merchandise assortment consisting of clothing, appliances, hardware and furniture. An example of such a store is Woolworths.

- **Discrepancy of possession, knowledge and/or ownership**. Intermediaries are also involved in the transfer of possession of the goods from the manufacturer to the customer. Discrepancies of possession, knowledge and/or ownership require that intermediaries provide information about the items and perhaps temporary credit, guarantees or adjustments to complete the sale to the consumer.

Specialisation in the distribution channel[6]

In the previous section, the discussion focused on the concept of numerous intermediaries who close the distance between manufacturer and customer. Another way to look at this issue is to investigate the specialised activities performed by intermediaries. For products to move from manufacturers to users, they must be handled, packaged, assembled, stored, shipped, displayed, sold and serviced. Each of these activities involves costs and is performed by firms operating in the channel based on their skills and efficiencies. Three main types of *specialised activities* may be identified:

'For products to move from manufacturers to users, they must be handled, packaged, assembled, stored, shipped, displayed, sold and serviced.'

- **Transactional activities** are involved in moving the goods through the channel, such as buying, selling, pricing, promoting and risk taking.
- **Physical activities** include warehousing, order-processing, storing, sorting, transporting and repairing goods.
- **Facilitating activities** ease the sale of the goods to end users by, for example, product grading, marketing research, providing advice on the product's use and assisting customers with financing of the purchase.

In most distribution channels specialist service providers have emerged that contribute to the success and efficiency of distribution channels by closing gaps between production supply and consumer demand and by performing certain activities. Two types of specialist service providers exist:

- **Functional service providers** are actively engaged in the day-to-day performance of the channel – moving, modifying or otherwise physically handling a product during the distribution process, or through direct involvement in the selling process.

- **Support specialists** are firms that facilitate overall channel performance by providing essential ingredients or services. Unlike the functional specialist, a support firm does not engage in actual selling or the logistics processes of the channel. Many support services are transparent to the physical path a product follows to market. However, they are essential to satisfactory completion of the overall distribution process.

Channel management

Cooperation and conflict[7]

Channel cooperation occurs when members share harmonious marketing objectives and strategies. Coordinated efforts by channel members whose marketing objectives and strategies complement each other reflect channel cooperation.

However, no matter how well channels are designed and managed, there will always be some conflict if for no other reason than that the interests of independent business entities do not always coincide. *Channel conflict* occurs when members cannot agree and it must be managed. Conflict exists when channel members have disagreements and an antagonistic relationship, often caused by the absence of a clearly identified locus of formal channel power or disagreements about common purpose or responsibility for activities. An example of channel conflict is when there is overproduction by the manufacturer, which results in an excess of products in the marketplace. Another example of channel conflict arises when there are newer versions of products, resulting in some channels stocking the outdated versions, whereas others have stock of the upgraded ones. Manufacturers increase conflict when they sell through image-oriented, full-price retailers and also through discount channels, thereby harming the retailer's ability to justify the higher price. This conflict has slowed many manufacturers in selling over the Internet. However, channel conflict may be beneficial to the system when it causes a more equitable allocation of resources, decision-making authority or stable functioning.

'Channel power is the ability of one organisation in a channel to exert influence over the other members, where the most powerful is the leader.'

Channel power is the ability of one organisation in a channel to exert influence over the other members, where the most powerful is the leader. Channel captains are able to exert power in a distribution channel. *Referent power* occurs when other members respect, admire and identify with the channel leader, for example, Coca-Cola.

'Vertical channel conflict means conflict between different levels within the same channel.'

Types of conflict

- **Vertical channel conflict**. This means conflict between different levels within the same channel. For example, Apple Inc. came into conflict with some of its authorised retailers and resellers when it started selling its computers through company-owned retailer, iStore.

Even as manufacturers continue to pump out thousands of new products, retailers seeking maximum productivity from their limited shelf space are able to collect *slotting fees* from manufacturers for stocking new products, *display fees* to cover space costs, *fines* for late deliveries and incomplete orders, and *exit fees* to cover the cost of returning goods to producers. In trying to regain power from retailers, manufacturers are expanding into alternative channels by placing more emphasis on market-leading brands and developing stronger links with important retailers through value-added distribution systems and programmes that benefit all members of the channel.

- **Horizontal channel conflict**. This involves conflict between members at the same level within the channel. For example, it may occur when a manufacturer sells goods via more than one retail store, and the goods are not represented the same way in both – one retailer may reflect a good image of the brand, whereas the other may reflect it poorly.
- **Multichannel conflict**. This type of conflict exists when the manufacturer has established two or more channels that sell to the same market. For instance, multichannel conflict can occur when a manufacturer sells its products through certain retailers, and then adds new channels. Tupperware, for example, started out by selling through independent direct salespeople, and then added selling via the Internet.

Physical distribution (logistics)

Logistics describes the entire process of moving raw materials and component parts into the firm, moving in-process inventories through the firm, and moving finished goods out of the firm. The following terms are important in this regard:

- The **supply chain** is used to describe all the organisations that regularly supply a marketing company and all members of the channel of distribution. It involves planning, implementing and controlling the efficient flow of both inbound materials and outbound finished products.
- **Supply chain management**, or **logistics management**, involves planning, implementing and controlling a chain of organisational relationships to ensure the efficient flow of both inbound materials and outbound finished products.
- **Materials management** is concerned with bringing raw materials and supplies to the point of production, and moving in-process inventory through the firm.
- **Physical distribution** is a term used to describe the broad range of activities concerned with the efficient movement of finished products from the end of the production line to the consumer. The purpose of physical distribution is to minimise cost while maximising customer service.

Reverse distribution

Backward channels of distribution are critical for ecological goals and the success of recycling efforts in a reverse distribution process. For example, some businesses sell many products packaged in valuable recyclable materials, but do not offer a recycling service. This may be seen as an irresponsible practice. When distributors agree to participate in a manufacturer's recycling efforts, they become part of a backward channel. Since this is not legally required in South Africa, other groups have taken the lead. Supermarkets sell cans and bottles because consumers purchase them, and evidence is conflicting as to the relative ecological impact. When consumers use their rand votes to support stores that do participate in recycling, supermarkets will quickly become socially responsible. Some will even decide to lead the way.

A cross-section of the physical distribution system

Physical distribution consists of several *activities* which include:

- **inventory management** – order timing and order quantities;
- **order processing** – receiving, filing and handling orders;
- **warehousing and storage** – accumulating, allocating and assorting, and readying goods for re-shipping to other locations;
- **materials handling** – moving items within the warehouse using standard pallets and forklift trucks;
- **protective packaging and containerisation** – providing appropriate protective covering, which is essential in reducing the incidence of damaged goods during movement in transit (also referred to as industrial packaging); and
- **transportation** – moving products, parts and materials into the production facility; moving semi-finished goods between production points; and moving finished goods to retailers or final consumers.

The systems concept is the notion that elements of a distribution system are strongly interrelated, and interact to achieve a common goal.

Managing the components of physical distribution

Physical distribution activities include five major areas of concern: *transportation, warehousing, inventory control, materials handling* and *order processing*.

'Physical distribution activities include five major areas of concern: transportation, warehousing, inventory control, materials handling and order processing.'

Transportation

Transportation decisions involve selecting the specific mode that will be used to move products physically from a manufacturer, grower, wholesaler or other seller to the receiving facilities of the buyer. The five major modes of transportation are road transportation, airfreight, water transportation, rail transportation and pipeline transport, which vary in flexibility, speed, reliability, tendency to damage goods and cost (see the advantages and disadvantages of different transport modes in the box below).

The advantages and disadvantages of different transport modes

- **Rail transportation** moves freight over long distances at low cost, especially when the shipment size is large. Railroads are therefore best at moving large, heavy or bulky items. As shipment size rises, railroads become more attractive to shippers. However, delivery is limited to places where tracks are in place, and railroads have a reputation for slow delivery and rough treatment of merchandise. Diversion-in-transit privileges, which allow a customer to specify a final destination after a trip has been mostly completed, are a useful feature of this type of transportation. In addition to diversion-in-transit services, railroads also provide some specialised cars and rates to appeal to certain users. When combined with containerisation, such as trucks on flat cars, rail transportation can be an efficient method for moving large amounts of goods.

Continue to next page

Continued from previous page

- **Road transportation** – motor carriers, trucks and the far less important 'bus freight' companies – is efficient at moving goods over short distances, is flexible, and has a far better record than railroads with less damage in transit for cartons, and on-time delivery. Trucks are more expensive to use than several competing transportation modes. They provide an effective array of specialised equipment; are fast, flexible and reliable; and have a good reputation in terms of breakage of goods; however, they cannot move the volumes of freight that railroads can. The greatest advantage trucks have is their flexibility. They can go anywhere with reasonable roads, requiring no particular specialised facility. They can go door to door with their cargo, and they are relatively safe as most large firms offer satellite tracking of trucks. For example, if a truck shipping goods is stuck or in an accident, and there is no communication with the driver, the truck's location can be tracked and assistance can be sent.
- **Airfreight** is fast but expensive. The primary advantages of airfreight are its speed and distance capabilities. Air transport is generally the most expensive of all modes, but rates near the top in terms of speed, reliability, the ability to span great distances and reach otherwise inaccessible areas, and gentle treatment of merchandise. The hub-and-spoke method, pioneered by FedEx, has greatly increased the cost effectiveness of using airfreight.
- **Water transportation** is inexpensive but slow. It is generally the least-costly mode of transportation, but its use is limited to places where ports and waterways are available. This mode of transport is suitable for easily protected, inexpensive, bulky products, but it is subject to the freezing of canals, ports and rivers in winter. Water transportation, compared to other modes, is thus not particularly reliable, and has a poor damaged-goods reputation. Internationally, water transport (sea freight) is much more common, particularly for goods that do not require a fast means of delivery.
- **Pipelines** are efficient movers, but can deliver only to specific terminals. Pipelines are the most specialised means of transport, designed to carry specific products. Once built, pipelines offer an inexpensive means of moving products such as oil and natural gas.

Warehousing

The holding and housing of goods between the time they are produced and the time they are shipped to the buyer refers to warehousing, or to the newer term *distribution centres*. Whatever the name, the emphasis is on moving, not keeping, the product. Note that warehousing, storage and bulk breaking are different activities. Warehousing involves the holding and housing of goods between the time they are produced and the time they are shipped to the buyer, and includes all the activities that take place from when the goods arrive at the warehouse until they are released for shipment. Warehousing involves many activities, both large and small, but taken as a whole, consists of two major activities: *storage and breaking bulk.*

'Warehousing is the holding and housing of goods between the time they are produced and the time they are shipped to the buyer.'

Storage consists of holding and housing goods in inventory. It is necessary because of the virtually inevitable discrepancies that almost always occur between the cycles of production and consumption. Note that storage can be part of production rather than distribution if storage is necessary before the product is bottled and sold, as in the

Reasons why organisations store goods in warehouses

- Irregular production facing regular demand, as with agricultural goods.
- Regular production facing irregular demand, as with air conditioners.
- The desire to postpone the sale of a product until prices are higher.
- The desire to have products ready to move when a planned promotional campaign begins.
- The need to have inventories handy to meet buyers' 'emergency demands'.
- The need to 'age' a product, for example wine, although this is technically a production activity.
- To gain a competitive advantage by being able to point to stocks of merchandise that competitors do not have.
- To ease problems associated with a 'rush season' by having merchandise already on premises.
- To deal better with channel members by handling some aspects of a storage problem.

case of wine or brandy. *Breaking bulk* involves converting large shipments of goods as they arrive at a warehouse into smaller quantities appropriate for customer needs. Warehousing strategy involves two basic decisions:

- determining the optimum number, location and types of warehouses needed; and
- calculating the proper levels of inventory to be stocked.

The 'best' plan is the one that maximises customer service, minimises costs and provides a strategic advantage.

Inventory control

Inventory control involves decisions concerning how large or small inventories should be and how overstocking of inventory can be weighed against costly stock-outs. Sales forecasts and knowledge of past requirements can be used to help determine the inventory level that provides proper service at 'minimum' cost. Three major costs of inventory include:

- **acquisition costs** – the expenses incurred in obtaining inventory;
- **holding costs** – the expenses incurred to keep inventory housed; and
- **out-of-stock costs** – the losses that occur when customers demand goods the marketer cannot provide.

Economic order quantity (EOQ) is a mathematically determined purchase order size that yields the lowest total order-processing and inventory holding costs. *International sourcing* refers to the reach of business increasing toward truly worldwide markets. The *inventory holding problem* is one of trying to balance the goals of minimising costs while satisfying customers. While acquisition costs, holding costs for warehousing and costs due to spoilage or obsolescence are significant, they also play off against one another when a firm increases order size or increases the frequency of smaller orders. More difficult to calculate is the cost in ill will, negative reputation or lost sales from out-of-stock situations.

Organisations perform *vendor analysis*, rating suppliers on attributes such as speed of delivery, quality of products and reliability of service. In recent years, *just-in-time (JIT) inventory systems* have been developed where the idea is to have supplies arrive as they are needed by an organisation, eliminating the need for stockpiling.

Materials management or handling

This component of distribution involves the physical handling and moving about of inventory – a process that is increasingly being mechanised and automated. *Materials management* refers to the activities involved in getting raw materials and parts to the point of production.

Order processing

Although most order processing is 'hidden' from the view of customers, the results of good and bad order processing are not. Order processing is the procedure followed to fill customer orders after these have been received by the company. The process begins when orders are received, and ends when merchandise has been shipped and bills sent to customers. Order processing is also becoming increasingly automated, and avoidance of error in the process is an important objective for many firms where expedient order processing can be to the advantage of the organisation.

Packaging is important to the product, price and promotion aspects of the marketing mix. Protection of the product in transit is a significant matter, but so is ease of handling. Shipments are therefore broken down into orders, while the use of colour coding may also ease handling difficulties.

Example (E)

The perils of poor order processing

Poor order processing proved to have costly consequences for a popular retailer in the North West, when the store ran out of their 'Christmas Day only' ready-cooked turkeys. Turkeys had to be bought from another outlet, but annoyed customers, who had ordered their turkeys in advance, refused to return later to the store to collect them, so the retailer had to deliver them.

Customer service

Customers want products, not excuses. In terms of distribution, customer service refers to how rapidly and dependably a firm can deliver what customers want.

Physical distribution provides maximum satisfaction to buyers while reducing costs. The central objective of physical distribution is to keep costs down while keeping the level of service up, yet improved service raises costs. Distribution managers must balance these two elements. The marketing concept suggests that managers determine what level of service will fit the buyers' needs and what prices are acceptable to them.

Quality is defined in terms of customer satisfaction. Quality is the company's performance to deliver customer satisfaction. Service quality therefore depends on expectations and perceived performance. Customer satisfaction is a marketing issue, and service quality assurance is an operational one.

Performance dimensions to analyse customers' desired service output levels[8]

Because the point of a marketing channel is to make a product available to customers, the marketer must understand what its target customers actually want, for example:

- **Lot size**. This is the number of units the channel allows a typical customer to purchase on one occasion. Engen prefers a channel from which it can buy a large amount of fuel, while a single-car owner would choose a channel that allows buying an amount suitable for one car.
- **Spatial convenience**. This is the level of accessibility the marketing channel delivers to the customers. For example, Standard Bank offers better spatial convenience than Capitec

'Spatial convenience is how easy the marketing channel makes it easy for customers to purchase the product.'

Bank, as there are far more Standard Bank outlets and ATMs geographically dispersed throughout South Africa.

- **Product variety**. This is the number of products provided by the channel. Generally, customers prefer a larger variety, which increases the chance of finding what they need. Relentless expansion of product variety is the special edge that has helped Amazon.com maintain its lead in Internet retailing.
- **Service backup**. This refers to the add-on services (credit, delivery, installation, repairs) provided by the channel. The greater the service backup is, the greater the work provided by the channel.
- **Cost**. This is always a concern, even for companies that compete primarily on some other dimension. In fact, in some industries, competition is so intense that firms are experiencing unrelenting pressure to reduce costs, even as their performance improves in other ways. Because operations and supply chain activities often account for most of an organisation's costs, they are natural targets in cost reduction efforts.
- **After-sales support**. This can be a critical performance dimension, especially if the purchased good or service has a high price tag or is critical to customers' success. For example, Mercedes- Benz offers an after-sales Internet portal and after-sales service centres for their customers, who expect this type of support, as Mercedes-Benz motor vehicles are expensive. At the individual level, a consumer's decision to buy a new car may depend in part on his or her previous experiences with the service department at the dealership.
- **Product availability**. This is the ability of the supplier to provide products on demand. It is measured in terms of the percentage of items or lines that can be filled from existing inventory or as the percentage of orders that are shipped complete.
- **Capability**. This refers to the length of time required to fill orders, the ability of the logistics system to adapt to special requirements, and the avoidance of errors such as damage or incorrect shipments.
- **Information support**. This is the ability of the logistics system to support a product throughout its life cycle, including the ability to handle situations such as installing, servicing, updating and product recall.
- **Waiting time**. This is the average time customers of a channel wait for receipt of the goods. Customers normally prefer fast delivery channels.
- **Quality**.[9] The concept of quality is a broad one that can be subdivided into the following categories:
  - **Functionality**. What are the characteristics or features of a product or service that determine how well it works? Products with many features or services that provide superior performance are often thought of as being of 'higher quality'.

WWW:

- http://www.capitecbank.co.za
- http://www.standardbank.co.za
- http://www.engen.co.za

'Product availability is the ability of the supplier to provide products on demand.'

- **Conformance**. Was the product made or the service performed to specification? Examples of conformance quality include degree of purity, the weight of a product and the amount of time it takes to perform a service.
- **Reliability**. Will a product work for a long time without failing or requiring maintenance? Does a service operation perform its tasks consistently over time?
- **Durability**. Can a product withstand adverse conditions, such as temperature extremes or rough handling? What is its expected lifespan?
- **Safety**. Was the product or service designed to be safe?
- **Serviceability**. If necessary, can the product be easily repaired or serviced?
- **Aesthetics**. Does the product/service appeal to the senses?

The relative importance of these quality dimensions will differ from one customer to the next. One buyer may be more interested in reliability and serviceability, another in performance and aesthetics. To compete on the basis of quality, a firm's operations and supply chain must consistently meet or exceed customer expectations or requirements on the most critical quality dimensions.

- **Delivery performance**. 'Today, many firms are requiring increasingly tighter delivery windows. Whereas in the past a delivery was considered to be on time if it was made within a few days of the promised date, the acceptable time frame is now as little as two hours – even for goods that are not perishable. One automobile manufacturer in the US charges suppliers a penalty fee of $10 000 for every minute delivery is late. This practice may seem extreme until one considers that late deliveries may shut down an entire production line. Delivery performance has two basic characteristics:
    - **Delivery speed** is the elapsed time from the receipt of an order to final delivery. A firm with superior delivery speed can "deliver more quickly than its competitors or meet a required delivery date when only some or even none of the competition can do so". Typical strategies for improving delivery speed include streamlining the order entry process, holding inventory at key points in the supply chain (in stores or regional warehouses), maintaining excess capacity with which to meet "rush" orders, and using faster transportation.
    - **Delivery reliability** refers to the ability to deliver products or services on time. Note that a firm can have long lead times yet still maintain a high degree of delivery reliability. Typical measures of delivery reliability include the percentage of orders that is delivered by the promised time and the average tardiness of late orders. Delivery reliability is especially important to companies that are linked together in a supply chain. Consider the relationship between a fish

Flexibility[11]

- An example of **flexibility in the service industry** is a full-service law firm that will handle any legal issue a client faces. (Some law firms specialise only in, for example, real estate transactions or divorce settlements.) A full-service hotel will go to great lengths to fulfil a guest's every need. A staff member at a well-known hotel once noticed a guest standing outside the gift shop waiting for it to open. The employee found out what the guest wanted, picked it up when the shop opened and waited outside the conference hall to deliver it to the guest.
- Flexibility has become particularly valuable in **new product development**. Some firms compete by developing new products or services faster than their competitors – a strategy that requires operations and supply chain partners that are not only flexible, but also willing to work closely with designers, engineers and marketing personnel. When the Vodacom network rebranded from blue and green to red, the colour of its UK parent, Vodafone, Cell C released an advertisement that mocked the move just days later, with comedian

Continue to next page

wholesaler and its major customer, a fish-processing facility. If the fish arrives too late, the processing facility may be forced to shut down. However, fish that arrives too early may spoil before it can be processed. Obviously, these two supply chain partners must coordinate their efforts so that the fish arrives within a specific time 'window,' usually a few hours.

- **Accuracy**. Another measure of delivery reliability is the accuracy of the quantity shipped. For example, a company may demand 95 % accuracy in stock deliveries from suppliers. If suppliers ship more than the quantity ordered, they are still considered to be in error. Some firms will consider a partial shipment to be on time if it arrives by the promised date, but others will accept only complete shipments, delivered within the scheduled window.
- **Flexibility**. Many operations and supply chains compete by responding quickly to the unique needs of different customers. Both manufacturing and service firms can demonstrate flexibility. Many manufacturers distinguish between different types of flexibility:
  - **Mix flexibility** refers to the ability to produce a wide range of different products.
  - **Changeover flexibility** is the ability to begin production of a new product with minimal delay.
  - **Design flexibility** refers to the ability to change the design of a product to accommodate specific customers.
  - **Volume flexibility** is the ability to produce whatever volume the customer needs.'[10]

Different types of flexibility may require different operations and supply chain solutions. Firms must decide which types of flexibility are important to their customers, and adjust their operations and supply chain efforts accordingly.

Supply chain management[12]

In the broadest sense, a supply chain starts from the origins of the raw material that is used in the production of the product and ends once the product has been discarded or recycled. Supply chain management has even been described as moving a product from 'cradle to grave' or from 'dirt to dirt'.

Supply chain management (SCM) is the integration of the logistics requirements of the supplier, distributor and customer into one cohesive process that includes demand planning, forecasting, materials requisition, order processing, inventory allocation, order fulfilment, transportation services, receiving, invoicing and payment. SCM also involves the management and control of all materials, funds and related information in the logistics process from the acquisition of raw materials to the delivery of finished products to the end user, as well as reverse distribution such as repair work and recall, product withdrawal, and discarding and recycling of products.[13] This all means that a supply chain extends from a firm's customer's customer to its supplier's supplier, and includes the primary decisions made in the supply chain, namely developing, planning, sourcing, manufacturing, warehousing and delivering of products:[14]

- **Developing**. New product development and design; product innovation; and/or product adaptation.
- **Planning**. Determining the quality of the final product; designing or adapting manufacturing processes.
- **Sourcing**. Choosing suppliers; locating suppliers; deciding how much raw materials to order; designing transportation channels.
- **Production**. Location of production plants (domestic and/or international factories); whether to make, buy or lease production facilities, plants and tools; deciding on the capacity of production plants; decisions about manufacturing products according to quality specifications and market focus (low cost leader, differentiation strategy).
- **Inventory**. How much inventory of raw materials, intermediate products, semi-finished products or finished products to hold (safety stock); deciding on whether the company should follow a JIT approach (just-in-time according to orders); how much to order; when to order.
- **Transportation logistics**. The best way to get the product to the customer (road, rail or air); mode of transport; shipment size; location of distribution centres to keep customer service high and costs low.

Some of the objectives of a supply chain manager include the following:

- Increase communication along all modes of the supply chain to create an uninterrupted flow of materials and products.
- Decrease inventory while still maintaining high customer service levels.
- Reduce the supplier base, and develop supplier relationships to reduce overall costs.
- Standardise parts as much as possible to reduce the amount of inventory to be carried to fulfil customer orders within an acceptable time frame.

Franchising

Franchising is the practice of using another firm's successful business format and trademark. Franchise systems can cover a wide variety of products and services, and can even extend across international and regional borders. In essence, the rationale for creating franchise distribution systems is that such systems make investment opportunities available to franchisees without their having to develop new products, create new companies or test the market. In return, the franchisee gives up some independence, and pays the franchisor a fee based on an agreed fixed sum or as a percentage of gross sales or turnover.

Continued from previous page

Trevor Noah saying: 'It takes more than a lick of paint to be SA's number one network'. Cell C's ability to react rapidly to Vodacom's rebranding displayed such quick-acting flexibility that Vodacom's advertising agency, Draftfcb, effectively accused its former executive creative director, Grant Jacobson, who had worked on their rebranding campaign, of sharing confidential information with Cell C.

DEFINITION

Supply chain

A supply chain is a system that includes all organisations, activities, people, information, technology and resources involved in the process of getting a product from the manufacturing phase to the final phase where it is sold to the ultimate consumer.

> **DEFINITION**
>
> **Franchising**
>
> Franchising may be defined as an agreement between a business owner and an independent individual to increase the business's geographic reach by releasing additional branches in separate areas. The owner of the business (franchisor) gives the right to the independent individual (franchisee) to operate his or her business, and terms and conditions are set which stipulate, among other things, how to maintain the same image of the brand throughout all branches, the support that the franchisor will give to the franchisee, and the fee that the franchisee will pay the franchisor for the use of its intellectual property.

WWW:

- http://www.fasa.co.za (FASA – Franchise Association of South Africa)
- http://www.franchisewebsite.com

The franchise agreement sets out how the market is to be served by the franchisee. The type of agreement signed, the level of control executed by the franchisor, and the commitment of and level of trust between franchisor and franchisee will eventually determine the level of satisfaction experienced by the end customer.

Franchising has the following advantages:[15]

- Franchise systems help provide advice on the best locations, customer trends and other market information so that consumer preferences, buying patterns and complaints can be reflected more quickly when planning marketing and production.
- The franchise system *provides needed investment incentives* by making substantial sales, service and management assistance available to potential franchisees. In return the franchisor expands his or her business operations, penetrates markets and contributes to economic growth as well as to customer choice and satisfaction in market areas.
- Franchising has also *opened up opportunities to empower members of disadvantaged communities* to own successful business formats.
- For many foreign companies, franchising has been the most successful way of *side-stepping state-controlled distribution systems* in those countries where few incentives exist to deliver products on time. With its own network and its own outlets, a franchisor can train franchisees in successful sales and business practices, and also control price and quality. In the process, the franchisor makes a valuable contribution to the economic growth of such a country and/or region.

Table 9.2 Services provided by the franchisor to the franchisee

Services offered at the beginning of the franchise endeavour	Services offered during the running of the franchise outlet
• **Facilities** Design and layout of the site, lighting, signage and banners, decor • **Training** Training for managers and staff to embed the culture of the business in their minds • **Operating advice** Operating manuals, market studies, business forms, merchandising methods	• **Business counselling** Ongoing advice on profitability (cost control and budgeting) and business activities (eg marketing, customer service and financial management) • **Image building** Ideas on how to build and maintain the image of the brand more effectively

Continue to next page

Continued from previous page	
• **Financing** Franchise fee, equipment, lease of building, service fees • **Market surveys** Trade area analysis, site selection, market forecasting	• **Supervision** Employee retraining and field supervision, advice on dealing with employee challenges • **Quality control** Regular inspections, maintenance of cleanliness, plans for improvement • **Sales promotion** Point-of-sale materials, competitions, free samples • **Product development and packaging** Upgraded products, new packaging

Table 9.2 illustrates that a franchisor not only offers services to the franchisee at the start-up of the franchise agreement, but throughout the period of the relationship. The effective and efficient distribution of products and services is therefore based on a continuous and contractual relationship between franchisor and franchisee. The wide range of services offered is often cited as the main reason why franchisees are willing to buy a franchise.

Vertical marketing system (VMS)

In a *vertical marketing system (VMS)*, members are owned outright by the controlling organisation to ensure cooperation and to increase effectiveness. In a *contractual VMS*, the members are linked by a formal contract. An *administered alliance* is composed of organisations that follow the lead of a channel leader. Another view is that vertically integrated marketing systems are networks of vertically aligned establishments that are managed professionally as centrally administered distribution systems.

In a VMS arrangement, primary channel intermediaries are interdependent. One of the members acts as channel leader because of its size and willingness to take risks. The main advantages of VMSs over conventional marketing systems are *cooperation and control*. A smoothly operating VMS may achieve technological, managerial, distributional, promotional and other economies of scale. Having one organisation in control ensures that things will continue to run smoothly. Let us now look at various types of VMS arrangements.

Types of franchises

- Franchises can be classified according to type of participants, type of business, or nature and extent of services exchanged.

Type of participants

- Between a manufacturer and a wholesaler – for example SABMiller and their seven bottling plants.
- Between a manufacturer and a retailer – for example a BMW dealership in the motor industry.
- Between a wholesaler and a retailer – for example Edgars, Zara and Mr Price in the clothing industry.
- Between a service provider and a retailer – for example Steers in the fast-food industry.

Type of business

- Fast food – for example McDonald's.
- Hospitality – for example Southern Sun Hotels.
- Education – for example Damelin College.

Nature and extent of services exchanged

- Full-format – for example Engen flagship garages.
- Product or trade name – for example Builders Warehouse.

Types of vertical marketing systems

Corporate systems

This type of VMS is characterised by *total ownership*. A corporate VMS is a single firm that owns and operates two or more consecutive levels of the distribution channel. Ownership connects two or more channel members with this system. For example, Pick n Pay may integrate backward and acquire a manufacturing facility to ensure quality control. Another example is HP, which manufactures and sells computer equipment.

Contractual systems

This type of VMS is characterised by a *legal relationship*. In a contractual VMS, dependency is defined in a formal contract (for example franchise, exclusive dealership, joint venture, etc). When channel coordination and leadership are specified in a contractual agreement, a contractual VMS exists. *Retailer cooperative organisations* are groups of independent retailers that combine resources and expertise to control their wholesaling needs through centralised buying centres. The *wholesaler-sponsored voluntary* chain is similar, but is sponsored by the wholesaler to service a network of loyal retailers. A *franchise* is a contractual agreement between a franchisor, typically a manufacturer or wholesaler, and a number of independent retailers or franchisees.

Contractual VMS arrangements such as franchises, exclusive dealerships, joint ventures and pacts between cooperative and voluntary groups are the most common today. Alliances in the form of partnerships and strategic arrangements are becoming increasingly widespread and important. So too are administered arrangements, which are dominated by major companies and are prevalent in certain business channels (for example retail mass merchandising).

There are three types of contractual VMS arrangements:[17]

- **Wholesaler-sponsored** voluntary chains organise groups of independent retailers to compete better with large chain organisations. Wholesalers such as Drug Guild work with participating retailers (for Drug Guild, independent pharmacies) to standardise their selling practices and achieve buying economies so the group can compete effectively with chain organisations.
- **Retailer cooperatives** arise when the stores take the initiative and organise a new business entity to carry on wholesaling and possibly some production. Members of retailer cooperatives concentrate their purchases through the retailer co-op, and plan their advertising jointly. Profits are passed back to members in proportion to their purchases.
- **Franchise organisations** are created when a channel member, called a franchisor, links several successive stages in the production–distribution process. Franchises include

manufacturer-sponsored retailer franchises (the way McDonald's licenses McDonald's outlet owners to sell its products); manufacturer-sponsored wholesaler franchises (the way SABMiller licenses bottlers – who are wholesalers – to buy its ingredients and then bottle and sell their product to retailers); and service-firm-sponsored retailer franchises (the way Hertz licenses participating car rental businesses).

Administered strategic alliances

This type of VMS is characterised by *strong leadership*. An *administered strategic alliance* is a vertical marketing system in which a strong channel leader coordinates marketing activities at all levels in the channel through planning and management of mutually beneficial programmes. In an administered VMS, the member firms acknowledge their dependence, and adhere to the leadership of a dominant firm. This dependence is based on the realisation by participating channel members that it is necessary to follow the leader if they desire continued participation in the administered arrangement.

An *alliance* VMS is a *voluntary* form of extended organisations typically not formalised by contractual arrangements. Examples include partnerships, vertical strategic alliances between factories and clothing stores, and horizontal strategic alliances such as Spar supermarkets that form a buying cooperative.

DEFINITION

Vertical marketing system (VMS)

A vertical marketing system (VMS) is a distribution channel arrangement in which all the main members of the channel work together in unity in order to satisfy consumer needs and generate profit, instead of the traditional channel where all intermediaries are working for themselves.

Introduction to franchising in South Africa[16]

- The Franchise Association of Southern Africa (FASA) is an industry body that regulates standards and the conduct of its members.
- The word *franchising* means 'privilege' or 'freedom', and in this sense it offers people the freedom to own, manage and direct their own business. It means being in business for oneself, but not by oneself. Franchising is an arrangement between the franchisor (the seller or grantor of a privilege) and the franchisee (the recipient or purchaser of a privilege). The franchisor owns the right to the name or trademark of the business, while the franchisee purchases the right to use the trademark and system of business.
- How does franchising work? Franchising is a 'business marriage' between an existing business (the franchisor) and the newcomer to business ownership (the franchisee). The franchisee buys licensed rights to clone the whole business package from the franchisor in a specific territory for a specific period. The franchisor provides a ready-made, established and tested business format including name, corporate power, knowhow, training and support services. The franchisee invests capital, time, effort and any relevant past experience to create its business, replicated from the franchisor's business formula or system. The franchisor gains a new outlet in a new territory with minimum capital investment in setting it up.
- The franchisee gets a safer way of moving into independent business. The franchisor expands its network cost effectively.
- One of the misconceptions of franchising is that the franchisee is buying a franchise. What a franchisee is really doing is investing assets in a system to make use of the brand name, operating system and ongoing support. All franchisees in the system are licensed to make use of the same elements. The business relationship is a commitment by all franchisees in the network to utilise the prescribed marketing and operating system of the franchisor to attract and retain customers.

CASE STUDY[18]

Who is Microsoft South Africa?

Microsoft South Africa is a subsidiary of the world's largest independent software and services provider, focusing on providing services, solutions and devices that assist government, people and businesses realise their full potential through technology. Microsoft SA has been recognised globally as a high-performance region. Its long-term sustainability is based on the contribution it makes to the local economy, both through its 7 000-strong partner ecosystem and its broad array of citizenship activities, for which it received the Best Corporate Social Responsibility award at the 2011 African Business Awards.

The Microsoft Equity Equivalence programme – a unique approach to BBBEE strategy implementation

In 2011, with the guidance and approval of the Department of Trade and Industry, Microsoft SA launched its Equity Equivalence programme, which will see the company spend R500 million over the next seven years in growing several sustainable, independent and majority black-owned software companies. To be eligible to apply for the programme, companies had to be in operation for a minimum of three years, have a maximum of 30 employees and turn over less than R10 million a year. The successful companies needed to demonstrate their track record in creating IP/software for specific market needs. They also had to specify what investment would be required to grow their IP/software solution into a global product by submitting a business plan. One of the cornerstones of the programme is that it creates a new model for entrepreneurship, and sets a new benchmark for developing talent in the South African technology industry. Through the success of this programme, it is hoped that the market will come to associate BBBEE with real entrepreneurship, job creation, business/enterprise development and skills enhancement. This investment directly addresses key challenges facing the government and South Africa, namely creating jobs, developing enterprises, building the local software economy and developing scarce technology skills. The first phase of the programme in early 2011 attracted the registration of 680 companies on the site, from which Microsoft selected the first four that would be part of its development programme. These were chosen through a process that included representatives from the investment group Here Be Dragons, the Black Management Forum and the Centre for Entrepreneurship. They are as follows:

- Chillisoft, from Pietermaritzburg, which creates public health software solutions that assist in alleviating service delivery bottlenecks
- Maxxor, from Cape Town, which creates consumer applications for mobile phones
- Johannesburg-based security solutions specialist BUI
- Home Grown Business Integrations, from Durban, which creates cloud-based software that boosts government service delivery to rural people.

Since then, a further two companies have been added to the programme:

- iSolv Technologies, which creates high-end security solutions for government and enterprises
- Mmapro IT Solutions, which creates law enforcement software for traffic authorities.

Microsoft is satisfied that its choices not only meet the letter of BEE, but also its spirit. While development is key, this is being balanced with commercial opportunities for all involved.

Continue to next page

Continued from previous page

The companies that grow out of this investment, and the software that they develop, will help Microsoft SA and its partners reach new markets. The investment should galvanise the local software economy and leave a legacy for other entrepreneurs.

The advertising campaign

Primary objectives

The primary objectives of the advertising campaign were:

- to launch and create awareness about the Microsoft Equity Equivalence Programme;
- to educate the target audience about the programme and drive them to apply to be part of the programme; and
- to associate BEE with entrepreneurship and, in turn, with Microsoft.

Secondary objectives

The secondary objectives of the advertising campaign were:

- to assist South Africans in understanding the role Microsoft is playing in inspiring and enriching a winning nation; and
- to build and entrench an emotional connection between South Africans and the Microsoft corporate brand.

Target audiences

The main target audiences of the advertising campaign were:

- Equity Equivalence programme candidates (black-owned independent software vendors);
- government and business;
- top Microsoft customers;
- top Microsoft partners;
- internal staff; and
- the South African public.

Creative idea

'We see things not as they are, but as they could be.'

Execution

Microsoft used a variety of channels in order to capture the attention of the diverse audiences. These channels included the following:

- Radio
- TV
- Intersection promotions on launch day
- Launch event
- Online
- Print – magazines and newspapers
- Website
- HTMLs

Continue to next page

Continued from previous page

- Internal desk drops
- 3D mailer.

All above- and below-the-line communication directed the audience to http://www.microsoftbee.co.za where more information on the programme could be found. Independent software vendors who wished to apply for the programme could do so online.

The results

The number of companies that registered on the website as a result of this advertising campaign are shown in the following table.

Number of registered companies	689
Number of completed profiles	473
Number of uploaded business plans	141
Number of uploaded supporting documents	141
Valid BBBEE submissions	215
Majority black-owned entities	455
Majority black-managed entities	454
Annual revenue less than R10 million	461
Entities with fewer than 30 full-time employees	457
Entities with the ability to create intellectual property and convert it into software solutions for South Africa and global markets	402
Entities that have been in operation for a minimum of three years or more	341
Existing independent software vendor/software development companies	327

Conclusion

The main features of the Microsoft Equity Equivalence programme are the following:

- It is a breakthrough approtach to implementing BBBEE objectives, and the first of its kind in South Africa.
- The programme demonstrated Microsoft's commitment to growing and empowering the industry.
- It is closely aligned to government's national priorities and provides support for them.
- It is helping South Africans move forward.

Summary

In this chapter, different types of channel participants were discussed. Wholesalers and retailers are important role players in distribution channels. Channel design aspects were highlighted and a wide range of channel activities was identified. Channel management was critically examined, and the various physical distribution activities compared. Customer service in logistics was examined and the supply chain was analysed. Channels for services and export were illustrated. Franchising and vertical marketing (distribution) systems or multilevel distribution were summarised.

References

1. Cole, R. 2013. *Differences between wholesalers, distributors, and retailers.* Chron. [Online] Available from: http://smallbusiness.chron.com/differences-between-wholesalers-distributors-retailers-30836.html [Accessed 2013-10-17].
2. Cant, M.C., van Heerden, C.H. & Ngambi, H.C. 2010. *Marketing management: A South African perspective.* Cape Town, South Africa: Juta & Co, p. 268.
3. Kottler, P and Keller, KL. 2009. *A framework for marketing management,* 4th ed. USA: Pearson p. 227.
4. Bikash, A. 2009. *Selecting and managing marketing channels.* [Online] Available from http://www.scribd.com/doc/19074725/Markt-Channel [Accessed 2013-10-17].
5. Lombardo, J. 2013. *Channel intermediaries: Definition and function in business.* Education Portal [Online] Available from: http://education-portal.com/academy/lesson/channel-intermediaries-definition-and-function-in-business.html [Accessed 2013-10-17].
6. Cant et al., op. cit., p. 276.
7. Ibid.
8. Kotler & Keller, op. cit., p. 235.
9. Kotler & Keller, op. cit., p. 235; Bozarth, C. & Handfield, R.B. 2008. *Introduction to operations and supply chain management*, 2nd ed. USA: Prentice Hall, Ch 2.
10. Bozarth & Handfield, op. cit.; [Online] Available from http://www.slideshare.net/Alistercrowe/download-it-4076906? [Accessed 2013-12-20].
11. Muller, R. 2011. *ASA rules against Cell C in Vodacom red case. MyBroadband.* [Online] Available from: http://mybroadband.co.za/news/cellular/19734-asa-rules-against-cell-c-in-vodacom-red-case.html [Accessed 2013-10-18].
12. This section was summarised from Lovejoy, J.L. *Principles of supply chain management.* [Online] Available from: http://www.techexchange.com/thelibrary/principles_SCM.html [Accessed 2005-07-20]; Supply Chain Today. 2013. *Supply Chain Refresher.* http://www.supplychaintoday.com/reflections.htm#SUPPLY%20CHAIN [Accessed 2005-07-20]; and Supply Chain Management. 1997. *Supply Chain Management.* http://eil.utoronto.ca/profiles/rune/node5.html [Accessed 2005-07-20].
13. Adapted from South-Western. 2003. *Glossary of key terms.* [Online] Available from: http://www.swlearning.com/quant/coyle/seventh_edition/glossary.html#s [Accessed 2013-10-18].
14. Ibid.
15. Adapted from the Franchise Council of Australia. n.d. *Advantages of the franchise system.* [Online] Available from: http://www.franchise.org.au/process/knowledgebase/knowledgeBaseAnswers.html?categoryId=225&answerId=1037 [Accessed 2013-10-18].

16. Adapted from The Franchise Association of South Africa. n.d. *What is franchising?* [Online] Available from: http://www.fasa.co.za/guidelines.php [Accessed 2013-10-18].
17. Kotler & Keller, op. cit., p. 240.
18. Adapted from Van Heerden, C.H. 2013. *Contemporary retail and marketing case studies.* Cape Town, South Africa: Juta & Co., p. 104.

CHAPTER 10

Marketing planning, implementation and control

✓ Learning objectives

After studying this chapter, you should be able to:

- explain the relationship between planning, implementation and control;
- explain what strategic marketing management is;
- describe the marketing planning process;
- discuss the importance of implementation; and
- describe the marketing evaluation and control process.

Introduction

All the best plans and strategies will come to nothing if they are not managed properly. This, by implication, means that the decisions made must be implemented, monitored and evaluated, and corrective action taken if needed.

The process of planning, implementation and control is the responsibility of marketing management and is not a once-off occurrence, but something that must happen on a continuous basis. It makes no sense to spend vast amounts of money and time on planning the marketing strategy of selected segments and not implementing what has been decided. In the same way, it does not make sense to implement a plan without monitoring it to see if the outcomes are met. These actions refer to the planning, implementation and control of marketing actions. Imagine all the planning that goes into the launch of a new washing powder aimed at housewives. To implement it, responsibilities must be allocated, time frames indicated, and launch dates set, etc. After the product has been launched, it must be established whether sales were as expected, whether they were made by the intended target market, what repeat purchases were like, and if targets were met. This chapter is based on Figure 10.1, which shows the relationship between the three main management functions of the marketing department.

'The three components of the strategic marketing process are:

- Plan;
- Apply;
- Assess.'

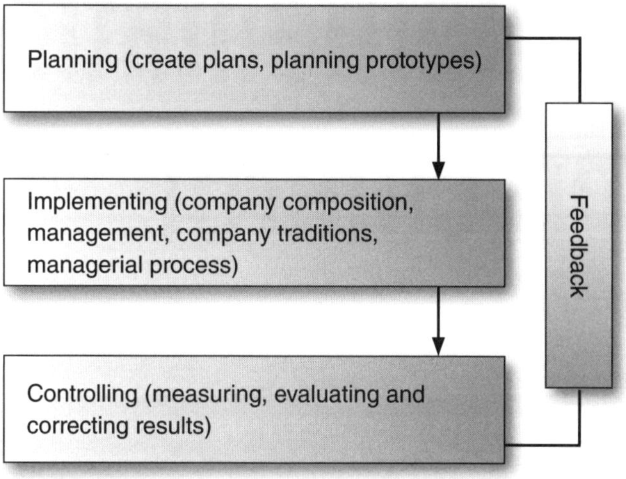

Figure 10.1 The relationship between planning, implementation and control

Strategic marketing management

The meaning of 'strategic marketing management'

The process of strategic marketing management involves in essence the following three steps:

- Plan
- Apply
- Assess.

A close relationship exists between these steps, which is clearly depicted in Figure 10.2.

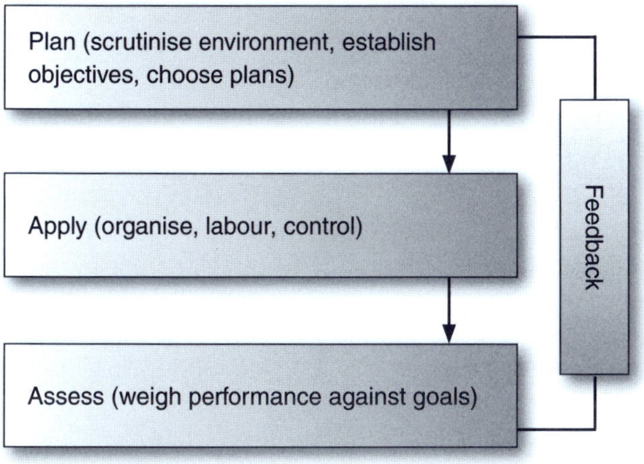

Figure 10.2 The marketing management process

Strategic marketing management implies that the above process takes place in a strategic context; in other words, with a long-term view towards achieving organisational goals, and integrating marketing goals and objectives with the overall goals and objectives of the organisation.

Strategic marketing management entails the decisions of the marketing department with a view to long-term growth and survival in a competitive environment. All the management tasks of planning, organising, leading and controlling are taken into consideration in the discussion in this chapter.

The three components of the strategic marketing process are discussed below.

Planning

The nature of planning

Planning is a central task of marketing and always starts with the gathering of information. At whatever level strategies are planned, information is gathered from the internal and external environments, interpreted and constantly monitored. A decision is only as good as the information on which it is based and therefore extensive marketing research and forecasting must first be done. Marketing managers must, for instance, do a detailed SWOT analysis to make plans to build on strengths and correct weaknesses.

Planning has many *advantages* for any business. These advantages include:[1]

- facilitating management by objectives;
- minimising uncertainties;
- facilitating coordination;
- improving employees' morale;
- helping to achieve economies of scale;
- facilitating control;
- providing a competitive edge;
- encouraging innovations

Because of the number and the uncertainty of factors influencing market success, a business must have a systematic way of analysing these factors, determining the impact of trends and designing a strategic marketing plan to meet present and future market conditions. The marketing planning process is the mechanism by which numerous organisations accomplish these tasks.

Through applying, the organisation turns the strategic and marketing plans into actions that will achieve its objectives. This is done by people in the marketing organisation working with others, both inside and outside the business. In order to assess the success of the marketing plans, it is imperative that the results of these plans are measured and evaluated. If necessary, the results of this procedure must lead to corrective action to ensure that the objectives are reached. Marketing analysis provides information and evaluations needed for all the other marketing activities.

> **DEFINITION**
>
> **Marketing plan**
> A marketing plan is a written document that states all the planned actions necessary to reach certain marketing goals.

The fact that planning is being discussed first does not mean that it always comes first, or that planning ends before marketers move on to other activities. Figure 10.2 also shows that planning and the other activities are all dependent on the results of preceding analysis.

The marketing planning process

The marketing planning process contains all guidelines for a business unit's marketing programmes and allocations over the planning period.

The need for planning is now almost universally accepted by managers, even though it is not as widely implemented in practice. Making use of a marketing plan can result in the following benefits for a business.[2]

- **Keeps marketing efforts aligned with corporate objectives**. Having a good plan can assist the business to identify what actions will best benefit it, and what actions are not worth it.
- **Makes sure marketing efforts remain proactive**. A plan can assist the business to act on emerging trends before they become full-blown, rather than the business being forced to change because of the trends.
- **Facilitates the process of evaluating new opportunities**. A solid plan will ensure that the business can identify which opportunities resulting from various trends will be good for their business.
- **Ensures all people in the business are on the same page**. With a plan, all people can be in agreement about the challenges, goals and tactics of the business.
- **Helps you to keep sight of the big picture.**
- **Boosts confidence**. A plan will provide a guide when the business is going through phases of uncertainty.
- **Facilitates measurement**. A plan provides a framework against which to measure performance.

Marketing planning is by its very nature a future-directed activity. Comprehensive and reliable information about all applicable environmental variables is necessary to make an educated estimate of what the future holds. Strategic decisions taken today may be implemented only at a much later stage. Marketing planning usually occurs in the short, medium and long term. In the short term (usually one year), it is reasonably easy to make forecasts. In the medium term (three to five years), it is more difficult, while long-term forecasts (five years and longer) are increasingly risky and uncertain. Nevertheless, all these planning phases are crucial for long-term survival and growth.

Analysing the environment is crucial to planning in a business. In many instances a marketing audit will form the basis of this environmental analysis. The ultimate goal of performing such an analysis is to identify factors that may have a significant impact on the long-term survival and profitability of a business. A technique that is particularly useful in the analysis of the material contained in the environmental scan is the SWOT (strengths, weaknesses, opportunities and threats) analysis. A SWOT analysis usually provides a graphical representation of the *internal* and *external* factors that affect a business:

- **Internal factors** refer to the strengths and weaknesses within the organisation. The internal variables in respect of resources, abilities and skills are discussed elsewhere.
- **External factors** refer to the opportunities and threats presented by the external environment. Information on these variables is systematised and kept up to date in a marketing information system, making it conveniently available for planning purposes and market forecasting.

A SWOT analysis can be described as a summary of the major findings of the organisation's current situation under the headings of strengths, weaknesses, opportunities and threats, as illustrated in Figure 10.3.

STRENGTHS Areas in which a company performs well that gives it an advantage over its competitors	WEAKNESSES The areas in which a company needs to improve, in which other companies have an advantage over it
OPPORTUNITIES Those aspects in the external environment of the firm that it can exploit to gain an advantage	THREATS Aspects in the external environment of the firm that threaten the long-term existence, profitability and market position

Figure 10.3 The components of a SWOT analysis

Implementation

The second step in the strategic marketing management process is implementation – without it, planning is useless to any organisation. Strategy implementation as discussed is outlined in Figure 10.4.

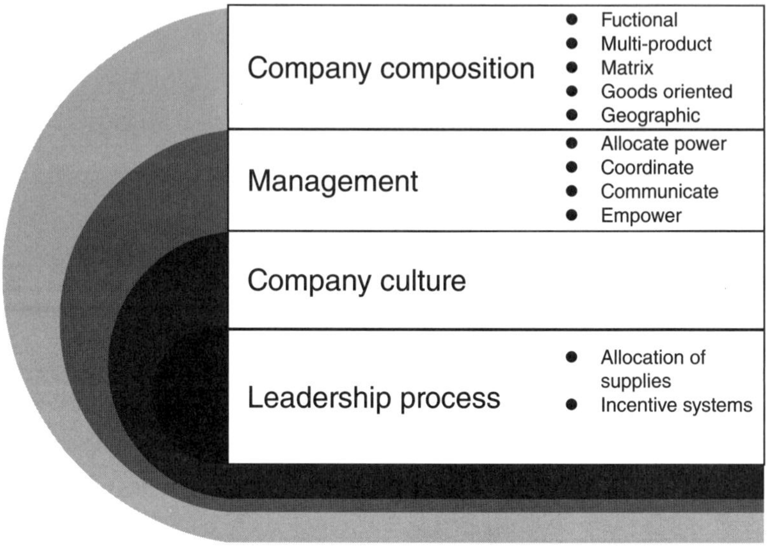

Figure 10.4 Important factors of strategy implementation

The importance of implementation

Implementation is one of the key routes to improved business performance, but is often recognised as one of the most difficult business challenges facing today's managers. Implementation is often recognised as one of the greatest Achilles' heels for all strategy initiatives.[3] Every business should be focusing more on implementing strategy than on creating it.

Companies no longer underestimate the importance of strategic intent and therefore, in a sense, know what to do. Their difficulties now lie in how to achieve the necessary changes. Implementation is the more difficult part of the process of strategy formulation and implementation, so now more focus is on ensuring the implementation of strategy than on creating it. Even the best-designed market and marketing strategies can fail without effective organising and structure, as well as good leadership. The implementation of marketing plans depends to a large extent on the organisational structure and the close cooperation of all marketing personnel under the leadership of the marketing manager. Planning and organising are thus closely linked.

Implementation strategies refer to the overall approach or framework for implementation. More simply put, the implementation strategy refers to *what* the organisation is going to do. Strategies are initiated and implemented in a strategic context, and various factors greatly influence the implementation process. Focusing on change in the organisation in a narrow, single situation results in the organisation not having a thorough understanding of environmental issues and their causes.

There are a number of frameworks for strategy implementation, but not one that is widely used or foremost. This has led to many organisations and their management failing to implement strategy effectively, as they do not have solid proven frameworks to base their tactics upon. A study done by Atkinson[4] states that there are several different implementation strategies but that there are similarities among them. For instance, they all consist of elements such as planning, resources, communication and monitoring.[5]

Implementation throughout the organisation

In a 'cascade phenomenon', goals and decisions flow down an organisational hierarchy much like water does from pool to pool in a Japanese garden. Strategic plans formulated at one level in an organisation are communicated to the level below, where they are interpreted and translated into actions undertaken to achieve the broader strategy. An organisation's design and management thus become critical factors in the successful implementation of any strategy.

Evaluation

The nature of evaluation

'True genius resides in the capacity for evaluation of uncertain, hazardous, and conflicting information.'[6]

During the process of evaluation, the organisation is able to identify and analyse errors made through previous actions. This will assist it to tweak those weaker areas and perform better in the future. The terms *monitoring* and *evaluation* are intimately linked, which has led to considerable confusion. The main differences are that monitoring is an ongoing analysis of the progress of a project toward reaching planned goals, done by *internal management*, that will lead to improved decision making; while evaluation is an assessment of the impact and sustainability of the actions of the project, usually done by *external agencies*, that leads to a provision of accountability.[7] The purpose of monitoring and evaluating information systems for key stakeholders includes:

- ensuring *project performance* through informed management decision making and control;
- demonstrating *accountability* through transparency and accountability; and
- promoting *organisational learning* through the testing of development hypotheses and the capture of lessons learned.

Assessing or evaluating is increasingly important as more and more stakeholders want hard evidence of the results of their project investments. One way of encouraging more evaluation and fighting the perception that it is such a time-consuming process is by applying only those tools.

CASE STUDY

KFC[8]

In 2004, KFC recognised that its position as market leader in South Africa was becoming the brand's Achilles' heel. While KFC was a strong brand, it needed to become an even stronger one if it were to sustain growth at the levels to which it had become accustomed.

Because KFC produced a universally loved product, it tended to create marketing that was just as 'universal'. The communication was traditionally aimed at one generic mass market, with a blanket approach focusing across the consumer spectrum – age, gender, race and income. The brand had become driven by product-led retail windows as opposed to consumer-led advertising. In addition, South African consumers were changing at a rapid pace, and because KFC was predominantly retail led, it had not kept up.

The solution was to transform a traditionally retail-led business into a marketing-led organisation by dividing KFC's massive market into new segments that could be individually targeted using age, income and gender to increase penetration across the board. It was to address each identified market segment individually, speaking to each group in its own language. The company adopted a new insight-driven approach to communication, which ensured that each piece of communication was not only relevant to the specific group's lifestyles and psychographics, but also addressed the business challenges in each segment. In addition, it communicated at least one functional product benefit of the product on promotion.

The new marketing-led approach, spearheaded by Ogilvy Johannesburg's communication strategy, has resulted in unprecedented growth for the brand.

This is a classic case study of good to great, of how a dominant brand should behave if it is to continue growing and thriving – by refusing to rest on its laurels and ensuring that the business constantly re-invents itself by focusing on its most valuable assets: its consumers.

KFC realised that, in order to connect with its audience, it needed to restructure its business around its consumers. The brand had always been a mass-market retail business with a very broad focus across the consumer spectrum. Admittedly, it segmented across race, dividing its target audience by 'emerging' and 'developed' – euphemisms for 'black' and 'white'.

The company divided that one mass market into the following new segments that could be individually targeted, using age, income, gender and product-usage occasions:

- **High-income families**. Young families with children, generally headed by 'mom'
- **High-income individuals**. Upwardly mobile high achievers, to be further segmented by gender divides – male and female

Continue to next page

Continued from previous page

- **Affordable-value consumers**. Families and individuals who are typically previously disadvantaged and very conscious of the cost of living, but would increase fast-food consumption if the price were right
- **Teen young adults**. Students and young adults with busy lives and limited responsibilities.

In summary:

- A radical new approach to business involved the identification of a selection of individual target markets.
- On a business level, the brand needed to increase market penetration, beat year-ago sales and meet same-store sales targets.
- On a marketing level, the KFC team was tasked with creating connections with consumers, increasing product sales and, ultimately, building one of South Africa's best-loved brands.

The campaigns

Moms and families

To capture the family segment, the team created a series of campaigns that positioned mom as the rightful hero in bringing the family together – with a little help from KFC. All of the campaigns tapped into the psyche of mom and the daily challenges she faces. For example, one campaign demonstrated how mom used KFC to persuade her headstrong and eccentric son to take off his superhero costume for the family meal.

High-income females

To communicate the arrival of the Twister range targeted at high-income females, the team developed a series of campaigns that illustrated the sophisticated and neat way to eat KFC. All of these campaigns resonated with young women because they tapped into the product usage insight that women do not like to get their hands dirty when they eat KFC and wanted to be seen to be projecting the right image when eating. One of the campaigns introduced the 'Twister Girl' who, in attempting to impress, chooses the Twister as an acceptable option.

High-income males

Males were targeted with offers that tapped into their need for filling food. All of the campaigns addressed the insight that for men, fast food is never enough on its own and they always feel that they need to add extra sides in order to satisfy their appetite. For example, in the 'In the dog box' advert they show a husband who needs to fill up because he does not know where his next meal will come from, as a result of insulting his pregnant wife.

Groups

Groups were targeted with the unforgettable: 'Your mom's quite nice' spot, which tapped into the insight that we let down our guard when our friends are around, possibly saying things we should not. The commercial also highlighted the product benefit of the meal, which was for sharing, encapsulated in the campaign line: 'Some things you should share, some things you shouldn't'.

Continue to next page

Continued from previous page

The youth and young at heart

To appeal to the youth, a selection of campaigns demonstrating the very real differences between teens and adults was created, such as the much loved 'Father and Son' advertisement that highlighted the generation gap by showing dad eating breakfast at the same time that his son was eating dinner.

The results

Short-term results

KFC's sales proved to be highly sensitive to the advertising. Upon launch of all campaigns, it was evident that advertising resulted in an instant spike in sales.

Long-term business results

The advertising achieved the business objectives. With the dramatic overhaul of the communication, KFC reversed the pitfalls of its leadership position – ensuring that as dominant brand it was still able to grow at an exponential rate, and increase penetration and relevance across the segments.

Marketing control can therefore be described as the *ongoing process of measurement and evaluation of the results of the marketing strategies and plans*, after which corrective action can be taken to ensure that marketing objectives are attained and competitors beaten. Control is the directing or redirecting of a company's actions to ensure that they meet objectives. Evaluation is a crucial addition to the control function, because actions need to be evaluated before they are controlled, in order to establish whether the results meet the goals that were set.

In marketing, control can be split into a product dimension and a corporate dimension.

Control at the corporate or small business unit (SBU) level is *strategic control* – that is, an attempt to keep the components of the strategic marketing plan on target and to redirect them when necessary. Control on a product-specific dimension is *product-marketing control* – that is, an attempt to keep the marketing plan on target.

Meeting the outcomes of a project is necessary, but this is not enough for reaching organisation goals, as managers have more complex issues to tackle, therefore performing all of the activities that are set out in the organisation's strategy is required in order to achieve desired outcomes.

An organisation must have a methodical basis according to which it evaluates and controls the marketing effort. Figure 10.5 displays a model of evaluation and control.

We will now discuss each of the steps in the process.

Steps in the evaluation and control process

Figure 10.5 Evaluation and marketing control process

Step 1: Set performance standards

Standards, as achievable objectives, can be determined for various marketing activities and are especially useful with routine activities, such as the number of calls or demonstrations per day expected of sales representatives. Standards can naturally also be laid down for once-off marketing projects, for instance activities involved in a specific corporate social responsibility (CSR) charity event.

Furthermore, standards can be set in quantitative and qualitative terms for the different marketing activities. Quantitative (or financial) standards consist of input, output and efficiency standards.

Step 2: Conduct performance forecasts

Once the company has established the criteria it will use to evaluate marketing performance, it develops performance projections for products and business units in the form of a profit-and-loss statement. For example, a company such as Dell could develop performance projections for a range of its laptops to increase sales by 40%. This would be at a product level. It could also develop a projection for its human resources department to decrease the rate of staff turnover by 20%. This would be at a business unit level.

To develop a profit-and-loss statement, management must establish a budget for a product or SBU that will provide cost and revenue estimates. Today, many companies are using a variation of an objective-task approach known as *zero-based budgeting* in which the budget is determined at the beginning of each year. Past sales or competitive expenditure are not considered. Instead, certain profitability goals are formulated. Management asks what actions are required to meet these goals, and then estimates the necessary expenditure.

Zero-based budgeting is popular as it provides a more objective basis for evaluating marketing performance. It simplifies evaluating product or SBU performance because expenditure is evaluated from a zero starting point. Many companies assess marketing expenditure by comparing it to expenditure in previous years. A company might say that a R5 million advertising budget for the year is 10% higher than the previous year, and evaluate advertising results on this basis. The fallacy here is that last year's budget might have been too high or too low to begin with. Zero-based budgeting overcomes this problem by assessing costs from a base of zero so that if R5 million is spent on advertising this year, the basis for assessing the value of this expenditure is the profit it produces without reference to past expenditure.

Step 3: Create marketing company

This step requires establishing a marketing organisation capable of implementing and evaluating marketing strategies.

Step 4: Create marketing strategy

The development and implementation of a marketing plan has previously been discussed. It is, however, important to realise that people are involved in the implementation of plans, and that conflict and resistance can arise. A critical requirement is therefore a corporate culture conducive to harmony in the company.

Step 5: Assess performance

Evaluation takes place by comparing the actual results with the formulated performance standards. Managers must analyse and evaluate whether or not the steps in the marketing plan are being performed optimally.

Strategic control points are established and overseen by people who have the required authority to exercise control. The product manager, the advertising manager and the sales manager, among others, are responsible for measuring and noting actual performance against the preset standards in their departments.

It has already been mentioned that evaluation is appropriate *before* the actual activity takes place, *while* it takes place and *after* it has been completed. The ideal is to evaluate before or at least while things are happening so that deviations from the standard can be spotted in time and changes made before money or time is wasted. However, this is not always possible, and marketing control is often required after the event has occurred. Then it is a matter of recovery management. The purpose of *recovery management* is to establish a basis for future planning and to prevent a repetition of the deviation in future – this

'The ideal is to evaluate before or at least while things are happening so that deviations from the standard can be spotted in time and changes made before money or time is wasted.'

points to *preventive management*. In large organisations it is often difficult for management to exercise effective control. Strategic control points are thus delegated to the lower levels, while only exceptional differences and deviations from the standards are reported to top management. This is referred to as *control by exception*. Where deviations occur, the nature and extent thereof and the reasons therefore have to be determined before corrective steps can be taken.

Step 6: Take remedial action

Where actual performances are below the standards set, steps can be taken to improve performance. If sales in the first quarter are lower than the norm set in the sales budget, then corrective measures can possibly entail an intensive marketing campaign. Remedial action can be taken in three areas: *territory decisions, product decisions* and *customer and order-size decisions*. For example, if the relative profitability of each product or group of products is known, informed decisions can be taken. For example, in the case of unprofitable models, sizes or colours could be eliminated; salespeople's compensation plans may be altered to encourage the sale of high-margin items; or channels of distribution may be changed. Even though specific actions are possible in each area, there are three broad guidelines that can be followed in terms of decision making, as described below.

When significant discrepancies have been detected between actual performance and the set performance standards, it must be decided whether the deviations warrant correction. These deviations can be dealt with accordingly by taking corrective action that eliminates the cause of the deviation, changing performance standards if it becomes clear that the standards set in the marketing plan are no longer realistic, or keeping the same goals and allowing the deviation from the plan to continue.

Where the deviation can be attributed to uncontrollable environmental factors (such as an economic depression), standards have to be lowered if they were initially set too high. In favourable circumstances, it is also possible that actual performance can exceed the standards laid down. Once again, standards will have to be adjusted. If sales in the first quarter are much higher than the norm set in the sales budget, an adjustment will have to be made to avoid stock problems in the second quarter.

'If sales in the first quarter are much higher than the norm set in the sales budget, an adjustment will have to be made to avoid stock problems in the second quarter.'

Information on deviations, the reasons for deviations and the nature of corrective action are used in the forecasting process to set more accurate standards for future periods.

Summary

The three components of strategic marketing – namely planning, implementation and control – direct the marketing task in the organisation. Marketing and market strategies are planned by marketing management, taking the internal strengths and weaknesses as well as the external opportunities and threats into consideration. The strategies are market driven, and consumer needs, demands and preferences, as well as the competitive position of the organisation, are considered. The main objective of the organisation, namely maximisation of profitability, can be realised only through aggressive marketing efforts, the creation of an effective organisational structure, the judicious application of resources and the establishment of an evaluation system through which performance standards are set and activities controlled.

References

1. Management Study Guide. n.d. *Advantages of planning*. [Online] Available from: http://www.managementstudyguide.com/planning_advantages.htm [Accessed: 2013-07-17].
2. Gastin, M. 2011. *Seven benefits of a strategic marketing plan*. [Online] Available from: http://www.mikegastin.com/content/seven-benefits-strategic-marketing-plan [Accessed: 2013-07-17].
3. Cant, M. 2010. *Marketing: An introduction*. Cape Town, South Africa: Juta & Co., p. 224.
4. Atkinson, H. 2011. 'Strategy implementation: A role for the balanced scorecard?' *Management Decision*, 44(10), pp. 1441–1460.
5. Markgraf, B. 2013. *Key elements of business strategy implementation*. [Online] Available from: http://smallbusiness.chron.com/key-elements-business-strategy-implementation-63668.html [Accessed: 2013-07-17].
6. OwlRE. 2008. *Top ten quotes on evaluation*. [Online] Available from: http://www.owlre.com/wordpress/wp-content/uploads/2008/01/factsheet_owlre_quotes.pdf [Accessed: 2013-07-14].
7. Aquaknowledge. 2004. *Main differences between monitoring and evaluation*. [Online] Available from: http://www.aquaknow.net/en/water-toolkit-trainings/monitoring-evaluation-and-audit-water-development-projects/monitoring-evaluation-and-audit-water-dev/15689 [Accessed: 2013-07-17].
8. Adapted from Van Heerden, C.H. 2013. *Contemporary retail and marketing case studies*. Cape Town, South Africa: Juta & Co., pp. 61–88.

Index